P9-CFX-316

WHAT IS *YOUR* RACE?

WHAT IS *YOUR* RACE?

The Census and Our Flawed Efforts to Classify Americans

KENNETH PREWITT

PRINCETON UNIVERSITY PRESS
Princeton and Oxford

Published by Princeton University Press, 41 William Street, Princeton, New Jersey 08540
In the United Kingdom: Princeton University Press, 6 Oxford Street, Woodstock, Oxfordshire OX20 1TW

press.princeton.edu

Library of Congress Cataloging-in-Publication Data
Prewitt, Kenneth.
What is your race? : the census and our flawed efforts to classify Americans / Kenneth Prewitt.
p. cm.
Includes bibliographical references and index.
ISBN 978-0-691-15703-0 (hbk. : alk. paper) 1. Ethnicity—United States—Statistics. 2. United States—Census—History. 3. United States—Population—History. 4. Demography—United States. I. Title.
E184.A1.P725 2013
305.800973—dc23
2012037528

British Library Cataloging-in-Publication Data is available

This book has been composed in John Sans Text Pro and Baskerville 120 Pro

Printed on acid-free paper. ∞

Printed in the United States of America

10 9 8 7 6 5 4 3 2 1

Dedicated to my grandsons, Benjamin and Jameson,
who are in the "transition generation"

CONTENTS

FIGURES AND TABLES

Figures

Tables

PREFACE

I WRITE THIS BOOK TO PRESENT COMPELLING REASONS JUSTIFYING A RADICAL change in how your government presumes to ask, What is *your* race? There is a story behind all books. My story starts in 2003, when I lectured to the Wildavsky Forum for Public Policy at the University of California–Berkeley, an event cosponsored by the Russell Sage Foundation. The Wildavsky Lecture was expected to address a policy issue that was getting insufficient notice—and it was expected to lead to a book-length publication. A decade later, this is that book. A year before the Wildavsky Forum, I spoke to officers of the MacArthur Foundation, reflecting on my recently completed tenure as director of the U.S. Census Bureau. I suggested that the option to "mark one or more" of the race categories on the 2000 census, sometimes called the multiple-race option, was a turning point in census history—but with consequences dimly understood. The MacArthur Foundation offered a grant with the understanding that I would study those consequences. Supported by the grant, I convened a small working group to help with the task. In 2007, as a resident Fellow at the Russell Sage Foundation, I started to write.

This combination of incentives—a named lecture that leads an author to think about a problem, foundation support, a writing residency—is not atypical and has fostered many a university press book in the social sciences. Also typically in the mix, and certainly present in my story, are various friends and colleagues who lend criticism along the way,[1] graduate students who argue with your ill-formed ideas, and academic audiences in various universities and professional settings who invite you to present a "work in progress" in the expectation (often wrong, in my case) that your ideas are more than half-baked. I won't name all of these colleagues and students, who number in the dozens, and the several very useful invited lectures and academic conferences, but do thank the many people who listened and then posed difficult questions that repeatedly delayed finishing this book. And, of course, I acknowledge with great appreciation support from the MacArthur and Russell Sage Foundations, and the team at Princeton University Press (especially the production group and two anonymous reviewers, whose smart critiques yet again delayed finishing the book—much to the benefit of its author and, I hope, its readers).

If a 2003 lecture launched this project, and the endeavor had so much support, why did it take a decade to publish? I could claim other duties and obligations as interruptions. The would be superficially true, but not true in any interesting way. The working group mentioned above can testify to the more interesting truth—they pushed me in ways that gradually made clear the difference between writing an academic book and writing something that has a chance of producing change.[2] The former is relatively easy; the latter devilishly difficult. In this book the former is an explanation of what is broken and what should replace it (chapters 1–9); the latter is recommending a feasible strategy to make changes (chapters 10 and 11).

When I began the Russell Sage residency, I understood what was involved in a historically analytic study of the census; it would explain how we got into the current mess of America's official ethnic and race statistics. It would argue that what is flawed should be fixed. It would identify needed improvements. It would, that is, say what many social scientists say: "My research is policy-relevant. People who make policy should pay attention." Had that been my only goal this book would have been published years ago. But I pledged to myself that I would work out the very specific steps that could change, for the better, America's "statistical races." I knew from my experience as U.S. Census Bureau director that these steps must be technically feasible—producing questions the bureau can efficiently and effectively administer, and that will work from Puerto Rico to the Bering Sea for a population unprecedented in its diversity. I also knew that new questions had to be politically acceptable—questions the U.S. Congress can agree to and that will attract political support to counter the opposition that was certain to emerge.

Academic literature on the U.S. government's race classification unanimously concludes that it is flawed, and offers numerous imaginative improvements—for example, the census should not ask your race, but "what color are you?" Or, the census should ask if you've been discriminated against because of your race or ethnicity, and, if yes, identify what your race or ethnicity is. The rationale for these and other proposals are invariably argued with strong sociological and psychological reasoning. But these two examples take no account of technical feasibility and political acceptability.

Driven by my brash pledge to meet the demanding criteria of technical feasibility and political acceptability, I wrote more than one recommendation-based final chapter, threw each away, and started on another. This went on for several years, and might still be going on had not two breakthroughs happened. One resolves the technical feasibility challenge. The Office of Management and Budget and the Census Bureau tested alternative race and ethnic questions during the 2010 census. One of the tested formats, though not in my view perfect, is sufficiently similar to what I do believe necessary that I strongly endorse it. Technical feasibility is no longer an issue if the Census Bureau, on the basis of extensive testing, adopts a question already worked out with the OMB.[3]

The second breakthrough alerted me to a way to conceptualize political acceptability. Though long in coming, it was a simple insight. Learning from the nation's experience with the "mark one or more" option introduced in the 2000 census—which upended basic ways of thinking about race *without* upending politically entrenched policies attached to the census question—I recommend a "no abrupt change" strategy. It strategically uses generational turnover to realize a radical change but prepares for this change with incremental adjustments stretching across several decades. What is today viewed as "radical" will not seem that way by the time it happens.

The necessary change may require a half century, even more. I dedicate this book to my young teenage grandsons. When I was their age (in the 1940s) I lived in a Jim Crow world, where my awareness of races other than Midwestern white was limited to lines from a Civil War hymn—with a political message that perhaps I unconsciously absorbed. It was a favorite of my Methodist bible school. "Jesus loves all the children of the world. Red and yellow, black and white. They're all precious in his sight." A decade later I was active in civil rights, and witnessed the shrinking of the segregated racial order of my childhood and the arrival of a racial order attuned to social justice. Now in my adult years I see changes unimaginable only a few decades back—the emergence of diversity, multiracialness, and even talk of postraciality, but also a resurgence of racism in some quarters.

The Jim Crow racial order, the civil rights movement, and the transformative demographic changes of our time still use the antique racial categories produced by an eighteenth-century science. The "five colors of mankind" serve us poorly for the challenges of the present. I hope my grandsons, when they reach my age, can look back on sixty years of successful policy erasing the color line that separates by race and the nativity line that separates by place of birth. America is deeply scarred by its racist and nativist past. It is a new generation—today's youth, the "transition generation"—that can, finally, erase the lingering effects of that past. They will need help from better national statistics than those available today.

PART I

What Are Statistical Races?

CHAPTER 1

INTRODUCTION AND OVERVIEW

There was a racial classification scheme in America's first census (1790), as there was in the next twenty-two censuses, which brings us to the present. Though the classification was altered in response to the political and intellectual fashions of the day, the underlying definition of America's racial hierarchy never escaped its origins in the eighteenth-century. Even the enormous changing of the racial landscape in the civil rights era failed to challenge a dysfunctional classification, though it did bend it to new purposes. Nor has the demographic upheaval of our present time led to much fresh thinking about how to measure America. It is, finally, time to escape that past. Twenty-first-century statistics should not be governed by race thinking that is two and a half centuries out of date. They poorly serve the nation, especially how it understands and manages the color line and the nativity line—what separates us as races and what separates us as native born and foreign born.

What Are Statistical Races?

On April 1, 2010, the American population numbered more than 308 million. When the Census Bureau finished with its decade population count it hurried to inform the president and the Congress how many of those 308 million Americans resided in each of our fifty states. The nation requires this basic fact to reapportion congressional seats and electoral college votes, allowing America's representative democracy to work according to its constitutional design (see chapter 2).

Immediately after this most basic population fact was announced, the Census Bureau told us how many of the 308 million Americans belonged to one of these five races: White, African American, American Indian, Asian, Native Hawaiian. The bureau reported that a few million Americans belonged to not just one of these five but to two or more. Simultaneously, the bureau reported how many Americans were Hispanics—which, the government insists, is not a race at all but an ethnic group. Incidentally, not all Hispanics got that message, because about half of them filled in a census line allowing Americans to say they belonged to "some other race." Hispanics, however, are not a race. Hispanics are expected to be Hispanics *and also* to self-identify as one or more of the five major race groups listed above (this is explained in chapter 6).

What perhaps puzzles the reader is why race statistics are so terribly important that they are publicly announced simultaneously with the population figures mandated for reapportionment. You may also be puzzled that the census form (fig. 1) dedicates so much of its space to the race and Hispanic question but has no space for education, health, employment, or marital status questions. Are such matters less important than the country's racial profile? We will examine such puzzles. It is important that we do so because the race and Hispanic questions used in the census have a very long reach. A version of these questions is used in hundreds of government surveys—federal, state, and local—and in official administrative record keeping that captures traits of Americans from the moment of birth to their death: vital statistics, military records, and education and health data. Further, because the statistics resulting from a voracious appetite for information in our modern nation-state are embedded in law, regulations, and policies, there are thousands of private-sector institutions—universities, hospitals, corporations, voluntary organizations—doing business with the government that collect matching race statistics.

America has *statistical races*. What they are, how we got them, how we use them, and whether today we want or need them are questions that shape this book. America's statistical races are not accidents of history. They have been deliberately constructed and reconstructed by the government. They are tools of government, with political purposes and policy consequences—more so even than the biological races of the nineteenth century or the socially constructed races from twentieth-century anthropology or what are termed *identity races* in our current times. Whether these biological, socially constructed, or identity races are "real" is a serious matter, but they are of interest in this book only as they condition what the government defines as our statistical races.

What, specifically, are statistical races? Organized counting of any kind—and certainly a census is organized counting—requires counters

→ **NOTE: Please answer BOTH Question 8 about Hispanic origin and Question 9 about race. For this census, Hispanic origins are not races.**

8. Is Person 1 of Hispanic, Latino, or Spanish origin?

- ☐ **No,** not of Hispanic, Latino, or Spanish origin
- ☐ Yes, Mexican, Mexican Am., Chicano
- ☐ Yes, Puerto Rican
- ☐ Yes, Cuban
- ☐ Yes, another Hispanic, Latino, or Spanish origin — *Print origin, for example, Argentinean, Colombian, Dominican, Nicaraguan, Salvadoran, Spaniard, and so on.*

9. What is Person 1's race? *Mark* ☒ *one or more boxes.*

- ☐ White
- ☐ Black, African Am., or Negro
- ☐ American Indian or Alaska Native — *Print name of enrolled or principal tribe.*
- ☐ Asian Indian
- ☐ Chinese
- ☐ Filipino
- ☐ Other Asian — *Print race, for example, Hmong, Laotian, Thai, Pakistani, Cambodian, and so on.*
- ☐ Japanese
- ☐ Korean
- ☐ Vietnamese
- ☐ Native Hawaiian
- ☐ Guamanian or Chamorro
- ☐ Samoan
- ☐ Other Pacific Islander — *Print race, for example, Fijian, Tongan, and so on.*
- ☐ Some other race — *Print race.*

Figure 1. Ethnic and racial categories on the 2010 census form.

to know what they are counting, which in turn depends on a classification scheme. Statistical races are by-products of the categories used in the government's racial classification. And what do the actual 2010 census categories produce? Though you cannot easily tell by looking at the census form, the categories are designed to produce two statistical ethnicities and five statistical races. The ethnicities are Hispanic and Non Hispanic, though this is not evident from a question in which the term *ethnicity* does not appear. The five statistical races are White, Black, American Indian, Asian, and Native Hawaiian/Pacific Islander, which we will learn in chapter 2 directly derive from a color-based division of the world's population by eighteenth-century natural scientists—white, black, red, yellow, and brown. With these basics established, the census form then unleashes the combinations that result from the "mark one or more" instruction. We will see later how these many combinations *have not*, as yet, been used to make public policy. They became part of the census to fulfill expressive demands for recognition. Then there is whatever appears on the "some other" line, though again these counts do *not* become statistical races. So, whatever you think might be going on in these census questions, the political and policy intent is to count the Hispanics separately from everyone else, and to then sort every American, including Hispanics, into five primary races. When I use the term *statistical races*, it refers to these five groups plus the Hispanic ethnicity.

If you are now confused, you are on your way to understanding why I've written this book. That statistical races are real there is no doubt. Law courts, legislatures, executive agencies, media, election campaigns, advocacy groups, corporate planners, university admission offices, hospitals, employment agencies, and others endlessly talk about "how many" African Americans, Asians, Pacific Islanders, American Indians, Whites, and Hispanics there are—and how fast their numbers are growing, how many have jobs, graduate from high school, are in prison, serve in the military, are obese or smoke, own their homes, or marry each other.

If the statistical races are real and important, why does the census form fail to make that clear? In fact, if you take a closer look at the questions you will be even more confused. You should be perplexed that one census-designated race—White—is simply a color. Nothing else is said. The next race is a color, Black (and Negro, which is another way to say Black), but also a descent group—that is, Americans whose ancestors are from the African continent—and in some respects an "ethnicity" as well. Today's immigrants from Ghana or Ethiopia also go into that category. Then color drops out of the picture altogether. A civil status enters.

American Indians/Alaska Natives belong to a race by virtue of tribal membership, which has a clear definition in American law; they can also belong to that race by declaring membership in a principal tribe, which is not a legal status but a self-identification. Look at the census question again. With Whites, Blacks, and Native Americans now listed, there follows a long list of nationality groups. If we read the question stem literally, each of these is a race. The Chinese, the Koreans, the Samoans are presented as if they are independent races. We are not, however, supposed to understand the question literally, but to understand that we become part of the Asian race or the Native Hawaiian/Pacific Islander race by checking a national origin or writing one in. Oddly, however, the term *Asian* only incidentally appears in the question, defining persons from India in a way that doesn't confuse them with American Indians, and inviting write-in responses, where the examples listed are again nationality groups.

With this nationality nomenclature in mind you might look back at the question on Hispanic/Latino/Spanish origin (terms used interchangeably), where you will see that it is similarly constructed. There is no box indicating Hispanic, but several boxes labeled with nationalities and a write-in space again guided by nationality examples. In a nation famous for its ethnic diversity, you might now be asking, is the census telling us that there are only two ethnic groups that matter (Hispanic and non-Hispanic) while ignoring all white European national origin groups (Swedes, Germans, Italians, Irish, Poles, and Russians, among others)? It seems so.

It's hard to find the underlying rationale for what appears, and what doesn't, in these two ethnoracial questions. We will discuss in detail the absence of a coherent rationale. As an astute scholar has written, the Census Bureau "has no choice but to rely on incoherent categories if it hopes to measure race in the United States" because, he continues, "race arises out of (fundamentally irrational) social practices."[1] A large part of the story told in the chapters to follow explains how "incoherent categories" result in incoherent statistical races, which derive not only from social practices but equally from policy goals.

It matters if America measures races, and then, of course, how the government decides what those races are. It matters because law and policy are not about an abstraction called *race* but are about races *as they are made intelligible* and acquire their numerical size in our statistical system. When we politically ask why black men are jailed at extraordinarily high rates, whether undocumented Mexican laborers are taking jobs away from working-class whites, or whether Asians have become the model minority in America, we start from a count of jailed blacks, the comparative employment patterns of Mexicans and whites, and Asian educational achievements. When our political questions are shaped by how many of which races are doing what, and when policies addressing those conditions follow, we should worry about whether the "how many" and the "which races" tell us what we need to know about what is going on in our polity, economy, and society. We should worry about whether we should have *statistical races* at all, and if so, whether we have the right ones. My answer, worked out in chapter 11, argues for incrementally transforming our racial statistics in order to match them with the governing challenges of the twenty-first century. This argument, and the tactical advice offered to realize it, makes sense only in the context of a historical account of statistical races.

Chapter 2 starts with basics that frame this American history. A German doctor in 1776 divided the human species into five races. Today, nearly two and a half centuries later, these are the same five races into which the U.S. Census divides the American population, making America the only country in the world firmly wedded to an eighteenth-century racial taxonomy. Embedded in this science were theories of a racial hierarchy: there were not just different races but superior and inferior races. American politics and policy held onto this assumption for nearly two centuries.

The next section covers the nineteenth century, showing how assumptions of racial superiority and inferiority tightly bound together statistical races, social science, and public policy.

Policy, Statistics, and Science Join Forces

The starting point—as is true of many features of American government—takes us to constitutional language (chapter 3). The U.S. Constitution required a census of the white, the black, and the red races.[2] The founders faced an extraordinary challenge—how to join the original thirteen colonies into a republic of "united states." They met this challenge with a political compromise that brought slaveholding states into the Union. Without this *statistical* compromise there would not have been a United States as we know it today. In the early censuses slaves were counted as three-fifths of a person, a ratio demanded by slaveholder interests as the price of joining the Union. Holding their noses, the northern states agreed. A deep policy disagreement at the moment of founding the nation was resolved in the deliberate creation of a statistical race. In this case, the policy need shaped the statistical practice.

Later in American history the reverse frequently occurred. Specific policies—affirmative action, for example—took the shape they did *because* the statistical races were already at hand. One of my major arguments, especially starting with chapter 8, is that we should learn a lesson from the founding period: start with agreement on public purposes and then design suitable statistics to meet policy challenges. Without clarity on *why* the nation should measure race, clarity on *what* to measure is impossible.

The political understanding in the nineteenth century that counting the population by race could do nationally significant policy work led naturally to a close partnership between race science and census statistics, setting the stage for what 150 years later we call *evidence-based policy*. It's a fascinating if also depressing story, resting as it does on the near universal assumption that there is a biologically determined racial hierarchy: whites at the top, blacks at the bottom, with the yellow, red, and brown races arrayed between. Chapter 4 tells the race science story, giving emphasis to features that mark American history to the present day. Among the more important was the shift from simply counting races, as was needed to make the three-fifths policy work, to investigating characteristics considered unique to different races. The policy goal was to determine who was fit for citizenship responsibilities: whites, certainly; the American Indian, probably not; the African, clearly not. The statistical races helped fix the color line in American politics, essentially drawing policy boundaries that gradually governed all aspects of life: schooling, housing, employment, marriage, travel, and—of course—political participation.

Drawing internal policy boundaries became more pressing when the Civil War ended slavery and presented the specter of four million free blacks in the society. Starting in the 1880s, the Jim Crow racial order sustained the color line initially put in place for slaveholders. Yet more complicated boundaries were drawn with the arrival of Chinese labor to the mines and fields of the western states in the mid-nineteenth century, and later in the century when massive flows of immigrants from southern and central Europe arrived as labor for the eastern states' factories. Chapter 5 covers how America continually readjusted its color line when the economy's need for workers resulted in immigration-driven population growth but the polity required a monopoly of power in the hands of the "right" whites—that is, European Protestants.

In the stressful half century starting with the Civil War, the social sciences entered the scene. Their methods and theories joined with the great resource of national census statistics lent the authority of a new science to the policy choices of the day, a *social* science that gradually displaced the biologically based race science popular earlier in the nineteenth century. In ways familiar to us today, the social sciences embraced the statistical races as a key to informing policy makers across a broad range of issues including, early in the twentieth century, stopping the flow of the "wrong" European immigrants—Catholic and Jewish—without interfering with immigration from the ancestral Protestant Europe. Statistical races at the time reflected assumptions of a color line but also of a nativity line, that drawn between the native born and the foreign born.

When You Have a Hammer, Everything Looks Like a Nail

The nation's statistical races were four as the twentieth century arrived: European White, African Black, American Indian Red, and Asian Yellow. They were put to policy work in restricting immigration in the 1920s and for racial segregation more generally until the civil rights challenge dramatically arrived in the 1960s. The simple version of what then happened, recounted in chapter 6, is how a policy instrument used to politically, economically, and socially *exclude* since the nation's founding made a 180-degree turn and was used to *include* the racial groups historically sent to the back of the bus—both literally and figuratively. It is a story of how proactive policies of racial justice were shaped with racial statistics never intended for the policy uses to which they were put. But the fit made sense. The policy tool—statistical races—could be shaped to match the policy goal of racial justice. It also made sense given the greater effectiveness of the Census Bureau at measuring population characteristics, and the availability of the social sciences to advise policy design at levels of detail previously unimagined.

Chapter 7 uses the metaphor "when you have a hammer..." to underscore that racial statistics can be misused by converting an issue or policy that is not about race into one inappropriately racialized. The first example is a census strategy to improve measurement of hard-to-count population groups. The second example, the case of genetic medicine, is more complicated and substantially more consequential. The statistical races now deeply embedded in American politics and culture are convenient shorthand for asking whether better health might be provided if treatment and medicines are targeted to the government's official race groups, thereby treating those groups as biological and not just statistical realities. The possible damage from this serious mismatch of the hammer at hand to the nail in view forces us to ask whether that is not reason enough to get rid of the hammer altogether.

The Statistical Races under Pressure, and a Fresh Rationale

Chapter 8 brings us closer to the present, introducing pressures that challenge the role of statistical races in today's policy environment. One pressure is *multiraciality* as exemplified in the "mark one or more" census option introduced in 2000. This option is a profound criticism of two centuries of American racial counting. There are not three or four or five races, each in its own census box; there are multiple combinations, permutations, mixtures. Millions of young Americans know and accept this, and they are increasingly impatient with a census that isn't better at recognizing it. A second pressure pulling in a similar direction is *diversity* as a policy goal, now widely embraced from the military to the corporation to the university. The complexities of the diversity agenda destabilize the racial classification. The third pressure is the *color-blind* movement. This is in response to the *dilemma of recognition*, a phrase indicating that making race groups beneficiaries of policy can itself intensify group identities. There is strong political sentiment that this contradicts basic American individualistic values—freedom, choice, mobility, and merit-earned rewards. In dismay over racial group–based policy, opponents are advancing color-blind proposals in law and politics.

These three pressures weaken the hold of statistical races and in so doing open up political space for fresh thinking about racial measurement. The founders confronted a policy issue of great consequence—the scope of the "united states" they were establishing—and then designed a simple statistical tool to ensure that the slaveholding South would join the Republic. Today's question is not dissimilar: What kind of United States will we become as the population inexorably shifts its racial center of gravity? What statistics are needed to understand and manage this shift?

Chapter 9 argues that the center of gravity is shifting because of an intricate interplay between America's color line and its nativity line. We use the color line concept to ask whether America has the right policy tools to fully erase the line that separated whites and racial minorities throughout America's history. We use the nativity line concept to ask whether America has the right policy tools to steer the nation toward the full integration of peoples now arriving from every world region. America's future is the future of these lines. If they merge—if immigrants are racialized—the future sadly repeats America's past. If, instead, America's population becomes so diverse and multiracial that the color line disappears, an altogether different future is in store, perhaps the promised postracial society. It is certain that millions of new Americans and their children will navigate the line between native born and foreign born. Not certain is whether this social process will strengthen or weaken a color line inherited from the eighteenth century, strengthened across the next century and a half, and then challenged but not fully erased by the civil rights movement of the mid-twentieth century.

The statistics needed to understand the dynamic interplay between the color line and the nativity line are not the ones we have. Chapter 9 offers a rationale for discarding today's statistical races, replacing them with a twenty-first-century architecture for a twenty-first-century challenge.

What We Have Is Not What We Need

At this point in the book I become an advocate for very specific changes in the census race and ethnic questions. The strategy I recommend depends on a close understanding of the political and technical landscape. Important technical details are presented in chapter 10. It is often the fine print that has to be changed to bring about change. In the case of census race questions the fine print is knowing exactly what is being asked by the Census Bureau, when it is asked, and on which of its many different surveys. Ignore this detail and the policy victory fades from view. Grasp it and a winning strategy can be shaped.

I do not underestimate the difficulty. Powerful political constituencies are wedded to the current statistical races, especially the well-organized African Americans and Hispanics. Commercial interests are organized around familiar race data, which they use for product placement and location of retail outlets. These and other sources of resistance contribute to what social science describes as the self-reinforcing tendencies of political and social institutions. Against these obstacles are aligned the pressures for change outlined in chapter 8 and, what I hope is obvious, the inability of today's statistical races to offer knowledge that can guide the nation as it faces the challenges of the color line and the nativity line.

Chapter 11 is about what, specifically, to change and how, specifically, to change it. The argument rests on several premises. Politics and policy don't like abrupt change, therefore introduce incremental modifications. Racial statistics create as well as reflect realities, therefore use the census to shape selected "realities" critical to effective use of racial statistics in the twenty-first century. Every generation opens up fresh possibilities, therefore design a strategy that takes advantage of generational turnover. Immigrants are much more likely to see themselves through a national origin lens than a racial lens, therefore add a fuller national origin dimension into America's statistics. Immigrant assimilation was not a major policy issue a half-century ago (when today's statistical races were firmly put in place), therefore add a second-generation question to the census.

Many of the specifics I recommend will be sharply criticized by friends and colleagues with whom I debated these issues in recent years. My question: Do you want the 2010 census question (see figure 1) to remain as it is for the rest of the twenty-first century? If so, defend it. (That won't be easy.) If not, offer a better version than the one I endorse, but it should meet two criteria: It must be technically feasible—that is, it has to work in the census environment. And it must be politically acceptable to the Congress—which, as the Constitution makes clear, controls the content of the census.[3] I have kept these criteria in mind. This book is written not as an academic exercise but as a policy brief.

CHAPTER 2

CLASSIFICATION BEFORE COUNTING: THE STATISTICAL RACES

CHAPTER 1 INTRODUCED THE TERM *STATISTICAL RACE*. AMERICA'S STATISTICAL races are created when its government bluntly asks: What is your race? and Americans check census boxes and fill in forms. These forms are ubiquitous. Birth and death certificates record race, as have school, employment, criminal justice, housing, military service, and such other records on matters of government and commercial interest.

But does the government and business need to know our race? And what is a race anyway? These and many related questions are our subject. We start simply. Statistical races are a product of governments and their policy-making chores, dating to colonial America and incorporated in the Constitution. It has been a taken-for-granted fact in American politics since.

A CONSEQUENTIAL CLASSIFICATION FROM THE START

Counting anything starts with classification. We start our story with one of the most consequential classifications in social history:

> *Americanus*: reddish, choleric, and erect; hair black, straight, thick; wide nostrils, scanty beard; obstinate, merry, free; paints himself with fine red lines; regulated by custom.
>
> *Asiaticus*: sallow, melancholy, stiff; hair black; dark eyes; severe, haughty, avaricious; covered with loose garments, ruled by opinion.

Africanus: black, phlegmatic, relaxed; hair black, frizzled; skin silky; nose flat; lips tumid; women without shame, they lactate profusely; crafty, indolent, negligent; anoints himself with grease; governed by caprice.

Europeaeus: white, sanguine, muscular; hair long, flowing; eyes blue; gentle, acute, inventive; covers himself with close vestments; governed by laws.[1]

So suggested an eighteenth-century Swedish botanist who, in the scientific fashion of his times, Latinized his name to Carl Linnaeus. Linnaeus is widely credited as the father of taxonomy. He first published his influential approach, based on the idea of a nested hierarchy, as a small pamphlet in 1735, under the title *Systema Naturae*; he enlarged it over a lifetime of collecting and classifying.

Linnaeus's classification is familiar from high school biology. He divided and subdivided all living things into ever more specific groups that students remember as "King Philip came over for good spaghetti," a mnemonic for *kingdom*, *phylum*, *class*, *order*, *family*, *genus*, and *species*. Mammals are a class, among which Linnaeus fixed the order Primates, the family *Hominidae*, and among them the human species. Linnaeus allowed for varieties within a species, and he presented the four human subspecies noted above.

Although there are references to different "kinds of people" or "races" in earlier ethnographic writings (many noting skin color), Linnaeus offered the first authoritative, systematic classification of human variation. Based on continental location and physical appearance, the classification favored skin color as the distinguishing trait.[2] In his classification, the privileged descriptive terms are those of color: reddish, sallow, black, or white. Other physical traits—hair texture or nostril shape—are applied less consistently.

In elaborating his racial classification, Linnaeus departed from his botanical expertise and turned anthropological, even amateurishly psychological. He told his readers that temperament and character systematically vary from one race group to the next. This essentialism—the idea that there are characteristics that any member of a given race must possess—imprinted public consciousness in ways we still struggle to overcome.[3] Race, more or less as we know it today, entered the scientific canon as a fact of nature.

This racial essentialism was powerfully influential because it occurred as Western science was coming of age. Linnaeus was not the first European to be fascinated with varieties of flora and fauna. Explorers of the newly discovered territories in the fifteenth and sixteenth centuries collected obsessively, and the collections became the basis for herbariums and natural history museums. These early scientific institutions categorized specimens so they could be compared, which in turn led to theories about the causes and consequences of variation in the natural world. A science of nature was born.

Why, then, could there not be a science of human variation based on the same comparative methodology? A taxonomy based on skin color could explain why one race was governed by custom and another by caprice, but only one, the white Europeans, governed by law, a self-evidently superior foundation for government. As Linnaean ideas took hold, European adventurer-scientists were making their way into the African interior. There, as in the Americas a century or two earlier, they confronted people with unfamiliar habits and beliefs, and concluded that their European culture was superior. Of course Africans came to the same conclusion about these new arrivals, whom they could see as ignorant and sickly.

In reducing human variation to four categories, Linnaeus created a typology based on common epistemological practice. In a scientific typology, each category consists of an internally coherent set of variables.[4] A well-known scientific typology is the periodic table of chemical elements. The chemical element hydrogen, for example, is distinguished from other chemical elements by its atomic weight, the temperature at which it freezes and boils, its specific gravity, its bonding properties, and other traits. All of these traits differ consistently and predictably from those same traits in helium or in any other chemical element.

Creating typologies in eighteenth-century botany, zoology, or chemistry made scientific sense. Using color as a category to explain human variation less so. A person's "color" will vary with climate and environmental conditions, and thus help explain food and clothing choice and even the belief that there are rain gods who must be worshipped. But to assume that color explained whether a person was gentle, indolent, avaricious, or obstinate had no scientific basis. These traits appear in all race groups; there was no evidence in the eighteenth century, and none today, showing those traits to systematically correlate with skin color or hair texture.

Of course, Linnaeus's classification was not innocent of politics. In moving from plants to people, and with respect to people, from physiology to moral worth, Linnaeus added the authoritative voice of enlightenment science to political doctrines that gave justification to slavery and colonial conquest; later, eugenics and ideologies of racial purity; and eventually apartheid and miscegenation laws, the latter not discarded by Americans until 1967.

I do not single out Linnaeus for special blame. He was one of many natural scientists in the eighteenth century (and many more in the nineteenth century, and, perhaps again even now in the twenty-first century) who proposed a rudimentary human classification scheme that conflated color and culture; he was hardly alone in imposing a rank order that assigned pride of place to his own race. Linnaeus's influence, however, was magnified; in Europe he was the preeminent classification specialist in botany and zoology. Among those influenced was the German medical scientist Johann Blumenbach, who in 1776 published the widely read and tellingly titled *On the Natural Varieties of Mankind*.[5]

Although Blumenbach avoided the moralistic terms embraced by Linnaeus, he offered the first explanation for the presumed superiority of the white race. He attributed racial differences to the influence of climate, diet, and living habits. He then ranked the races, finding that the Caucasian race was favored and the other races, in varying degrees, were degenerate by virtue of less favorable habitat. His scientific reputation helped to establish racial rank ordering as a fundamental principle of eighteenth-century human sciences.[6] Blumenbach's rank ordering is a classic instance of a scientific error leading to a moral wrong. We have yet to escape fully the habits of thought rooted in the flawed assumption that deep cultural traits can be predicted by superficial physiological traits—the shape of a nose, the pigmentation of the skin, the texture of hair.

Blumenbach's racial taxonomy differed from the Linnaean taxonomy in its presentation of five rather than four races, making the Pacific Islanders a race separate from Linnaeus's Asiaticus. Blumenbach's taxonomy, as he labeled and rank-ordered it, was: Caucasian, Mongolian, Malay, American Indian, and Negro (Ethiopian). This taxonomy bequeathed to Western science and culture the all-too-familiar color-denominated racial pentagon: white, yellow, brown, red, and black.[7] We now fast-forward more than two hundred years, from the mid-eighteenth century to the late twentieth century, and from European science to the American census.

The American Government Catches Up

An extraordinary thing happened two hundred years after Blumenbach announced that the world's population should be divided into five race groups distinguished by skin color. The United States government agreed.

There is much to say about the racial classification used in America's official statistics—how it came to be, what its consequences are, where it is going—but here let us briefly consider what happened to America's official statistics in 1997. Updating an earlier directive addressing how race should be tabulated, which (echoing Linnaeus) had listed Asian/

Pacific Islander as a single category,[8] the Office of Management and Budget (OMB) removed the slash and separated the Pacific Islanders from the Asians. This was in anticipation of the 2000 decennial census, which then used the five primary Blumenbachian races. Thus, for its census on the eve of the twenty-first century, the American government applied a racial taxonomy dating to the eighteenth century.[9]

In the government's rationale there is no echo of Blumenbach's climate theory, let alone any hint that one race might be superior to another. But eighteenth-century biological essentialism and its associated racial rank-ordering had become deeply entrenched in America's racialized political order in ways that follow and haunt us into the twenty-first century.

The 2000 census question, which now serves as the basic taxonomy for all federal race statistics and administrative records, inserts Blumenbach's color pentagon into congressional debates, social science, public health research, political campaigning, identity politics, media coverage, marketing strategies, and, of course, law and policy. And also, with consequences too early to comprehend, into modern genetic medicine (see chapter 7).

Here I offer one example of the reach of this classification; many others will follow.

Blumenbach's taxonomy was universal and totally inclusive. Every living person on earth could be assigned to one of its five categories. A consequence of employing a universal classification system in the American census is that *any* new immigrant arriving from *any* corner of the world will be put into this preexisting taxonomy—whether or not he or she seems to fit. Recently arrived Ethiopians, for example, are counted in the census as African Americans, though the former are Nilotic in ways unfamiliar to the African Americans. The politics of numbers that infuse the fractious present-day debate over immigration, as well as election strategies and much else in our political life, is shaped accordingly.[10]

Early science taught that humans, no less than plants and animals, could be scientifically categorized into distinct subsets. It is at once ironic and deeply worrying that a human classification based on a now thoroughly discredited racial essentialism continues to structure how the American population gets counted at the beginning of the twenty-first century. This merits explanation, starting with the role of classification in public life.

The Imperative to Classify

We cannot reason or behave without classification. The earliest humans quickly learned the difference between things they could eat and things that could eat them, and why it made sense to chase the one but run from the other. We need not get deep into cognitive neuroscience to appreciate that classification is as natural and indispensable as breathing. Nor need we get into ontology to make the commonplace observation that reality is comprehended through systems of classification. Whatever may be the status of "reality" outside those systems, it is not available to us.

Categories, without which there are no classifications, are a form of commonsense theory building. These theories tell us what kinds of characteristics go together, and how persons in one category differ from those in another. These theories are more or less coherent, more or less complete, more or less formalized. How carefully or even consciously theories are constructed is not the issue. Even if unconscious or unexamined they work as frameworks for explaining what we encounter in the normal course of living. "These theories provide subjective explanations that structure the social environment and define the partitions the perceiver imposes upon it. They explain what a given group is like, what attributes the group members share, and, more importantly, why they share these attributes."[11]

If science proceeds through classification, so does the state. The state is a boundary-drawing project—creating territorial boundaries, of course, but also demographic boundaries. "Every state must draw lines between kinds of people and types of events when it formulates its criminal and civil laws, levies taxes, allocates benefits, regulates economic transactions, collects statistics, and sets rules for the design of insurance rates and formal selection criteria for jobs, contracts, and university admissions. The categories adopted for these institutional purposes do not float above society in a 'superstructure' of mental life. They are sewn into the fabric of the economy, society, and the state."[12] In the modern nation-state statistical categories are deeply entrenched in policy making. The size and distribution of various demographic groups frame social problems and lead to policy responses: school dropouts, veterans, homeowners, the unemployed, and on and on.

This much is obvious. Not obvious is why race groups have such a prominent place in the human sciences and why they play so centrally in politics and policies. A race or ethnic classification, for example, appears today in about two-thirds of the censuses around the world.[13] Why so frequently? Then again, why only two-thirds? Does this mean that elsewhere there are no such groups to be measured?

Ethnoracial counting is widespread but not universal; it is a choice, and we want to understand what goes into the choosing. France (see the appendix) refuses to count by race or ethnicity in the name of solidarity and national integration. On its independence from British rule,

India dropped the caste-based classification used by its colonial rulers. Today it is having a vigorous argument over reinstating the caste-based classification in its census. In the many national censuses that do count "race," terminological choice is exercised. *Race*, *ethnicity*, *nationality*, *ancestry*, *indigenous people*, and *tribal status* are among the various terms that appear in censuses that measure group membership based on descent. The actual term *race* itself is not common; it is found in only thirteen censuses around the world—eleven of them former slaveholding countries.[14]

The United States has been especially, perhaps uniquely, persistent in its use of a racial classification in its science and its policy making. From the beginning there was a color line. Race appears as a category in colonial censuses and administrative records. The practice continues with the founding of an independent nation. The first national census was taken in 1790. This initial census made distinctions based on civil status. Free and slave provided a count of whites and Africans; the taxed and untaxed distinction separated the American Indians living among the settled white population from those living outside of settled areas and thus not subject to taxes. From this primitive starting point, various racial distinctions and taxonomies came and went over the next twenty-two censuses, but never was there a census without a racial classification. In the 2010 census, the relevant question used the specific term *race* four times, as if to emphasize that the government is really serious in asking, What is *your* race?

Across America's long history of racial counting, there were two core political principles at stake: creating a racial hierarchy and separating outsiders from insiders—that is, the vertical and the horizontal positioning of Americans.[15] We will return often to these two principles and find, somewhat unexpectedly, that even the civil rights revolution in the mid-twentieth century did not lessen the importance of counting by race, though it did certainly reorient its policy purpose. An issue in the twenty-first century is the future of the color line, complicated by the fact that America has also always had a nativity line—one separating the native born from the foreign born. In later chapters we review how these two lines have at times been reinforcing and at other times pulled in separate directions.

Coterminous with the centrality of racial statistics in American politics has been its central place in American social science. We might think of science and politics as analytically separate spheres, but wherever and whenever race is prominent in one of these spheres it is prominent in the other. What gave rise to this seemingly inescapable feature of modern science and politics in America? To understand the origins of racial classification based on skin color, why we count by race in contemporary

America as we do, and what we might do about it, we need background on how race entered our consciousness.

Is Making Racial Distinctions a Hard-Wired Human Practice?

You might think that making racial distinctions starts with human history itself. Not true, in the judgment of historians. Ancient civilizations paid little attention to color. The Egyptians and Nubians, "had for centuries been accustomed to the gradations in skin color among the inhabitants of the Nile Valley and hence saw nothing unusual in their differences."[16] Similarly with Greco-Roman civilization, where color prejudice familiar to us today did not exist: "Greeks and Romans did not establish color as an obstacle to integration in society."[17]

It is not that the classical world made no distinctions among population groups, with, as always, those in charge of classifying assigning themselves to the superior group. The distinctions that mattered focused on customs and religion, which separated the civilized from the barbaric. Whether one was civilized or barbaric was not taken to be inheritable, was not biological, was not essentialist. The Greeks saw themselves as civilized and superior because of their institutions of government—not because of some biological trait labeled "Greekness." In Rome, if barbarians accepted Roman law and learned Latin, they were no longer barbarian but became citizens with full rights.

The ancients knew about slavery. It was, in fact, widespread. But it was independent of race or color; "by far the vast majority of the thousands of slaves [in antiquity] was white, not black."[18] Christians and Muslims enslaved peoples without regard to their color, language, customs, or nativity—with only the restrictions that, theoretically at least, Christians did not enslave other Christians and Muslims did not enslave other Muslims.

This began to change in the late Middle Ages, when religious difference was racialized and used to administer systems of forced group separation. In his compelling book *Racism: A Short History*, George M. Fredrickson situates early racism in the massacres of Jews during the First Crusade in 1096. He writes, "The notion that Jews were collectively and hereditarily responsible for the worst possible human crime—deicide—created a powerful incentive for persecution."[19] Persecution took different forms depending on whether it was believed that Jews could be saved from their false beliefs through conversion to Christianity or were "intrinsically and organically evil."[20] By the thirteenth and fourteenth centuries, folk mythology demonized Jews—putting them "outside the pale of humanity."[21] Demonizing Jews became the foundation for a racialized anti-Semitism that by the latter centuries of the Middle Ages sanctioned systematic discrimination and ghettoization.

If treatment of Jews provides an early instance of religiously sanctioned and state-imposed racial classification, color-coded classification—the form in which we are interested—comes later, with the Atlantic slave trade and European colonization of Asia, Africa, and the Americas. Prior to the slave trade and colonization there is little evidence of color prejudice in Europe. In describing European attitudes in the fourteenth and early fifteenth centuries, Fredrickson writes that, with the exception of the Iberian Muslims' attitudes toward Africans, there is little anticipation of the antiblack racism that was soon to explode.[22]

These cursory paragraphs give emphasis to the fact that a color-coded classification arrived as a conscious political strategy. The Western Christian world needed to justify slavery and colonization, and it did so by describing black Africans not simply as different but as inferior. This, of course, is a long, complicated story that starts with Arab enslavement of Africans centuries earlier. Its European roots date to Portugal's exploration of Africa's west coast, with 1441 generally cited as the year African slaves were first delivered to Portugal.

The North American chapter in the transatlantic slave trade dates almost from the beginning of European colonization of the continent. In 1619, a British pirate ship sailing under a Dutch flag tied up at Jamestown, Virginia, where the captain traded twenty Africans he had captured from a Portuguese slave trader. His bounty was tobacco, already being grown by America's earliest settlers.[23] Devout Christians that they were, the Jamestowners—and the many who followed them in establishing the slave plantation economy in the seventeenth and eighteenth centuries—had to invent a racialized classification system to justify their slave economy. They turned to a biblical passage neatly fashioned to this purpose. No one seriously challenged this justification until the antislavery movement gained political strength in the late eighteenth century.

A Detour: The Biblical Origins of Race and Their Application

At one point in time most Americans of European descent knew the sequence of Genesis by heart. Things have changed, however, and not everyone has read the Bible or heard its stories. Those who have can skip this section. Those who haven't (or at least haven't done so recently) may want to read on, as they may find some twists even for those who think they know the story.

The creation story of man in the image of God takes a turn when the serpent tempts Eve to eat of the tree of knowledge (of good and evil—another example of basic classification). Eve, finding the fruit tasty, shares it with Adam. Banned from the Garden of Eden for this forbidden act, the two multiply (apparently with help from some other people whose origins are murky), but wickedness spreads across the face of the earth. And wickedness—as it often does—gets out of hand.

Contemplating a new start, the God of the Old Testament finds a good man in Noah. Following the successful aquatic adventure in the Ark, Noah's three sons repopulate the earth. According to the text, Shem engenders the Semitic (Asian) people, Japheth the Japhetic (European) people, and Ham the Hamitic (African) people. These descendants of Noah formed the different peoples of the earth who, at first, shared a common language and culture.

The Tower of Babel marks another turning point in the biblical account of human history. A prideful group built a tower, "whose top may reach unto heaven" (Gen. 11: 4). This displeased God: "Let us go down, and there confound their language, that they may not understand one another's speech. So the Lord scattered them abroad from thence upon the face of all the earth" (Gen. 11: 7–8). This scattering explains to the Bible's readers why the earth is inhabited by peoples with different languages and cultures.

How does race get into the biblical picture? It appears in the fateful curse of Canaan, caused by an act of his father, Ham, Noah's youngest son. Ham's mistake was his audacious gaze upon his father's drunken nakedness as he slept. Noah "awoke from his wine, and knew what his younger son had done to him. And he said, 'Cursed be Canaan; a servant of servants shall he be to unto his brethren'" (Gen. 9: 24–25).

It's not clear why Noah's grandson Canaan was cursed for an act of his father, nor why Canaan alone of Ham's children was singled out. However, at a time when virtually everyone of European descent knew the basic biblical narrative, a self-serving (and biblically suspect) interpretation transferred this curse of slavery—a "servant of servants"—from Canaan to the Hamitic people of Africa—the putative descendants of Ham.[24]

It's this specious interpretation that served America's early tobacco growers so well. As the "curse of Canaan" moved from scripture to the political economy of slavery, Christian slave owners found it a handy justification for the Atlantic slave trade. It was continuously deployed by southern slave owners in their nineteenth-century debates with abolitionists.[25] Even the end of slavery did not diminish its political usefulness. It was routinely cited to defend racial segregation; as late as 1964, Senator Robert Byrd of West Virginia famously read it in its entirety into the *Congressional Record* as he filibustered against the Civil Rights Act.[26]

CHAPTER 2

Justifying Policies

Counting by race is a purpose-driven political practice that, in America, has its origins in slavery as conveniently allowed by the Christian Bible. Racial counting, of course, outlived slavery. To understand how and why requires an account of its use more broadly in the context of democratic politics, the focus of the next three chapters. Democracies emphasize rule of law, citizen rights, transparent governing processes, periodic elections, and probationary office holding. Underlying these institutional arrangements is the core democratic principle that power cannot be arbitrary. Laws and policies have to be justified. Democracy is reason-giving. In a democracy—unlike an autocracy—leaders cannot simply say, "Fight this war, pay this tax, obey this law." The norms of democracy oblige its leaders to give reasons for promulgated policies. The design and justification of policies nearly always includes subdividing the population into different groups, for it is only by separating the young from the old, the veteran from the nonveteran, or the employed from the unemployed that a targeted policy can be fashioned.

What preoccupies us in the chapters to follow are the policies and their justifications that required America to give such a prominent role to racial classification—starting in 1787 with a constitutional compromise without which there would have been no union, continuing in the nineteenth century with pro- and antislavery policies that culminated in the Civil War and then underpinned the apartheid Jim Crow policies. These are the policies that gave America its color line. Other policy debates emerged—how to classify and therefore to treat new immigrants and then how to restrict immigration in a manner that would preserve the country for its Anglo and Protestant legacy. These are the policies that gave America its nativity line (see chapter 9 for discussion of the color line and the nativity line). America became a nation at a time when "races" and "aliens" emerged in world history as issues of intense political and scientific interest. This shaped the American experience of nation building, and shaped the social theories available to guide and explain what kind of nation to build.

The mid-twentieth century brought the civil rights era, which posed the political question—should race-sensitive policies be used to undo the legacy of racism? Other policy issues now take shape around multiculturalism, identity politics, diversity, and a color-blind movement. The late-twentieth-century immigration surge returned policy debates to an earlier preoccupation with protecting the unique American racial character by closing borders. As we enter the twenty-first century, the genetic revolution introduces new complications, leading to worries that the country could return to biologically based race distinctions. This march of race-sensitive policies from the nation's founding to the present never answered a key question, as addressed in the next section.

Is Race Real?

Phenotypic variation is real. There is variation in skin color, facial features, hair texture, and other physiological traits. These variations are continuous. Biologists use the term *cline* to describe the tendency of variable traits to grade into one another—a continuum of gradual change rather than sharp, distinct change. The people who live at the source of the Nile River (today's Ethiopians) are noticeably darker than those who live at its end point (today's Egyptians). But along the river, the skin color of one neighbor is hardly distinguishable from another. This is true of other phenotypic traits used to describe races. Nor can we get a tidy division by using combinations of traits. Racially described trait distribution is discordant. Hair texture does not necessarily predict skin tone.

Blumenbach himself wrote that the "[i]nnumerable varieties of mankind run into each other by insensible degrees."[27] His categories were arbitrary abstractions, but his correct view on this did not prevent him from declaring that humankind was divided into five races any more than a much more sophisticated science of phenotypic variation prevents us from doing so today. Blumenbach's arbitrary distinctions took something that is biologically real (phenotypic variation) and made something that is biologically suspect (five races). A folk taxonomy became a biological fact. In the eighteenth century in some parts of the world, the Americas included, this biological fact became a political fact.

Under what conditions does *race* become a politically or economically useful principle of classification? Although the conditions have varied across American history, there has never been a moment when a race classification was not thought useful. Conservative political forces used racial classification in the nineteenth century and early decades of the twentieth; progressive political forces appropriated it to their purposes in the second half of the twentieth century. For whom today does a race classification matter? This question we ponder in the final chapters.

Statistical Races

This book, then, is about a very particular way of thinking about race. It is a way of thinking made available only because the American government has created a constitutionally derived racial classification system. Americans, because of their putative membership in various race groups, are treated differently in political, economic, and social policies.

For the policy maker, groups become real when they are counted; and, they are counted only if initially identified as units in a classification scheme.

To put this in the bluntest terms, there is no such thing as a "race" without a classification scheme with more than one race category. If there is only one race—the human race—there is no classification, and there is no way to govern different races differently. With classification comes enumeration, more or less formalized and more or less precise. Those issues will interest us later, but here the point is more basic: a profoundly important way to understand race is to examine the purposes and practices that create statistical races.

The study of race, therefore, "should be directed at the *principles* which render groups intelligible. It should be directed at the *practices* through which groups are 'racialized' (or framed, if you will, in 'racial' terms). And it should be directed at the *processes* by which, in a variety of different contexts, groups are made, unmade, stratified, or divided."[28] It is the study of these principles, practices, and processes that allows us to see historic patterns of racial discrimination and exclusion and then to understand the effort to compensate for that history with antidiscrimination and inclusiveness policies. And it allows us to ask what principles, practices, and processes associated with racial classification are likely to—or should—fashion policies in the twenty-first century.

When framed in this manner, it is clear that there is more to America's race history than the nineteenth-century assertion that "race is biology," or the effort to displace this assumption in the twentieth century with the assertion that "race is a social construct" or the contemporary claim that "race is an identity choice." Statistical races persisted across America's history, and in law and policy trump biology, social construction, or identity politics. A government that asks, "What is your race?" in order to know how many belong to what race constructs statistical races. There are two principal venues in which this occurs—in the courts,[29] and in government record keeping and census taking.[30]

I have not yet acknowledged the problematic nature of taxonomies in general and racial taxonomies in particular. There is nothing straightforward about racial counting. It is plagued by fuzzy boundaries, inconsistent definitions, causality (did the American census "create" Hispanics?), hybridity, self-assignment versus assignment by census takers, and confused terminology—*race*, *ethnicity*, *national origin*, *descent community*. I will postpone discussion of these problems until the end of the book. The next four chapters treat racial statistics as if they did what their designers intended—accurately represent members of America's races. Because my topic is the application of racial statistics in broad policy making and not whether they meet reasonable standards of measurement reliability and validity, this suspension of methodological skepticism is not fatal to our historical overview. It does matter when recommending how to improve statistics, as we see in chapters 10 and 11.

The historical overview is necessary to my concluding recommendations. The statistical races that emerged from the most recent decennial census in 2010 were not fresh products. They came out of a deep political history. Categories accumulate: "We neither ordinarily think about nor act upon the categories of social life: we act and think within them. At any given time, the legal and other official categories are like geological deposits, with layers of varying age, bearing traces from their period of formation."[31] But unlike geological deposits, statistical classifications are subject to political forces and social mobilization, a process that unfolds within "the system for adjudicating conflicting claims, its rules, presuppositions and organizational form."[32] My treatment will reveal both historical precedent and the play of ongoing politics in how America's population is racially classified.

The historical overview is derivative, wholly dependent on the work of other scholars. No new research is offered. If my treatment of familiar material has any claim to originality, it is perhaps in the insistence that statistical races are a unique lens for examining a large number of issues at the intersection of race and public policies, as well as underpinning the science that reveals deep patterns in the racial conditions made either better or worse by those policies.

Postscript

As will become evident, I am guilty of what Herbert Butterfield famously critiqued in *The Whig Interpretation of History*—viewing the past as a progressive process leading to Western democracies: "The study of the past with one eye, so to speak, upon the present is the source of all sins and sophistries in history. . . ."[33] The "pathetic fallacy" of the historian, he observes, is found in abstracting from the historical context those snippets on which to base judgments about the present. My sin is perhaps even greater, because I practice history without a license. Writing as a political scientist, I have imposed a tidy sequence from the nation's first census in 1790 to its most recent in 2010, making stops that suit my several theses—the links between statistical races and public policies, earlier mechanical counting leading to the measurement of group traits as the basis for policy; an early marriage of census taking with social science steadily lending authority to both partners; earlier policy coherence based on a generally accepted racial taxonomy giving way to today's policy confusions, which in turn are used to justify my recommendations.

I admit to the sin Butterfield describes. The book is not written to tell American historians something they don't already know. It is written to tell today's policy makers how we got into the current mess, and what we should do to escape it.

PART II

Policy, Statistics, and Science Join Forces

CHAPTER 3

THE COMPROMISE THAT MADE THE REPUBLIC AND THE NATION'S FIRST STATISTICAL RACE

THE NUMBER OF BLACK SLAVES COUNTED IN THE 1790 CENSUS DETERMINED the outcome of the nation's first contested presidential election and the congressional balance of power between the North and the South, with great consequences for how the country was governed across its first half century. The infamous three-fifths constitutional clause produced a statistical race without which the Union might never have been established.

In recounting this early moment in America's history I stretch the term *statistical race* to apply it to enslaved people enumerated not as full persons but as three-fifths. This momentous statistical policy set the stage for a parade of statistical races that reach to the present. The policy did so

- by requiring the census count of a specific group, America's enslaved population, and using the statistical result to shape the balance of power between free and slave states; and,
- doing this with little reflection on the deeper implications of making "race" a feature of government; and in this,
- serving as a bridge between eighteenth-century natural science and nineteenth-century race science as elaborated in American political life.

The three-fifths clause was the new nation's initial step in connecting race, policy, and science into one interdependent bundle.

Why a Census so Early in the New Republic?

The three-fifths clause is bound up in a larger question: Why did the newly formed government make the census one of its very first tasks? Would not a new nation have many higher priorities—establishing a functioning administration, electing a Congress, creating a taxation system to raise public funds, appointing diplomats and federal marshals, coining money, securing borders, deciding on citizenship criteria, and other such pressing nation-building tasks? The census, nevertheless, was one of the earliest uses of federal power in the nation's history. This bears explaining.

Census taking was familiar. In colonial times, reasoning that no one can manage the unmeasured, the British Crown routinely took local population and economic censuses in its colonies. It sent instructions to collect "minute information" on the number of slaves on sugar plantations, the better to ensure that "a proper balance should obtain between the free and unfree." These "periodic reports on numbers of masters and slaves, or barrels of sugar, or militia and arms" allowed these quantities to be adjusted "if they were found to deviate from some ideal conception of how things ought to be."[1]

In these instructions we see a fresh idea associated with statecraft: measure the population in order to ensure that its size and composition match policy objectives. This was nothing short of radical in its implications, but it could hardly have arrived on the scene had not a brilliant new star illuminated seventeenth- and eighteenth-century science: statistics. Today most people's eyes glaze over whenever statistics is mentioned, but our nation's founders didn't see this as dry science. Manipulation of quantities was exciting and it was useful for governing. Along with territorial mapping and boundary setting, regular compiling and analyzing of statistics became a defining characteristic of the modern nation-state.

America was the first nation to conduct a census on a fixed ten-year schedule. It was the statistical centerpiece of what the political sociologist Aristide Zolberg eloquently labels "designing a nation" by trying to influence the size, distribution, and characteristics of that nation's population.[2] Only with this basic idea firmly in mind can we see why, when, and how statistical races first entered America's population policy.

Foreshadowing Independence: The Right to Leave

Britain's colonial empire had a population policy. Its American colonies were, in part, a place to dispose of its vagrants, religious dissidents, and criminals. From the early seventeenth century on, criminal emigrants were relocated from England, Scotland, and Wales to the American colonies. It was lucrative business. The British government sold convicts to middlemen, who profited by reselling them as cheap labor to overseas employers.[3] In addition to profit, this policy shaped Britain's population in a desirable way: get rid of convicts and the poor but keep the law-abiding and the productive. This will sound familiar to readers who today follow immigration debates.

Of course, in colonial times what served the interests of Great Britain did not serve its American colonies. Though many an eventually prominent family had a horse thief or similar undesirable in their past, Americans resented having the criminal and the poor foisted upon them. They wanted the law-abiding and productive workers, as we do today.

Disputes over population policy played out against a much larger issue. From Britain's perspective, the colonies were essentially a revenue source and not much more. Pre-independence Americans did not see the colonies that way at all. They had their eye on an ambitious civic project, nothing less than creating a new kind of government. These conflicting perspectives led to different judgments about population composition. If colonies were primarily a British economic project, their population composition was of consequence only in terms of economic policy. But if to people living on this side of the Atlantic, the colonies were political "communities in the making" perhaps to become "a single political entity,"[4] a heterogeneous population, larded with too many troublesome characters, was worrisome, especially so to visionaries beginning to imagine America as independent from the mother country.

The convict issue faded in the 1770s, when the Australian coast became an alternative dumping ground for Britain's criminals. The political question remained: What principles and practices should guide population policy in colonial America? Americans wanted rapid population growth based on the "right kind" of immigrants—those who could farm, mine, and timber the vast, largely unpopulated territories that spread westward. Securing these lands involved military capacity as well. The indigenous Indians resisted expansion into their hunting and fishing grounds. Furthermore, the French and Spanish were determined to control the waterways that were indispensible for trade, such as the lucrative fur industry. This threat needed tending to. Given these challenges, the colonies needed a growing population of fighters, farmers, explorers, and tradesmen. And these new Americans should, of course, be loyal to the great civic project of building this new country.

Natural fertility was the preferred way to population growth, and though strikingly high in the eighteenth century it was not supplying the numbers needed. Happily, however, at least as seen from the colonies, there was a ready supply of people eager to migrate to America—not the criminals Britain wanted to export but talented and adventuresome subjects who wanted to depart the British Isles for opportunities in a promised land. This introduced a radical idea, one that again pits interests of the American colonies against those of the British Crown. Immigration policy, argued colonial leaders, should be decided by the receiving, not the sending, country.

Benjamin Franklin, in the inimitable style that would serve him and the new nation so well, fixed upon a flowery syllogism: "God has given to the Beasts of the Forest and to the Birds of the Air a Right when their Subsistence fails in one Country, to migrate into another, where they can get a more comfortable living." Franklin then made the grand leap: "shall Man be denyed a Privilege enjoyed by Brutes, merely to gratify a few avaricious Landlords?"[5] This was indeed a consequential leap; treating the "right to leave" as a natural right. Franklin upped the political stakes: people born under the British Crown did not thereby owe the king a lifetime allegiance. President Reagan had this in mind when at Berlin's Brandenburg Gate he famously challenged the leader of the communist USSR to "Tear down this wall," a massive stretch of concrete then enclosing West Berlin. There was a right to leave an oppressive state.

This principle was invoked by Thomas Jefferson in *A Summary View of the Rights of British America* (1774), a document that served as a trial run for Jefferson's Declaration of Independence. Allegiance is a matter of consent, he argued. This lofty philosophical point became very practical in an early draft of the declaration. Among his litany of grievances against the crown, Jefferson accused the imperial King George of suppressing the population growth that Americans considered essential: the king "has endeavored to prevent the Population of these States; for that purpose obstructing the Laws for Naturalization of Foreigners; refusing to pass others to encourage their migration hither. . . ."[6]

Although a fuller assertion of the right to leave as a justification for rebellion did not appear in the Declaration of Independence, Jefferson continued to expound it as American political doctrine. It contributed to the spirit of revolution fostering the War for Independence,[7] and later to permissive immigration policy. The desire of the English—but also the Dutch, the Germans, and other northern Europeans—to migrate to America gave the revolutionary leaders confidence that an independent America would be strong militarily and economically. Those agitating for independence "used demographic data to show that the infant United States had a large and growing population and could withstand war with England for many years." In contrast, Britain at the time was experiencing population decline.[8]

Indeed, as the War for Independence got underway, statistics served more than propaganda purposes. During the war years America's leaders made repeated population estimates through which to assess war readiness and capacity to fight, including numbers of potential soldiers and available resources that could be taxed.[9] After independence was realized, John Adams continued to cite population size as a warning to European powers that they not underestimate America and be tempted to imagine that they could ever again rule it: "The Americans are, at this day, a great people, and are not to be trifled with. Their numbers have increased fifty percent since 1774. A people that can multiply at this rate, amidst all the calamities of such a war of eight years, will in twenty years more, be too respectable to want [i.e., lack] friends."[10] Meanwhile, Jefferson, serving as ambassador to France, promoted the argument that the new nation's growth made it an expanding market for French goods: "For every article of the productions and manufacturers of [France] then, which can be introduced into the habit there [in the United States], the demand will double every twenty or twenty-five years."[11]

Population growth was integral to how America envisioned itself. Echoing Jean-Jacques Rousseau, Jefferson observed that the most certain sign of the prosperity of a political association and its members "is the number and increase of population."[12] Jefferson boasted that Virginia was doubling its population every twenty-seven years; Franklin made similar claims for Pennsylvania, and Jeremy Belknap for New Hampshire.

Population growth was to be expected given the unique attractions of the New World. Anticipating the claims that enticed Europeans in the nineteenth century, and perhaps sounding a bit like a salesman, Franklin attributed population growth to the "salubrity of the air, the healthiness of the Climate, the Plenty of good provisions, the Encouragement of early Marriages by the certainty of Subsistence in cultivating the Earth."[13]

Jefferson had his theory of high fertility rates, claiming that men multiply not to become happy but because they *are* happy, and that a flourishing population was "a product of and a tribute to the blessings which America enjoyed—blessings not only of Nature, but of government, economy, and society."[14] For Jefferson, it was all of a piece. The nation was good because it multiplied; it multiplied because it was good.

When the 1790 census counted a population just shy of four million, President George Washington was disappointed. He had hoped for a number closer to that of England's eight million. Washington attributed the lower count to uncooperative citizens and indifferent census takers. The "authenticated number", he asserted, would be far greater "than has ever been allowed in Europe, and will have no small influence in enabling them to form a more just opinion of our present growing importance. . . ."[15] Secretary of State Jefferson did his part by circulating edited census reports to America's diplomats, indicating in red ink his own population estimates, higher than those officially reported.

The Blessings of America—Selectively Enjoyed

We now turn to the dark underside of early population policies.[16] In the consensus that population size and composition should be controlled in service to economic and civic goals, nations want to keep and attract the "right kind of people" but to keep out or deport the "wrong kind of people."

This distinction has time and again been difficult to implement. Labor needed for economic growth does not always produce what prevailing political thought takes to be the "right kind of people." For America's civic life, put bluntly—Negro slaves, Chinese coolies, Mexican guest workers or today's undocumented have been good for the fields and factories but not, presumably, for citizenship.

America's indigenous population, resident for thousands of years before Columbus made landfall in 1492, posed the issue in one way, the enslaved Africans in another. The "Indian question," as it was known, was framed by Jefferson in 1803: the Indian would either incorporate peacefully or be forcibly removed west of the Mississippi River. Incorporation, he wrote, "is certainly the termination of their history most happy for themselves." They would be allowed to become Americans! But if they refused this generous offer, wrote Jefferson, "our strength and their weakness is now so visible that they must see we have only to shut our hand to crush them."[17] The American cavalry did, in due course, shut its hand and crush them, though the Indian Wars lasted for decades. The great Apache warrior Geronimo surrendered in 1886, and four years later the Massacre at Wounded Knee effectively ended the Indian Wars.

Jefferson did not argue for forcible relocation of the Indians on racist grounds. He celebrated the culture, intelligence, and spirit of Indians, describing them as a noble race faced with an unhappy fate. His romantic respect for the "noble savage" notwithstanding, Jefferson was no early multiculturalist.

If the red race could be assimilated, the black race could not: Jefferson wrote in his *Autobiography* that "nothing is more certainly written in the book of fate than that these [slaves] are to be free." This sounds promising until it comes out that he was just as certain that "the two races, equally free, cannot live in the same government. Nature, habit, opinion has drawn indelible lines of distinction between them."[18] It would be necessary to create "an asylum to which we can, by degrees, send the whole of that [African] population from among us, and establish them under our patronage and protection, as a separate, free and independent people, in some country and climate friendly to human life and happiness."[19] That asylum could not be the American West, for Jefferson had marked the West as the frontier where free white men and women would nourish republican values. Jefferson's opposition to relocating even freed blacks to the West rested on his belief that the African was simply not fit for the American experiment in self-government.[20]

Jefferson certainly grasped that the nation he imagined required population growth and territorial expansion. The territory, he expected, would be added to peacefully through treaty and purchase, and would eventually spread to the Pacific coast. Free and equal states would join the Union as quickly as population numbers dictated. Despite both population and territorial expansion, the new nation would avoid fragmentation because its people would have a common language, a shared love of liberty and republican principles. The westerly expansion Jefferson anticipated did come to pass, as did a common language (even though waves of immigration threatened that particular unity at different times), but it came about through a mixture of nationalities unprecedented in world history. We will get to that story below.

This brief treatment of colonial America and the early independence period introduces ways of thinking about statistical races. Nation building is necessarily an exercise in controlling who belongs to the nation, an issue that time and again tested America's political ingenuity. Belonging came to be parsed differently from one group to the next—for some implying citizenship and full civic involvement; for others, the right to sell their labor but not much else; for yet others, not even that. Many of the boundaries separating one type of belonging from another were racially constructed. Counting by race was there from the beginning.

The 1790 census is one of a series of examples we consider, each shedding additional light on how statistical races came to be intricately connected to public policy. But let us first review the extraordinary experiment of establishing a polity based on democratic representation, with particular attention to the role of the census.

The Census: Indispensable to Representative Democracy

The year 1790 brought something entirely new to census taking. Although the ancient purposes of a census—creating a system of taxation and assessing military preparedness—were among the reasons for America's census. The census of 1790 was different from all previous censuses in history because it was embedded in the unprecedented idea that citizens would select their own leaders. This familiar story merits brief review.

The framers faced two challenges unique to a representative republic at the edge of a vast, sparsely populated continent—federalism, or how to assemble a unitary government while granting substantial autonomy to its parts; and imperialism, or how to avoid the dangers an empire posed to democracy.

The Americans of the Revolutionary generation, Henry Steele Commager explains, "took the idea of federalism, which had never worked successfully, solved its most complex problem of the distribution of powers, and its most importunate problem of sanctions, and created the first successful and enduring federal government."[21]

Federalism was facilitated by separating law-making powers between two legislative houses, with the Senate based on equal representation for each state and seats in the House of Representatives allocated in proportion to population size. Without this compromise (one of many) there would have been no Union, no Republic. What was needed, of course, was a way to determine the size of the population for each of the thirteen new states so that seats in the House could be apportioned depending on their respective share of the nation's population—and the solution was the initial census of 1790, mandated by the U.S. Constitution.

Article I, Section 2 of the Constitution states that seats in the new House of Representatives "[s]hall be apportioned among the several states which may be included within this Union, according to their respective Numbers. . . ." The counting would begin three years after the first Congress met, and thereafter, every ten years.

Why require American census every ten years, the first regular decadal census in world history? It could solve the problem of imperialism, which had undermined efforts to establish a government founded on the consent of the governed since the days of the Greek city-states. The framers of the Constitution were familiar with political theories holding that a republic could not coexist with imperialism. A nation that treated some of its subjects as noncitizens contradicted the basic premise of a republic. Unrepresented Indians and African slaves, colonized groups within the state, were incompatible with the idea of a republic, as the framers well understood. They effectively sidestepped that issue, putting its resolution off for more than a half century.

Imperialism was not taken to be an issue of black slavery or of the American Indians. It was something more difficult: Would the western territories enter the Union as independent states or as colonies subject to the control of a central government? The settlers moving into the vast, rich, and sparsely settled lands beyond the Allegheny mountain range were demographically like those living along the East Coast. The vision of a nation stretching to the Pacific posed a division-of-spoils issue even as it presented a nation-building opportunity.

During the debates at the constitutional convention, New Jersey's Gouverneur Morris pushed for annexing western territories as colonies, suggesting that "the rule of representation ought to be so fixed as to secure to the Atlantic States a prevalence in the National Councils."[22] Those along the Atlantic coast could reap riches by exploiting the mineral, timber, and agricultural resources of the areas not yet granted statehood. Morris did not prevail.

Jefferson was in Paris and not Philadelphia that hot summer of 1787, when the founders sweated—literally and figuratively—drafting the Constitution. But Jefferson's view prevailed: he had earlier argued the dangers of an empire, believing that it would lead to a strong central government ruling its empire by force of arms and keeping its constituent units weak. It was the tyrannical British imperial system that motivated Jefferson's Declaration of Independence. Why replicate it in America? The imperial danger would be avoided if the new states were all republican, "independent of each other and the world yet bound together in perfectly harmonious and consensual union."[23] To put this in today's terms, Jefferson defended state's rights against a central government, and the nonimperialistic response to territorial expansion was the gradual addition of separate new states, each with the same powers as the original thirteen.

If "the Old World imagined the Enlightenment and the New World realized it,"[24] the political procedure behind it was a simple census. It blended theory and practice: the idea of an expanding federal republic composed of republican states and the institutional means of realizing these aims. Measuring population growth and its westward movement regulated the pace at which territories became new states.

"Just as the regular and periodic elections would provide smooth mechanisms for adjusting the shifting political power within the nation, so too would the periodic census and reapportionments adjust the power and burdens among the people."[25] This reference to "burdens" is another dimension of early census taking. Having no experience with a national, periodic census, and yet making it so central to the success of the republican experiment, the founders were anxious about whether it would work. The Republic could falter if the census was not judged to have produced accurate population counts for each state.

Accuracy faces two challenges. If the census conferred benefits, such as seats in the new Congress, every state would push for the highest number, by whatever device might work. If instead it conferred burdens, the lower the number the better. What better way to assure an accurate census than to balance benefits with burdens? In the new Constitution, the founders tied taxation to population counts. Large states would carry a heavier burden of the taxes needed to pay off the war debt and to create the necessary government programs, from diplomacy to standardized weights and measures needed for commerce. By linking census counts to the benefits of congressional power and the burdens of taxation the census became immune to the temptation to inflate or deflate the state-by-state counts.

With representation and taxes linked to the proportionate size of each new state, another issue emerged. Was is just the population size of a state that mattered, or was it also its wealth? An early attempt in the preindependence period to tax the wealth of a state, using land as the indicator of wealth, had failed. There was no satisfactory way to calculate the respective value of improved versus unimproved land, of fertile soil versus barren areas. As a substitute, the idea of counting slaves as wealth was broached. Though never implemented under the Articles of Confederation, it found its way into the constitution as the three-fifths clause. The constitutional passage establishing the census declares that the count "shall be determined by adding to the whole Number of free Persons, including those bound to Service for a Term of Years, and excluding Indians not taxed, three-fifths of all other Persons." Translated, this census clause included free persons and indentured servants as part of the free persons count (whites all), limited the count of Native Indians to those living in the settled regions along the Atlantic Coast who could be taxed (the second race), and then "all other Persons"—that is, black slaves, but at only three-fifths their actual numbers.

With this the Constitution guaranteed that population growth *of each race* was equally important to the population growth of each state.[26] The now infamous three-fifths clause had enormous policy and political consequences. Those who demanded and those who detested the clause were clear that "all other Persons" included the slave population in the count. As Madison observed, the "Constitution therefore, decides with great propriety on the case of our slaves, when it views them in the mixt character of persons and property. This is in fact their true character."[27]

Policy Making in the Shadow of the Three-fifths Clause

Northern interests initially resisted the three-fifths clause, arguing that it would include slaves in apportionment of congressional seats even though they were excluded from the nation's political life. But the northern states reluctantly agreed, in a great victory for slaveholding states, because the Union itself was a stake. A North Carolina delegate to the constitutional convention, William Davie, "was sure that North Carolina would never confederate on any terms that did not rate [slaves] at least as three-fifths. If the [northern] states meant therefore to exclude them altogether, the business [of union] was at end."[28] As Alexander Hamilton observed, "Without this indulgence, no union could possibly have been formed," and his cosigner of the Constitution, Gouverneur Morris, agreed, asserting, "The states in which slavery is prohibited ultimately, though with reluctance, acquiesced in the disproportionate number of representatives and electors that was secured to the slaveholding states. The concession was, at the time, believed to be a great one, and has proved to have been the greatest which was made to secure the adoption of the Constitution."[29]

Jefferson came to be called a "Negro president" by his Federalist opponents when they pointed out that his political career rested on the arithmetic of power that was the purpose and consequence of the three-fifths clause. The arithmetic is simple enough. For purposes of apportioning power, a Massachusetts farmer was counted as one, a Virginian farmer with 100 slaves was counted as 61 (himself, plus 100 slaves multiplied by .6). This arithmetic gave to the slaveholding states one-third more congressional places than warranted by the size of their free population—47 seats in Congress instead of 33 after the 1790 census. The slave bonus was not a one-time event. After the 1810 census, slaveholding states had 76 instead of 59 seats, and after the 1830 census, 98 instead of 73.[30]

Additional seats in the Congress translated into additional votes in the Electoral College. These bonus electoral votes were the margin of victory in Jefferson's election to the presidency, and the bonus would favor southern slaveholder presidential candidates for decades to come. Three Virginians—Thomas Jefferson, James Madison, and James Monroe—controlled the presidency from 1801 to 1825, and with few interruptions were followed by slave-owning presidents. All told, for fifty out of the sixty-two years from the presidency of George Washington to 1850, the White House was home to slave owners.

Similar dominance occurred in the other two branches of government. The powerful and longest-serving Speakers of the House were slaveholders. Eighteen of the thirty-one Supreme Court justices were slaveholders. The party patronage system that controlled appointments to federal offices, including federal judgeships, tilted toward southern leadership: distorting the North's representation in party leadership and making it far too small in proportion to its larger free population. "From the inauguration of Washington until the Civil War, the South was in the saddle of national politics."[31] A consequence was a great number of policy victories protecting slavery in the South and extending its reach into the new western territories.

There was strong opposition to policies that protected and extended slavery, and Federalists tried many times to undo the three-fifths clause. Massachusetts senator Timothy Pickering, the most consistent and vocal critic of the three-fifths clause, noted, "The inequality of representation which existed when the Constitution was formed has increased and is increasing by the gradual or entire abolition of slavery in one portion of the Union and by the importation and natural multiplication of slaves in the other."[32]

Various political maneuvers to undo the clause were tried, but none succeeded. A proposed constitutional amendment in 1803 reasoned that the balance necessitated by conditions in 1787, though relevant to forming the Union, was not relevant to how it should continue to govern itself. The amendment went nowhere, nor did later argument that the three-fifths clause should not be applied in new states because it was "tailored *only* to the specific balance of the thirteen original states."[33]

The Three-fifths Clause in Broader Perspective

It is likely that the census would have counted the slaves even in the absence of the three-fifths clause, if not in 1790 then certainly in the censuses that soon followed, as statistics grew important to governing. Even in 1790, James Madison—responsible for this inaugural census—ushered through the Congress census questions that went beyond a basic population count. The questions separated by gender, and within the male gender, by age. This ensured a separate count of the group that most mattered to the new government: adult white males—that is, those who voted, paid taxes, owned property, and, if needed, could defend the country militarily.

Madison, in fact, wanted a more expansive census. He urged an occupational classification of farmers, manufacturers, and tradesmen. In support he offered the commonsense rationale that "to accommodate our laws to the real situation of our constituents, we ought to be acquainted with that situation."[34] When the Senate rejected the proposal, Madison wrote to Jefferson that it had been dismissed as "materials for idle people to make a book."[35]

Jefferson shared Madison's interest. In 1800, when as secretary of state he supervised the census, he submitted a proposal to collect "useful knowledge" beyond the bare minimum needed for congressional apportionment. He recommended a nine-part occupational classification, a more detailed set of age categories, and a question on immigration.[36] Jefferson fared no better than Madison, and the 1800 census largely replicated that of 1790 in its sharply limited focus.

It is telling to compare the ease with which a racial classification was included in the earliest census and an occupational classification was rejected; the latter, Congress concluded, would do political mischief. Congress's counterargument was a profound insight into the power of the measurement system. Classification is arbitrary. It creates differences where there would otherwise be fuzzy boundaries and overlapping groups. After all, argued the opponents of an occupational classification, the American who farmed but also manufactured and sold nails on the side could not be assigned to only one of the occupation groups. He was a farmer, manufacturer, and tradesman. The whole exercise was artificial.

This artificiality, opponents maintained, would erroneously signal that society was made up of separate interests. Measuring the relative size of different economic interests "conflicted with the traditional principle of a common good that embraced the entire community. The object of wise governmental policy was to foster the happiness of society as a harmonious whole," a view "that arose from eighteenth-century ideas of an organic society."[37]

Because Congress so clearly grasped the political implications of sorting the population into different economic groups, its unhesitating use of a racial taxonomy is all the more telling. Members of Congress were educated in the natural science of race summarized in chapter 2, with its small number of distinctive races. A Congress that recognized blurred boundaries across occupational groups refused to see that blurred boundaries might be true of racial groups.

Counting by race but not by occupation was building on the eighteenth-century lessons taught by Linnaeus and Blumenbach. The earliest assessments of how rapidly the new American population was growing generated statistical tables *by race*, initiating a practice that still persists in the way government statistics are presented, dividing the public into different racial groups.

The nation's first census, one of the largest, most visible, and significant undertakings of a brand new government, told its people that it was necessary to pay attention to the size of its enslaved black population. Racial discourse would have existed in 1790 even if no census had been taken, but in meaningful ways the census structured that discourse. A few censuses later, this first step toward a "statistical race" became a much more elaborate statistical edifice, distinguishing slaves from free blacks, and both, of course, from whites. By the fourth census (1820), the black population, free or enslaved, was also classified by age and gender. This more fully measured statistical race became increasingly important in the nation's heated debate over slavery, as we will see in chapter 4.

Conclusion

The census was necessary to apportion political representation—and for a brief period taxation—proportionate to population size across the new states. Particular features of the census could be debated, but taking a census itself could not. From the beginning, however, the census-based apportionment was caught up in the strife that dominated national politics until the Civil War resolved the issue of slavery. A census that counted slaves at .6 of a person was an early lesson that a racialized statistical system could be a policy tool.

The lesson was well-learned. From the 1790s to the 1990s no political constituency seriously questioned the fact that America would sort its population into a small number of discrete, seemingly fixed races as articulated by the natural sciences. For two centuries the resulting statistical races were deployed on behalf of countless policy initiatives, large and small. The next three chapters review three especially significant instances, each furthered by new scientific tools and each addressing a policy issue central to America's political history. Looking back at this history prepares us for a remarkable development in our own time—the emergence of a political movement intent on dismantling the edifice of statistical races altogether. Whether this will happen, and whether it should happen, occupy us in the final section of the book. First, however, we need a clearer understanding of why America has time and again taken for granted that policy requires a scientifically validated count of the relative size of its racial groups.

CHAPTER 4

RACE SCIENCE CAPTURES THE PRIZE, THE U.S. CENSUS

THE RELATIVE SIZE OF DIFFERENT RACE GROUPS MATTERED IN THE FOUNDING of the Republic, so too the way size was measured. A census that separately counts the enslaved as if they were only three-fifths of a person, bizarre as that sounds today, determined who had political power and how they used it. This set the stage for even more bizarre treatments of race statistics in the nineteenth century. Census taking matured because census results were used in designing public policy.

The way the government gathered race data, the methods used to interpret them, and the influence the science of the nineteenth century had upon that process is the topic now at hand. A new form of race science emerged, one that carried eighteenth-century natural science features forward to the twentieth-century social sciences. We will see that this new race science wormed its way into census taking and from there into government policies, again serving as bridge between statistically primitive eighteenth-century governing and statistically saturated twenty-first-century governing. Citizens inside and outside government in the eighteenth century championed changes that affected statistical use and nudged it toward professionalism. Growing professionalism, however, did not include letting go of race as a feature the census could measure. To the contrary, it embedded racial counting ever deeper into the process of governing. Some of those who shaped the discourse in this period and, consequently, in its later iterations as well are Adam Seybert, a former congressman with a statistical bent; Samuel George Morton, who measured skulls; and Josiah Nott, an Atlanta physician. However forgotten they may be today, each wrought changes in the straightforward process of census-taking. Each influenced the development of the census as a professional undertaking that steadily piled up racial distinctions.

Early in the nineteenth century, political and intellectual leaders "began to talk about perfecting a 'science of statistics,' in which unimpeachable data would reveal the laws of political action."[1] State governments issued gazetteers. The common citizen developed an appetite for almanacs. The teaching of arithmetic grew apace. Arithmetic "not only improved the logical faculties of the mind and prepared young boys for commerce; it also opened the doors to useful political knowledge in the form of statistics."[2] Even popular board games helped. One taught players how to garner electoral votes by answering quantitative questions about population and commerce. "The object of the game was to win the presidency; the lesson of the game was that statistical knowledge leads to political power."[3]

An enthusiastic believer in the science of statistics was an ex-congressman from Pennsylvania, Adam Seybert. To persuade his fellow legislators to become more statistically literate he published *Statistical Annals* (1818), a compendium of statistics about the growing nation. In a formulation that anticipated the social indictor movement of the late twentieth century, Seybert noted that statistical trends offer proofs of the quality of government, writing, "The state of civilized society and the resources of nations are the tests by which we can ascertain the tendency of the government. It is to the condition of the people, in relation to their increase, their moral and physical circumstances, their happiness and comfort, their genius and industry, that we must look for proofs of a mild and free, or a cruel and despotic government."[4] Congress bought 500 copies of Seybert's eight-hundred-page treasure trove of data. Whether or not the Congress paid close attention to its former colleague, Seybert certainly set an example of thoroughness, broad scope, and a taste for statistical data that would find its way into census policy in his century.

Many lawmakers and other influential people bolstered their political positions with newly developed statistical data as the century moved along. Of course, no one needed statistics to convince American political leadership that whites were superior to black people. Laws and policies based on that conviction stretched back to colonial times. Nonetheless, professionals and politicians often request statistical research that can support their preconceptions, and it's the use of those data that concerns us here.

Today Americans take for granted large-scale empirical investigations of society that use the methods and theories of the social sciences. These draw heavily upon data provided by the Census Bureau and federal statistical programs in health, education, employment, and other sectors of the society and economy. More than descriptive, these investigations offer causal explanations for why behaviors and characteristics vary from one race or ethnic group to another and similarly vary by age, gender, occupation, and region. Law-makers move from explanations of group variation to policies to intervene and shape consequences. Today, beyond the government's own efforts, there are thousands of think tanks, advocacy organizations, for-profit consultant firms, corporations, university centers, and private foundations that carry the social science research forward. Working together, government agencies and these nongovernmental groups labor on behalf of evidence-based policy.

Although *evidence-based policy* is a recently coined term, something resembling it took shape in the early nineteenth century as race science. It has had a long, strong march through American political thinking and policy. Anxieties over the presumed superiority of one race over another and the question of what to do about it remained open, especially in political argument about the dangers lurking if slavery were abolished. The supposed catastrophes certain to follow if slaves were freed first brought statistically argued causal theories to the fore. They provided fodder for successful policy argumentation. As we note below, a particular hypothesis advanced by proslavery interests was logically flawed, and the data marshaled were seriously misused, but this did not prevent the "evidence" being argued on the floor of Congress—not the last time statistics have been misused there.

Specious or not, this kind of argumentation only occured once leaders realized that the census could measure how one group differed from another and that these measures could be used for policy purposes. This important step beyond the eighteenth century's simple quantification of group size put something new into the political mix. The three-fifths clause required only counting slaves. It made no demands on assessing slave characteristics or behaviors. Nineteenth-century policy interests, however, required something beyond mere mechanical counting. Policy makers went in search of statistically argued causal hypotheses about how groups differed in their traits or behaviors. Not surprising, race groups were at the center of this critical step in policy making. Statistical races were elaborated from raw counts to clusters of traits that differed from one race to another in ways that invited policy attention. To understand how this happened requires reaching back to the question sidestepped by the founding fathers—what to do about slavery.

The Political Voice of Early Statistics

It's no surprise that slaveholders turned to the growing science of race in search of fresh arguments to prop up their case. By 1830 the slaveholding states needed a convincing explanation for why it would be dangerous to free slaves, and were nervously watching the uneven rate of population growth between their own and the free states. Notwithstanding the bonus awarded by the three-fifths clause, the South's hold on national politics was weakening. Up to this time, white racial superiority was asserted scripturally (the curse of Ham) or as a condition of nature. Now something else could be brought into the picture: scientifically gathered data.

Decades earlier Thomas Jefferson had seen this coming. Rather than treat racial inferiority as a truth of scripture or of nature, the science-minded Jefferson had repositioned inferiority as an empirical hypothesis to be tested. "[T]he blacks," he wrote in 1781, "are inferior to whites in the endowments both of body and mind." However, he went on to ask: were blacks "originally a distinct race, or made distinct by time and circumstances?"[5] If time and circumstance determined racial characteristics, time and circumstances could change them. Jefferson left it to a future science to determine whether the source of racial inferiority was an essential trait or a contingent human condition—was caused by biology or social circumstances.

The Future Arrives: Science in a Brain Pan

The science foreseen by Jefferson arrived as phrenology and craniology—"measuring heads," as Stephen Jay Gould has put it. The scientist-doctor who stands out in this effort is Samuel George Morton. He started collecting skulls in the 1820s, and by the time he died in 1851, he had assembled more than 1,000 skulls. Upon his death the *New York Tribune* claimed that "probably no scientific man in America enjoyed a higher reputation among scholars throughout the world."[6] Skull collecting was not an idle pastime for Morton. Notes Gould, "He had a hypothesis to test: that a ranking of races [an indisputable given] could be established objectively by physical characteristics of the brain, particularly its size."[7]

Morton measured cranial capacity by pouring lead pellets into skulls. It was then a simple matter to compare brain size and, by inference, intelligence across Johann Blumenbach's five races (which we will meet again and again). In 1839 he published his findings in *Crania Americana*. In this lavishly produced volume summarizing decades of pouring pellets into brain cavities, Morton reported that, indeed, Caucasians, blessed with the most capacious skulls (averaging eighty-seven cubic inches), led all other races in intelligence, followed by the Mongolian, Malay, and American Indian, with Negroes and selected aboriginal groups (with skulls averaging only seventy-eight cubic inches) on the lowest rung. Yankee America took special pleasure in the additional finding that, among whites, the Anglo-Saxon and Teutonic people ranked above Jews, who in turn ranked above the Hindus. Morton's science was deeply flawed, of course. He offered no independent assessment of intelligence. He selected samples, made classification errors, and used dubious statistical treatments. Gould documented all these flaws over a hundred years later,[8] but in his time Morton's influence was substantial. The largest collection of skulls in the world offered objective facts to show black inferiority—welcome if not surprising news for slave owners.

If cranial measurement helped establish a science of racial and gender inferiority, social statistics took the argument to a new level when the censuses of 1840 and 1850 put into play a number of facts that proslavery forces gleefully paraded. The accuracy of these facts was quickly disputed, but that did not prevent many proslavery partisans from citing them widely in the policy battles leading to secession and the Civil War. A vociferous din overrode reason in policy argument, not for the first time and certainly not for the last in American politics.

Preparation for the 1840 census saw a critical step toward embedding the science of race into the count. We have seen that fifty years earlier Madison had been rebuffed when he proposed that the census include a question on occupation. But Madison was subsequently vindicated as political thinking began to catch up with his views on the value of statistics in governing. In the 1820 census an occupation measure was embraced by a government increasingly understanding that it had a responsibility to foster economic growth.

Respect for the quantitative gathered momentum, and had by the mid-1830s "created buoyant expectations for the upcoming decennial census of 1840. The idea took hold in several quarters that the census could become a full-dress inventory of the greatness of America and that even statistical information that had no bearing on legislation could legitimately be collected."[9] It was this embracing attitude that allowed an unusual item to slip into the 1840 census, one not focused on any particular law or policy but that—and not for the last time in census history—produced an unexpected statistical result of great political weight.

Race Science and Insanity Join the Debates over Slavery

Slow-building census professionalism didn't guarantee accurate results, of course, but new data, even if not good data, could provide politicians more fuel to stoke the heat of debate. Congress stipulated that the 1840 census count the "insane and idiots" and do so in a manner that could track those characteristics by race. The census office carried out this instruction and then, providing no definition of the condition because presumably everyone knew it when they saw it, reported epidemic rates of insanity among free Negroes, compared to only a trace among enslaved Negroes. In the free state of Maine, for instance, 1 in every 14 Negroes was "insane," compared to 1 in every 5,650 Louisiana slaves. "Overall the rate of insanity or idiocy among Northern blacks was 1 in every 162." "This compared to the astounding superior finding among Southern slaves of 1 in 1,588."[10]

Here was a statistical finding that a slave-state politician could celebrate: freedom makes black people insane. In the bitter battle over the future of slavery, the census insanity results confirmed "that Negroes were naturally inferior and thus uniquely suited for servitude and subjugation."[11] The census results were immediately trumpeted by proslavery forces in the Congress, bolstered by the southern press reporting that the census had presented a basic truth about the catastrophe awaiting the country if slavery were abolished. The insanity data were linked to other statistics that showed high rates of poverty, incarceration, and general ill health among the free black population. Emancipation was a risky proposition for the nation, maybe especially for the slaves themselves. When members of the newly formed American Statistical Association argued that on this matter the census was in serious error (which subsequent analysis confirmed), their report was ignored.

Debate about the meaning of these statistics moved to the floor of Congress. John Quincy Adams, having been the nation's sixth president, strenuously argued for congressional investigation of the quality of the statistics being cited. He and his similarly skeptical colleagues were outmaneuvered by powerful South Carolina senator John C. Calhoun, who found the data too politically useful to allow its close examination. The goal foremost in Calhoun's congressional politicking was statehood for Texas; he wanted it to enter the Union as a slave state. Calhoun was quick to see in the insanity data an opportunity to argue that slavery "was actually a blessing to blacks."[12] The senator continued, "[T]he census and other authentic documents show that, in all instances in which the States have changed the former relation between the two races, the condition of the African, instead of being improved, has become worse."[13] In the Northern states, he claimed, Africans had "invariably sunk into vice and pauperism, accompanied by the bodily and mental afflictions incident thereto"; but in the Southern states, where the "ancient relation" between the races was preserved, Africans had "improved in every respect—in number, comfort, intelligence, and morals."[14]

Calhoun's reference to the "ancient relation" cleverly called to mind the ideas that shaped Morton's monographs on craniology, based on the spurious proposition that racial inferiority could be traced to antiquity.

Statistics joined with the prevailing race science was considered powerful evidence justifying black slavery, and the slave states made the most of it. Equally important, and anticipating the growing importance of a "social" science in policy making, was multiple variable analysis. Partisans could assert free blacks were not just prone to insanity; they were also unproductive, immoral, and given to vice.

Significantly, if perhaps inadvertently, Calhoun was making a social, not a biological, argument. That is, it was the slave/nonslave distinction and not the black/nonblack distinction that "explained" differential rates of insanity. To put this in conventional scientific terms, the independent variable and the dependent variable are both social. It is ironic that Calhoun was anticipating what would become commonplace later in the century—arguing policy on the basis of social science evidence—and did so before we even had the label *social science*.

It might be supposed that this (mis)use of the 1840 census would raise doubts about the wisdom of racial counting, but no sign of it appears in the historical record. To the contrary, in a move that would surprise no one familiar with contemporary policy debates, antislavery circles felt that the best way to counter proslavery arguments was to answer statistical arguments with contrary statistical arguments. Writing prior to the Civil War, a moderate congressman from South Carolina hoped that statistical comparison of the North and the South would persuade slaveholders to give up their irrational attachment to their slave-based economy. After all, he pointed out, the South was failing to keep up with the free states. Comparing economic productivity and population growth, he noted that "the South has nothing left to boast of; the North has surpassed her in everything, and is going farther and farther ahead of her every day."[15] Although this statistical argument—again social scientific in its formulation—got little political traction, it provided antislavery groups their own reasons for race counting.

Counting the Mulatto Race

The 1850 census greatly extended the political reach of nineteenth-century race science. A prominent southern physician, Josiah Nott, was certain that biracial children born of black-white racial mixing would constitute a feeble and probably infertile "race." In an unprecedented partnership of the census with prevailing scientific opinion, a new statistical race—mulatto—was introduced in the 1850 census, to continue for the next eight decennial censuses.

"It is well settled by anatomists and physiologists that the brain of the Negro compared with the Caucasian is smaller by a full tenth, that its nerves are larger, the head differentially shaped, the facial angle less, and the intellectual powers comparatively defective."[16] Nott, however, wanted to go beyond this standard argument of race scientists. He practiced medicine in Atlanta, where he treated a number of mixed-race patients. Racial hybridity, especially the mulatto, became his scientific specialty. Compared to the "pure races," whether European or African, the mulatto, Nott believed, was less fertile, more susceptible to disease, and lived a shorter life. His thesis was widely circulated in the *American Journal of the Medical Sciences* in 1843, dramatically titled "The Mulatto a Hybrid—Probable Extermination of the Two Races if the Whites and Blacks Are Allowed to Intermarry."

Nott was enough of a scientist to admit that his view was speculative, based on small patient samples: "I am well aware that my assertions would have much greater weight, *if they were supported by statistics*."[17] He returned to his argument a few years later, writing, "I hope I have said enough to make apparent the paramount importance of *negro statistics*. If the blacks are intellectually inferior to the whites—if the whites are deteriorated by amalgamation with the blacks—if the longevity and physical perfection of the mixed race is below that of either of the pure races, and if the negro is by nature unfit for self-government, these are grave matters for consideration."[18] These few sentences are among the most consequential in all of nineteenth-century race science. Framing his argument as "if-then," Nott made it science. Population statistics were the best-equipped science for testing his hypothesis.

Nott got his wish. In congressional discussion leading up to the 1850 census, a Kentucky congressman asked for a mulatto category on the census form. His reasoning? Dr. Nott, reported the congressman delicately, "said that he believed that a certain class of colored people had fewer children than a certain other class; and he believed that the average duration of the lives of the darker class was longer than that of the lighter colored class, or mixed. And it was for the purpose of ascertaining the physiological fact, that he wanted the inquiry made."[19] Remarkably, and without precedent, the 1850 census was enlisted on behalf of Nott's scientific inquiry. The census office instructed enumerators to separately record blacks and mulattoes, marking B for the former and M for the latter.

This was a key moment in the political reach of statistics in general and of race science in particular. In preparation for the 1850 census, a Census Board was appointed—marking the first time that Congress turned to outside experts to decide what should be covered by the decennial census. The census form was greatly expanded. "The 1850 census proved to be a watershed, not only because (social) scientists were marshaled in its service, but because they brought with them, as scientists, their thinking about race. This census boldly ushered in the inextricable and enduring link between census categorization, racial scientific thought, and public policy in the United States."[20] Twenty years earlier the 1830 census schedules had seven items. In 1850 the schedules covered 138 items, including commerce, agriculture, crime, religion, and manufacturing. This was also the first census that collected data not just on the household but on each individual in the household.

In a nation enamored of statistics and increasingly embracing secular science over religious authority, the 1850 census gave race science a much grander stage than that available to Morton with his skulls or Nott with his patient records. Capturing the census for Nott's mulatto theory moved into new scientific territory. The census was marshaled to explore a sociological hypothesis about why and how a "hybrid" race differed from the "pure" races.

If this was new scientific territory, it was also new policy territory. The measure of racial characteristics—fertility or premature mortality—could be used to make race-specific policy, or so it was assumed. Viewed from the perspective of today's social science with its boundless appetite for census and survey data on the characteristics of different race groups, putting a single item on the census form is not extraordinary. But because the 1850 census predates the empirical social sciences by several decades, it is highly significant that the marriage of the census and sociological thinking first occurred in the context of race science.

Group Traits Enter the Count

The Mulatto category stayed on the census through 1920. These eight decades of data never confirmed Nott's hypothesis; nor, as a matter of fact, were the data ever seriously analyzed. But in maintaining the mulatto question the census continued to feed the nation's fervid anxieties about racial mixing between whites and blacks leading to mulattoes, and mixing of whites and Indians leading to "half-breeds."

A more subtle consequence of the introduction and persistence of the Mulatto census item is its implicit message. The census racial classification was available to policy making in ways that relate not just to group *counts* but also to group *traits*. As noted above, the political work carried by the three-fifths clause since 1790 needed only to count slaves. The argument that a hybrid race was fragile required more statistical sophistication. Was a mixed race different in some politically important way from pure races? The Mulatto category kept this sociological question around at a time of increasing use of the census for policy purposes. The mulatto counts were in this sense important, but in fact did not themselves ever shape a policy, as will be explained below.

CHAPTER 4

The Census Goes to War and Beyond

The four-year-long Civil War that started in April 1861 was, of course, fundamentally about slavery and race. The most current statistics available, from the 1860 census, influenced both military policy during the war and postwar thinking. This influence frequently incorporated race data. The census office, for example, compared the military strength of the Union to that of the Confederacy as the war started, reporting to President Abraham Lincoln the regional distribution of white males of fighting age; nearly 70 percent were in the free states and only 9 percent were in the states that had seceded—a ratio that would continue to favor the Union even if all the other slave states joined the Confederacy.[21]

In January 1862, Congress passed a resolution on war statistics that instructed the superintendent of the census, Joseph Kennedy, "to report data directly to the War Department."[22] The census office reported not only statistics but in a major innovation also prepared county-level maps. Thus "northern commanders had data on the number of whites, free blacks, and slaves for each county. They also knew the amount of improved land, the number of horses and mules, and the amount of wheat, corn, oats, and other crops produced in the county."[23] General William Tecumseh Sherman's infamous march through Georgia drew heavily from these data. Explaining how the Union Army could move fast and without supply lines, Sherman wrote to his daughter, "No military expedition was ever based on sounder or surer data. . . ."[24]

It is in this context that policy makers called "on the Census Office and on census data to address the most fundamental question raised by the war: What was to become of slavery and the slaves?"[25] President Abraham Lincoln had initially hoped that the southern rebellion could be put down without freeing the slaves, or, if that proved difficult (as obviously it did), that freed slaves could be relocated outside the United States. Lincoln quickly discovered that he needed support from militant antislavery interests and he needed black soldiers.[26] These considerations made moot the question of whether emancipation was necessary or whether the emancipated slaves could be moved abroad (as Jefferson had proposed decades earlier).

The basic information provided by the census proved its immediate worth in war planning and execution. But census superintendent Kennedy wanted to make more ambitious claims. In his initial report of the 1860 census results, he promised that the country would quickly recuperate when the war was over, citing indicators of a vibrant economy. The report offered that "the truth as presented by the census, will teach us the importance of the Union and harmony, and stimulate a proper pride in the country and people as one and indivisible."[27] The union that Kennedy had in mind was that between northern and southern whites—not, of course, between whites and blacks. The report that waxed so enthusiastic about the future of the country reassured northern whites "that the future of the Union would not include Negroes."[28] Kennedy's final report on the 1860 census has this stunningly racist paragraph:

> That corruption of morals progresses with greater admixture of races, and that the product of vice stimulates the propensity to immorality, is as evident to observation as it is natural to circumstances. These developments *of the census*, to a good degree, explain the slow progress of the free colored population in the northern States and indicate, with unerring certainty, the gradual extinction of that people the more rapidly as, whether free or slave, they become diffused among the dominant race.[29]

The conclusion drawn by the superintendent of the census, echoed the putative 1840 census result that free blacks were slow to progress, and it echoed Nott's theory that racial mixing resulted in a hybrid race without a demographic future. The "colored population," wrote Kennedy, "is doomed to comparatively rapid absorption or extinction," concluding that his duty as superintendent of the census had been accomplished "in developing the facts, as the figures of the census reveal them respecting the past."[30] Kennedy's report demonstrated again that the racial classification system in the census could be used to support racist political purposes based on hypotheses about the characteristics of different statistical races.

Surprisingly, especially for a superintendent of the Census, Kennedy offered no statistics to justify his conclusions. The hybridity theory was not tested with either the 1850 or the 1860 census data. When an independent scholar skeptical of Kennedy's conclusion asked for a breakdown of mortality rates by race, he got nowhere. Kennedy replied that because there were only two data points—1850 and 1860—"it is not yet easy to determine how far the admixture of races affects their vital powers."[31] This did not prevent Kennedy from asserting it. The census office was not yet the fully professional and nonpartisan agency it would become in the twentieth century—by then, a census director who opined as irresponsibly as Superintendent Kennedy did would find himself out of office, and probably out of town, within hours.[32]

Because, in Kennedy's argument, two data points were insufficient to test the hybridity hypothesis, more data were called for, and Nott's theory lingered in the census world for decades. When preparing for the

1870 census, the chair of the relevant congressional committee, James Garfield (later elected president of the United States), sought outside expertise from the American Statistical Association. The expert, Edward Jarvis, had been rebuffed in his efforts to get racially disaggregated data from the prior census and, still intent on testing Nott's hypothesis, Jarvis now reiterated his plea that the census distinguish between blacks and mulattoes. The census did so. Instructions to census takers were specific, declaring that the Mulatto category should be understood in its generic meaning—that is, to include "quadroons, octoroons, and all persons having any perceptible trace of African blood." The instructions urged care in this enumeration because "[i]mportant scientific results depend upon the correct determination of this class."[33]

Still in search of an answer to the question raised in 1850 whether fertility and mortality did differ between the "pure" and the "mixed" races, the 1880 census repeated the categories and the instructions used in 1870. The 1890 census asked for more detail. Joseph Wheeler, a Georgia congressman who had been a general in the Confederate States Army, wanted the census "to ascertain and exhibit the physical effects upon offspring resulting from the amalgamation of human species. . . ."[34] Wheeler went on to call for specific counting of "Chinamen, Indians, and half-breeds," among others. The congressional bill setting forth the plans and purpose for the 1890 census replicated Wheeler's full request:

> To ascertain and exhibit the physical effects upon offspring resulting from the amalgamation of human species. Be it enacted by the Senate and House of Representatives of the United States of America in Congress assembled, That the Superintendent, or officer in charge of the Eleventh Census be, and is hereby, authorized and directed, in making the enumeration provided by law, to take such steps as may be necessary to ascertain, report, and publish the birth rate and death rate among pure whites, and among negroes, Chinamen, Indians, and half-breeds or hybrids of any description or character of the human race who are found in the United States, as well as of mulattos, quadroons, and octoroons.[35]

The census form that emerged from the congressional discussion reflected the sentiments in this bill but differed in some particulars. It added Japanese as a second Asian group and did in fact instruct census takers to count blacks, mulattoes, quadroons, and octoroons with this guideline: "The word 'black' should be used to describe those persons who have three-fourths or more black blood; 'mulatto,' those persons who have from three-eights to five-eights black blood; 'quadroon,' those persons who have one-forth black blood; and 'octoroons,' those persons who have one-eighth or any trace of black blood."[36]

The statistics produced from the 1890 census made no report of these fine-grained distinctions; in any case, they produced useless data. The resulting mortality tables, however, persuaded an expert on social statistics that America's race problem would disappear—blacks were dying off at a higher rate than whites. In his influential publication by the American Economic Association, this insurance industry statistician offered "a concise tabular statement of the facts," that showed, "Of all the races for which statistics are available . . . the Negro shows the least power of resistance in the struggle for life." Not content to let the absence of tabular data on mulattoes deter a judgment, the author, citing Nott, concluded that the mulatto was in every way "inferior to the black, and of all races the one possessed of the least vital force."[37]

The Policy Significance of Counting Blacks in the Late Nineteenth Century

Long before insanity was tabulated or Mulatto became a census category, there were so many racial laws on the books—and not just in the slaveholding states—that the Supreme Court could declare that it would be tedious to recount all the laws testifying to the inferiority of the black population. Nevertheless, in *Dred Scott v. Sandford* (1857), which ruled that free blacks could not become citizens, the court was tedious in documenting that colonial law and policy, the Declaration of Independence, the Articles of Confederation, the Constitution, and more than a half century of subsequent federal and state law show "the fixed opinions concerning that race, upon which the statesmen of that day spoke and acted." These fixed opinions unarguably showed, wrote the Court,

> that a perpetual and impassable barrier was intended to be erected between the white race and the one which they had reduced to slavery, and governed as subjects with absolute and despotic power, and which they then looked upon as so far below them in the scale of created beings, that intermarriages between white persons and negroes or mulattoes were regarded as unnatural and immoral, and punished as crimes, not only in the parties, but in the person who joined them in marriage. And no distinction in this respect was made between the free negro or mulatto and the slave, but this stigma, of the deepest degradation, was fixed upon the whole race.[38]

It was not science or statistics that disputed the court's ruling; it was the Civil War followed by constitutional amendments that overturned the court's reasoning in the *Dred Scott* case. But the war that ended legal slavery could not erase the nation's belief in white racial superiority on which slavery was based. It was this belief that sustained government-sanctioned segregation and discrimination for another century.

By far the most consequential policies for the black population in the post-Reconstruction period were Jim Crow policies, a term summarizing how the southern states, beginning in the 1880s, systematically used law and the "separate but equal" constitutional provision to subordinate the black population. Legalized segregation in schools, housing, the workplace, and transportation was fully in place by 1910. Literacy tests and poll taxes shut down access to the ballot box. When law was an insufficient deterrent, violence and intimidation were used, most notably in public lynchings that numbered in the thousands.[39] Northern states were less deliberate in institutionalizing white supremacy, but millions of white children could grow up in the North without ever seeing any black child in their classrooms or churches or neighborhoods (see the preface for a case in point, circa 1950). With some exceptions in the area of public health, official race statistics were marginal to the establishment and enforcement of legalized segregation and disenfranchisement—but not thereby inconsequential.

The Symbolic Significance of Counting Blacks

Counting slaves at three-fifths between the nation's founding and the Civil War seven decades later was hugely significant in American politics and policy. From the end of the Civil War to the civil rights era a century later, statistics on black Americans were less significant in the making and implementing of specific policy. But, no one asked if the census might stop telling America how many belonged to its statistical races or questioned their basis in a scientific reality. Decade after decade, the census office sent out its enumerators to visually ascertain who was White and who was Black, Red, and Yellow. It was simply assumed that statistical races had a role to play in the governing process. More specifically, the census signaled that real and distinct races existed and that every person in the country could be assigned to one or another of them. This initially rested on the prevailing science that declared race to be biological, evident in the introduction of the Mulatto category at midcentury, and subsequently in debates over how to count the Chinese and Japanese in the late nineteenth century (the topic of chapter 5). Even when census officials finally admitted that the mulatto category produced useless statistics and removed it from the 1930 census form, the enumerator instructions still made clear that blood quantum mattered. "A person of mixed white and Negro blood should be returned as a Negro, no matter how small the percentage of Negro blood," it read. "Both black and mulatto persons are to be returned as Negroes, without distinction. A person of mixed Indian and Negro blood should be returned a Negro, unless the Indian blood predominates and the status of an Indian is generally accepted in the community.... Any mixture of white and nonwhite should be reported according to the nonwhite parent."[40] The Census Bureau did not invent hypodescent —"the one-drop rule"—but in these instructions to its census takers it signaled to the country that racial purity was a measurable trait.

The political weight of the census in matters such as signaling that blood quantum mattered and could be measured visually by census workers was enhanced by the growing professionalization of census taking. It may seem counterintuitive to suggest that this depoliticization of the census enhanced its political influence, but that is precisely what happened. The credibility of impartial professional government statisticians rested on distancing themselves from partisan and social reform interests. The first Bureau of Labor Statistics, established by Massachusetts in 1873, made it quite clear that government statistics could "command the cordial support of the press and the body of citizens" only if it did not take sides in the raging debates over how much government regulation was appropriate in a free market economy.[41] The trend toward professionalism in the social sciences, of which statistics were a part, was consistent with the broader argument that a combination of objectivity and neutrality was the best platform for establishing a credible voice in the important issues of the day.[42]

By the twentieth century national statistics had become too important to leave to an intermittent arrangement, and in 1902 the permanent Census Bureau was established. Responsibility for census details, including question wording and enumerator instruction, shifted from Congress to career professionals in the bureau. It came to be believed (or at least asserted) that counting the population was an administrative rather than political function, and that if the Census Bureau needed advice it should turn to the statistical expertise found in universities rather than to politicians.

Ironically, the professionalization and depolitization of the Census Bureau granted—and grants today—political weight to its view on racial classification. What the census counts is taken to be socially real and important to government. The census enterprise addresses every conceivable policy issue—including, of course, race relations, but also public health, child welfare, crime, employment, and much more. But, excepting age and perhaps gender and income, no demographic variable is as central to an effort to "inform the policy maker" as is race.

What the statistician Walter Willcox observed in 1904 is even more the case today: "there is no country in which statistical investigation of race questions is so highly developed . . . as in the United States."[43] Chapter 11 will ask whether we should still want that distinction among nations.

CHAPTER 5

HOW MANY WHITE RACES ARE THERE?

THE PROMINENT PLACE OF STATISTICAL RACES IN AMERICAN POLITICAL LIFE DID not end when slavery was abolished and with it the three-fifths clause. Quite the contrary, the next half century extended the number of statistical races. The Chinese and Japanese immigrant workers initially entered the census as nationalities—which, of course, they were. Their census identity, however, was gradually converted from one of national origin to one of race, with Asian becoming the fourth statistical race enshrined in the American census. By the end of the nineteenth century the census had become Linnaean in its four races: White, Black, Red, and Yellow. The fifth race would arrive late in the twentieth century (see chapter 6.)

Converting nationalities to a race took a second, even stranger turn at the end of the nineteenth century. Aliens from white Europe posed a threat to America's self-image as racially pure, and presented to policy makers the unexpected challenge of distinguishing "good" whites from "bad" whites. This challenge stretched the census in ways unimaginable to the founders who had so casually introduced three statistical races into the census process a century earlier.

The problem arrived with immigrants streaming to America's eastern port cities in the late nineteenth and early twentieth centuries. Though "white," they were not at all like the Anglo-Protestants who had migrated to the Eastern Seaboard, settled the country, fought for its independence, founded the Republic, and felt America was their country. The newcomers arrived not from the ancestral Northern European countries but from farther East and South, bringing with them suspect languages, cultures, and religions. They were Polish Jews, and Irish and Italian Catholics.

Facing two invasions, then—the "yellow peril" from the west and the alien cultures from the east—the nineteenth-century census was pressed into service, once again to draw internal boundaries when demands for cheap labor required porous external borders. If immigrants were fit for factories and fields they were not fit for the voting booth. Policies to allow workers but not voters needed new ways to account for the nativity line and the color line where they overlapped. Eventually, the foreign born were racialized. I tell this story for two reasons. It is a major chapter in the history of "statistical races"; but, more important, it parallels a twenty-first-century issue: will today's immigrants from Africa, Asia, Central and South America, the Middle East, and around the globe be racialized? I address that question in chapter 9, and then, in chapters 10 and 11, urge that the government dismantle its eighteenth-century classification so ill-suited to today's challenges.

But first the earlier story: with the Civil War behind it, and major industrialization underway, America's market economy needed workers. For many Americans the new immigrants from Asia and Europe threatened America's civic nationalism. But what the economy needed, politics had to manage. Internal borders were erected that controlled marriage, property, and certainly civic participation. Census data proved useful but did not often convince anyone of things they did not already believe. They did buttress policy arguments in ways that moved political agendas forward.

In this chapter we explore the shift that occurred in the census as the nineteenth century progressed and as the early twentieth presented new issues. I note how race measurement shaped social policy and consider the perspectives that a maturing social science brought to those policies. The latter becomes particularly clear in the task of differentiating *within* the white European race. It was this task that most fully joined the counting-by-race project encountered in the first half of the century with the measuring-group-traits feature that would emerge in the second half. By the first decades of the twentieth century, measuring group characteristics produced felicitous policy outcomes otherwise unattainable. This immigration story and the role of the census in it start with the fate of Chinese laborers.

Counting Asians in So They Could Be Counted Out

President Abraham Lincoln, in an 1863 message to Congress, urged that "a system for the encouragement of immigration" be put in place, one that would redress the "still great deficiency of laborers in every field of industry, especially in agriculture and in our mines." Lincoln may also have had in mind the heavy use of Chinese labor in constructing the Central Pacific Railroad in California. A Sacramento businessman, Leland Stanford, a founder of this railroad, was elected governor of California in 1861. His inaugural speech took one view: "To my mind it is clear, that the settlement among us of an inferior race is to be discouraged by every legitimate means."[1] His economic interests pointed in another direction. By 1863 his railroad was bringing thousands of working-age Chinese men from the Pearl River Delta. Chinese eventually made up 90 percent of the labor force that built the Central Pacific Railroad, the westernmost spur of the trans-continental railroad completed at Promontory Point, Utah, in 1869. Stanford got very rich, and was later to establish and name Leland Stanford Junior University after his son.

Constructing railroads, mining gold, planting vineyards and orchards, and otherwise building California's economy needed labor. China was the preferred source, offering workers considered more reliable and docile than the Irish alternative. By the 1870s, Chinese made up 9 percent of California's population, "but since nearly all of them were adult males, they amounted to one-fifth of the economically active and probably one-fourth of all wage workers."[2] Stanford's "inferior race" had arrived, and with them internal borders no less aggressively established than those that denied full citizenship rights to newly free blacks in the Jim Crow South and in segregated neighborhoods and work places farther north. Zolberg points out that treaties with China, which established labor flows but limited naturalization rights, created "an institutional limbo, populated by a mass of permanently segregated noncitizen workers," adding, "[This institutional limbo] constituted an idiosyncratic solution to the recurrent dilemma posed by the contradiction between economic rationality and racial exclusiveness: the erection of an internal boundary between the general population and a special category of human beings, identified as 'workers' rather than as persons on the basis of membership in an ascriptive or nationality group. . . ."[3]

The internal border was codified in a series of laws, especially in California. When these failed to stop the flow of Chinese labor that the economy demanded, the external border was closed as well, notably by the 1882 Chinese Exclusion Act suspending the importation of Chinese labor. The justification was a mixture of racism and labor policy (save the jobs for true Americans). Theodore Roosevelt, looking back at the treatment of the Chinese worker, opined that he, from an alien race, was properly excluded "because the democracy, with much clearness of vision, has seen that his presence is ruinous to the white race."[4]

That this early victory of immigrant restrictions was framed in racial terms is but one small indicator of what is described as America's racial nationalism, in contrast to its civic nationalism. Civic nationalism is the enduring creed that America is "a divine land where individuals from every part of the world [can] leave behind their troubles, start life anew, and forge a proud, accomplished, unified people."[5] This is the promise of life, liberty, and the pursuit of happiness drawn from the founding documents of the new nation and repeated time and again across American history. Those who migrated to American shores viewed America "as a transforming nation, banishing dismal memories and developing a unique national character based on common political ideals and shared experiences. The point of America was . . . to forge a new *American* culture."[6]

Racial nationalism is a sharply different political ideology. It "conceives of America in ethnoracial terms, as a people held together by common blood and skin color and by an inherited fitness of self-government." This ideology, too, dates to the founding as in 1790 the new government ruled that only free white persons could become naturalized citizens.[7] Clearly no slaves, but also no free blacks or American Indians were deemed fit for self-government. These groups were joined by the Chinese in the mid-nineteenth century.

Nationality Becomes Race

Amalgamating the Chinese in this way with blacks and Indians raised a new question. Were they a race in the same taken-for-granted way in which African slaves, Native Indians, and Europeans were? The Chinese had an indisputable national identity; in fact, their arrival was regulated by treaties between the United States and China, the latter an empire boasting a highly accomplished civilization and a three-thousand-year history comparable to Europe's. A crucial issue was posed to the census taker by the Chinese: "what a race actually is, and who should be allowed to join the insiders of American society rather than being excluded or remaining on the margins as perennial foreigners."[8]

The Chinese became the first instance in American census history of a nationality group appearing in the census as a race. Chinese was listed along with the prior race groups—White, Black, and Indian in 1870. The population report from that census makes clear that the census office had in mind Asians more generally, indicating that the term Chinese "was held to embrace Japanese."[9] In racializing and lumping together Asian nationalities, the census was taking sides in an intense political argument then underway, one that echoed the earlier debate about whether Native Indians or freed slaves could aspire to citizenship.

By denoting the Chinese and Japanese as races—the latter getting its separate census race category in 1880, as did immigrants from India, under the label "Hindoo"—the census made Asians categorically different from whites, who remained the only population group fit for self-government.

In this the census was echoing and amplifying the prevailing sentiment. In a Senate report of the period, the Chinese were an "indigestible mass in the community" who "do not desire to become citizens of this country, and have no knowledge or appreciation for our institutions."[10] There was a brief and futile attempt to treat the Japanese differently—they, after all, were Christian and therefore cultivated; Japanese could "conform to our customs [and] have become Americanized," claimed a congressional report.[11] This more tolerant view gave way as the number of Japanese immigrants increased, approaching the size of the Chinese immigrant population. Despite considerable taxonomic confusion over who belonged to the Asian race,[12] by the end of the century, the census had added its authority and its statistics to the consensus that the Asian, a member of a distinct race, could never have a permanent place in White America.

This racialization of nationality became a "form of surveillance, a mechanism for imposing order and racial clarity on the proliferation of an ambiguous alien."[13] The ambiguity was resolved by the simple expedient of creating a new census category. By making Asians a statistical race, the politics of exclusion familiar from the treatment of Native Indians and African Americans could be applied. Internal borders redefined the color line, adding a yellow race to the black and red races.

When growing numbers of Asians made internal border enforcement difficult, external borders were erected. Asians were counted in so that they could be counted out. The Chinese Exclusion Act of 1882 made Chinese immigration illegal; anyone caught bringing Chinese into the country was fined and, under criminal law, could be imprisoned. The Chinese already in the country were registered, becoming permanent aliens with no prospect of citizenship. The 1882 act was not repealed until 1943, when the United States and China joined forces in World War II.

Immigration from Japan was curtailed by a "gentleman's agreement" between the United States and Japan in 1907, and then further restricted by harsh immigration controls in the 1920s. Not until 1965 did American immigration law treat Japanese on an equal footing with Europeans, when, legally, the racialization of nationality groups finally came to an end. Its legacy, however, is the statistical race group currently labeled "Asian," and the awkward wording of the census question (see fig. 1) that is, in fact, a nationality and not a race question.

Who Was "Really" White? The White Race Faces Division

The "yellow peril" could be contained on racial grounds but matters became more complex when the nation's anxieties turned to immigrants who were undeniably European and white, even though they seemed darker skinned than their Anglo or Teutonic neighbors. Admittedly it is a stretch, though a suggestive one, to view the racialization of the Asian nationality groups as a practice run for what was looming as a greater test for racial classification. Could the census classification distinguish not just whites from nonwhites, but within the white population separate those to be allowed in and those to be kept out? In the late nineteenth century the Asian race seemed evident. After all they had, along with the African and the Indian, been separated from the white race by Linnaeus, Blumenbach, and their legion of successors. But those authorities provided no guide for distinguishing among groups that were indisputably Caucasian. The immigration restrictionists needed something fresh, which as we see later in the chapter, was provided by twentieth-century social science.

By 1884, recently arrived European labor was being described on the floor of Congress as a class of immigrants who "care nothing about our institutions . . . are ignorant of our social conditions . . . do not become citizens, and are certainly not a desirable acquisition to the body politic."[14] The civic nationalism project was too weak to accommodate this new immigrant flow. But it took four decades of political debate and false starts before the government figured out how to count these undesirable Europeans separately and restrict their entry into the country. As this lengthy process unfolded, the labels shifted from race to national origin and mother tongue—a shift made necessary because those who threatened American virtues and those deemed to embody them were clearly of the same race. This label shift, however, left in place the basic logic and methods of racial exclusion. Some groups, *as groups*, did not belong. The census could classify and count these groups; social science could show them to be morally or mentally deficient or criminally inclined; Congress could write laws to exclude them. The race science of a half century earlier had put the model in place, and exclusionary immigration forces made full use of it.

Aliens from Outer Europe

The demography and politics of European immigration from 1884 to 1924 is too complex to summarize here even briefly. The following treatment is selective, focusing only on those features that bear most pointedly on the argument advanced in this book—the creation and use of statistical races to design significant policies at key junctures in American history.

The 1880 census is our starting point. Its superintendent, Francis Walker, like his predecessor, Joseph Kennedy, felt that directing the census equipped him to pronounce on the main issues of the day. If Kennedy in the 1860s reassuringly reported that white America need not worry about the Negro, who would fade away, Walker twenty years later alarmingly reported on the demographic threat to white America posed by the growing foreign-born population, recorded at 13 percent in the 1880 census. This alien element, if unchecked, would corrupt and degrade white Anglo America.

Elaborating this theme, University of Chicago professor Edward Webster Bemis titled a prize-winning essay "The Evil Effects of Unrestricted Immigration." Bemis, soon to be popular on the lecture circuit, shocked the nation with his (mis)reading of the 1880 census data. Half of white America was now in the problematic category of foreign born or children of the foreign born, he claimed. From immigration, wrote Bemis, "there is great good, but in another large measure there is equally great evil." It was the evil that most caught his eye. Immigrants, Bemis reported in his sweeping indictment, were overrepresented among the insane and criminally convicted. They "indulge in most of the mob violence in time of strikes and industrial depressions." The economy suffered from their presence: the foreign born "lower the standard of living and wages, increase unemployment . . . and through this incalculable injury to our wage-earners depress their purchasing power, and consequently affect the prosperity of all other classes." Some of this, no doubt, sounds familiar to those who follow contemporary immigration debates. Even American political institutions were put at risk, he said. Immigrants obstruct "needed improvements in legislation and administration" and could not be trusted in the voting booth because "by their votes keep our worst men in power."[15]

The statistician Richman Mayo-Smith, in his widely read newspaper series titled "Control of Immigration," continued this political reasoning (and anticipates arguments voiced today about Mexican Americans; see chapter 8): "The thing we have to fear most," wrote Mayo-Smith, "is the political danger of the infusion of so much alien blood into our social body that we shall lose the capacity and power of self-government, or that the elements of our national life shall become so heterogeneous that we shall cease to have the same political aspirations and ideals and thus be incapable of consistent political progress."[16] Citing 1880 census data, Mayo-Smith even tried to sort out the difference between the foreign born and southern Negroes, concluding that the former were an "alien element" but the latter "who speak our language and have no other institutions and customs than those acquired here" should not be classified as alien but instead "simply as a lower" element.[17]

Bemis and Mayo-Smith were but two of the many social science voices drawn into the immigration debates. Others included the prominent sociologist from the University of Wisconsin, E. A. Ross, who found an outlet in popular magazines for his view that America's general intelligence would deteriorate as its racial stock changed and John W. Burgess, Columbia University's influential political scientist, who shared the view that democracy was put at risk from unchecked immigration.[18]

In parallel with contemporary evidence-based-policy reasoning, prescriptions were forthcoming from social inquiry in the 1880s. Walker, for example, became a spokesman for a sharp increase in the immigrant head tax. Bemis thought a literacy test might be the policy answer, because it was not likely to exclude the English or Swedes or Germans but "the Italian, Hungarian and Polish emigration would fall off fully fifty percent."[19]

These and other minor policy prescriptions floated in and out of political debate without providing the resolution that restrictionists were seeking. These small-scale policy recommendations were not politically irrelevant for they marked the fuller and more complex entry of the newly established social scientists into the major political debates of the day. Many of the arguments put forth echoed earlier scientific assumptions that members of certain groups, *because* they were of these groups, had some inborn deficiency—thus justifying their exclusion. Census data were repeatedly exaggerated and distorted to advance these claims. Statisticians skeptical about these uses of the census raised concerns, but the political pressures for restriction—which then, as now, made selective use of the available social science—drowned them out.

The stage was set for the policy answer to America's anxiety about uncontrolled flows of alien races to its shores—an immigration quota system that could exclude the unwanted without interrupting immigration from the European ancestral lands. By the beginning of the twentieth century, social scientists and statisticians met the policy challenge of fashioning this new kind of border designed to preserve America's racial nationalism.

Before turning to the quota system, we pause to consider something else new to the census in this period: nationality groups began to have some say in how they were counted. In 1790 it would have been unthinkable to ask slaves whether or how they wanted to be counted in the census. At midcentury no one asked mulattoes if they wanted to be a race category. There were debates about how to include the Chinese and Japanese in the census, but the terms of their inclusion were not negotiated with them. The race classification left no doubt about who was white, and those counted as nonwhite were not consulted in the matter.

It was different with European immigrants. They had views about how they wanted to be counted, made demands to census authorities, and often got the results they wanted. Immigrants from the Austro-Hungarian Empire did not have a European nation-state to point to, but they viewed themselves as belonging to distinctive cultural and linguistic groups. Because they did not emigrate from a recognized nation, they insisted that the mother tongue of the foreign born be added as a census question, and in 1910 their demand was met. Neither could Jews, having migrated from Russia, Germany, and the Austro-Hungarian Empire, be easily identified on the basis of geographic origin. They appear in the 1910 census as an ethnoreligious category. Paul Schor describes various efforts by European groups to control how they were counted as "purely prestige-oriented mobilizations" in contrast with the late twentieth-century pressures on the census motivated by material benefits.[20] What might be viewed as a benefit at one time—the pride and prestige of census recognition—might turn sour in another time, as we now see.

The Census-Based Quota System

A congressionally appointed Immigration Commission in 1908, chaired by the strongly "keep-them-out" senator Charles Dillingham and drawing on the expertise of leading social scientists and statisticians, assembled a wealth of information. When consolidated and published in forty-two volumes, the *Report of the Commission* (1910) provided "an authoritative analysis of these data that allowed of no other conclusion than that, however much ongoing flows might contribute to the American economy, they severely challenged the country's absorptive capacity and entailed unacceptable social and political costs. Hence, immigration must be limited."[21]

The commission initially favored a literacy test "as the most feasible single method of restricting undesirable immigration" but it also broached the idea of a quota system. It's worth noting, in the context of arguments that will be made in chapter 11, that the commission clearly and casually defined national origin and language as a matter of race, a division of humanity far finer than Blumenbach's five races. The literacy test had congressional support but, when passed, was vetoed by President William Howard Taft and, when later passed, was again vetoed by another president, Woodrow Wilson; in each instance the presidents were persuaded by business lobbyists claiming the need for immigrant laborers.

In 1913, Dillingham, whose literacy test had now been twice vetoed, resurrected the alternative proposal from his commission, which was a quota system based on census statistics. The commissioners defined this as a ratio, "a limitation of the number of each race arriving each year to a certain percentage of the average of that race arriving during a given period of [prior] years."[22] Specifically he proposed that immigration from any country be limited to 10 percent of the foreign born from that country as counted in the census of 1910. Here was a new role for census data, one that would take advantage of the earlier collection of national-origin statistics. As it happened, shortly after Dillingham advanced this policy idea, the outbreak of World War I in August 1914 pushed aside the immigration debate. The war, in any case, effectively stopped immigration, which dropped from a million migrants in 1914 to less than 10 percent that number the following year.[23]

Despite this sharp decline brought about by wartime conditions, public concerns did not fade. Fueled by a heightened patriotism, new anxieties about the political loyalties of the foreign born came to the fore. The prime target of xenophobic attacks, German Americans, some from families dating to the colonial era, defensively Americanized their surnames—Schmidt to Smith, Müller to Miller. Adding to the patriotic fever were fears that peace in Europe would unleash a huge flow of European immigration as thousands tried to escape their war-torn homelands. Congress rushed to pass a literacy test. Again Wilson vetoed it, but now Congress had the votes to override the president, though even among its congressional supporters there were doubts about its effectiveness. The argument that immigration could be more effectively controlled through a statistically based quota system still had political life.

The feared postwar surge did occur; European immigration jumped to more than 650,000 in 1921. Yet higher numbers were expected in 1922, perhaps returning immigration to the peak year of 1907 when 1.3 million had passed through Ellis Island. Wilbur Carr, head of the U.S. Consular Service, warned that the country was at risk of an "unprecedented wave of Polish Jews who were 'filthy, un-American, and often dangerous in their habits.'"[24]

Stirred by such alarms, Congress applied quotas, reducing immigration by 50 percent in 1922. The following year the numbers were again reduced by half. For all practical purposes, European immigration from other than the ancestral countries of the founding generations was finished. Italian immigrants, a third of the 650,000 immigrants in 1921, numbered fewer than fifteen thousand annually for the rest of the decade. Polish immigration dropped as sharply. Asian immigration was stopped altogether.

The focus here is not immigration history itself as much as the policies that so efficiently closed it down in the 1920s. New social science theory underpinned these policies, a development made possible by a radical change in the social sciences themselves. Between 1884, where this account of immigration started, and 1924, where it concluded, *social* science largely displaced nineteenth-century *race* science.[25] Social science did not neglect race—quite the contrary. But it found a way to talk about race in which *social* explanation took preference over *biological* explanation. The new sciences of anthropology and sociology pushed aside Samuel George Morton and his pellet-filled skulls and Josiah Nott and his theories about racial hybridity to make room for new theories that blended national origin into the racial classification system.

The anthropologist William Z. Ripley and the sociologist W. I. Thomas were among the more influential representatives of the new social science disciplines; both used the term *race* in a way that seems strange today but it caused no raised eyebrows in their time. In *The Races of Europe* (1899), Ripley explored the consequences of a distinction framed by Columbia University professor Franz Boas, recognized as the father of anthropology. Boas argued the need "to distinguish the concepts of race and culture, to separate biological and cultural heredity, to focus attention on cultural process, to free the concept of culture from its heritage of evolutionary and racial assumption, so that it could subsequently become the cornerstone of social scientific disciplines completely independent of biological determinism."[26]

Working in the service of this radical idea, Ripley argued that by separating race and environment "[w]e may discover what are the distinctive social peculiarities of the three [European] races whose history we have been outlining (Teutonic, Alpine, and Mediterranean); and we may form a definite idea of the class of remedies necessary to meet the peculiar needs of each community . . . for it is quite obvious that social evils due to inherited tendencies require very different treatment from those which are of recent origin, the product of local circumstances."[27] Inherited tendencies were, self-evidently, harder to treat than those produced by local circumstances—such as poor schools, unhealthy diet, or unsafe working conditions.

Thomas, a famed University of Chicago sociologist, took as his task the shaping of a "science of man," also based on distinguishing the biological from the social. In an influential 1907 article, "The Mind of Women and the Lower Races," Thomas reasoned that because "one race has advanced farther in culture than another does not necessarily imply a different order of brain, but may be due to the fact that in one case the social arrangements have not taken the shape affording the most favorable conditions for the operation of the mind."[28]

Thomas turned his formidable sociological skills to the social institutions—family, religion, education—that influenced mental and moral development.[29] Differences between men and women or whites and blacks had nothing to do with biology and everything to do with what today we call institutional sexism and racism. If excluded groups could fully enter and absorb "the world of modern intellectual life [that] is in reality a white man's world" argued Thomas, we then would "be in a position to judge of the mental efficiency of women and the lower races." Until then, he concluded, "we seem justified in inferring that the differences in mental expression are no greater than they should be in view of the existing differences in opportunity."[30] What Thomas "originally thought of in terms of 'race' he came to see in terms of 'culture.'"[31]

By loosening the hold of biology and giving prominence to social and cultural explanation, social science provided critical theoretical grounds for the quota-based immigration policy. The northern, southern, and eastern Europeans could each be racially white yet differ radically in their fitness for membership in American society. The cultural habits and ways of thinking the southern and eastern Europeans brought from their benighted regions were cause for closing the borders against them. Converting this scientific argument into policy took active help from the Census Bureau.

The Reapportionment That Never Happened

The 1920 census mattered in the politics leading to the restrictive immigration quotas that determined America's demographic destiny for the next half century. To understand this policy success, we first we have to take note of a lesser-known story about the 1920 census.[32] It is the only census in American history that did not result in a reapportionment of Congress, the very reason the Constitution mandates taking the census in the first place. The refusal to reapportion occurred because powerful interests in Congress did not like the implications of what the census reported.

The 1920 census statistics revealed the striking and unsettling fact that America had become more urban than rural. This was disturbing to a country still politically and culturally comfortable with its virtuous, white, rural, and Protestant self-image. The shock was especially felt in the South and West, where demographic realities still largely match that traditional self-image. Viewed from these regions, population growth in the North and Upper Midwest industrial cities meant that labor unrest, socialism, political corruption, and loose morals were growing. It also meant too many alien immigrants, the supposed carriers of these many social ills.

The 1920 census would normally have led to a reapportionment of congressional seats and a new pattern of Electoral College votes. This had occurred following every census from 1790 to 1910, but across these thirteen decades the political impact of population growth and its regional redistribution was moderated by continually enlarging the size of the House of Representatives. Adding seats to Congress in one region did not necessarily subtract them elsewhere. In 1912, the final two continental states—New Mexico and Arizona—were added to the Union. Congress then fixed the size of the House of Representatives at 435. Henceforth, differential rates of growth would inflict a political loss upon the slow-growing regions. When it suddenly became clear after the very next census, in 1920, that eight urban states would gain eleven congressional seats at the expense of ten rural states, it was too much for rural America to stomach. A conservative coalition in Congress successfully stalemated the reapportionment process for a decade. For the only time in American history, the census did not shift power from the slow-growing or shrinking regions of the country to the rapidly growing regions. The advantage this gave to conservative interests lasted only a decade, not nearly as long as the slave bonus, but it did influence restrictive immigration policy.

Shortly after the 1920 census data were available, emergency legislation was introduced to restrict immigration. The "emergency" was based on high unemployment and a concern that postwar immigrants would take jobs away from deserving Americans. Once again, many policy rationales from the past are echoed in today's immigration debates. The emergency legislation was the first to apply an immigration quota based on national origin. Congress passed immigration levels set at 3 percent of the size of each nationality as reported in the 1910 census, capping immigration at approximately 350,000 annually.

This policy victory was fairly easily won, partly because it was proposed as a temporary emergency measure. Its opponents, especially business lobbyists, were confident that Congress would shortly be reapportioned, and that this would shift congressional voting strength in favor of more lenient immigration when the emergency measure expired. They miscalculated. Reapportionment did not happen after 1920, and more restrictive legislation was on its way. As anti-immigrationists marshaled their forces, they renewed the emergency legislation with the long-term goal of passing an even more restrictive and permanent law.

A Vanderbilt University political scientist hit upon the idea of moving the baseline denominator for nationality quotas from the 1910 to the

1890 census.[33] This would reflect America's population before the turn-of-the-century surge from eastern and southern Europe, and thus more effectively allow only immigrants who would strengthen America's colonial stock. A bill doing so was introduced in Congress, but restrictionists felt they needed a rationale that was not overtly racist. This they located in a Census Bureau report prepared several years earlier on "vitality" across different nationality groups, as measured by their rate of population growth. The somewhat tortured argument taken from this report hypothesized that America's colonial stock had historically been especially fertile, but that this reassuring birthrate had slowed toward the end of the nineteenth century. In a throwback to Nott's mulatto theory, it was posited that fertility among these whites dropped if there was intermarriage with eastern or southern Europeans, even if the latter were second- or third- generation Americans.

This became justification for restricting European immigration more generally but still allowing it from countries representing the same bloodline as America's original settlers. Only in this way could the descendants of the founders be assured that their bloodline could retain "vitality," and with it, numerical superiority. The Census Bureau report became a stock reference for the Nordic supremacists who held that "the decline in the native White birth rate in the late nineteenth century was an 'abnormal' and reversible condition."[34] Flaws in the census data and its dubious analysis, debated for the rest of the decade, did not lessen its political usefulness.

Testimony from an influential lobbyist urging quotas based on census numbers is but one of many resting on this argument: "With full recognition of the material progress which we owe to the races from southern and eastern Europe, we are conscious not only that these people tend to depress our standard of living, unduly charge our institutions for the care of the socially inadequate and criminal, but also that they can not point during a period of seven centuries since Magna Carta to any conception of successful government other than a paternal autocracy."[35] Once again, questionable statistical analysis of the national origin data lay behind the legislation, but this seems to have had no effect on Congress. The Johnson-Reed Act (known as the National Origins Act) passed nearly unanimously in 1924, setting a limit on European immigration at 165,000. Using the 1890 baseline, the quota for Polish immigrants was set at 6,000 and for Italians at 4,000. Political squabbles continued, but a turning point in American history had been reached. Only six senators and a handful of representatives voted against it. One Congressman voting nay, Immanuel Cellar, spent the next forty years of his fifty-year career in the House fighting to repeal the act. He succeeded in 1965.

The success of the National Origins Act was part of a broad "racial and ethnic remapping of the nation during the 1920s," one taking place in demography, economics, and law.[36] The first step was placing the nonwhite races. Here conventional color-based racism was sufficient. Preexisting law excluded Asians from citizenship, and the National Origins Act simply applied that criterion to prevent any additional Asians from immigrating. Then, in a formulation breathtaking in its espousal of racial nationalism, the act ignored the presence in the 1890 census of non-European ethnicities and nationalities from the counts that were to be used for setting quotas. This neatly eliminated anyone who had originally come from the Western Hemisphere, along with descendants of slaves. That is, the existing Latin American or African populations living in the United States in 1890 could not become a quota for immigration from their original homelands. This spectacular redefinition of eligibility reaffirms a basic rule in statistical policy making: if you control the denominator, the numerator will take care of itself.

With the nonwhite population out of the way, the remaining issue was distinguishing the desirable from the undesirable among the white European population. The census provided a mechanism for this; in 1890 for the first time, it had asked parents' place of birth. Answers to this question made possible a classification constructed on national origin. Congress put it to use and the white population was defined as both native stock and foreign stock, the former being descendants of the original settlers and the latter being descendants of immigrants arriving after the founding period. It was this distinction that fit comfortably with social science theories declaring that nationality groups differed in their ability to become true Americans. Native stock was safe, foreign was suspect. If the social sciences offered a rationale for national origin quotas, the "census data gave the quotas an imprimatur that was nearly unimpeachable."[37]

Zolberg points out that, in practice, America was not as restrictive as the draconian 1924 policy implies. The Congress so intent on preserving America for the "whitest" European stock also bent to economic realities and left the back door unlocked for cheap Mexican labor: "The emerging distinction between a main gate tightly regulated in keeping with the 'national interest' (as determined by the guardians of the country's 'Nordic' character) and an informally managed 'back door' where agricultural employers ruled supreme, was thus institutionalized into a long-lasting feature of American immigration policy."[38]

From the racist perspective that determined the entire immigration debate, the irony of closing down European immigration while quietly tolerating Mexican immigration did not go unnoticed. The leading academic spokesman for the quotas complained to Congress that "to admit peons from Mexico—while restricting Europeans and excluding Orientals is not only ridiculous and illogical—it destroys the biological, social, and economic advantages to be secured from the restrictions of immigration."[39] But inconsistency is a consistent feature of congressional politics.

A further consequence of leaving the back door open was, predictably, a surge of migrant workers from Mexico. By the time planning for the 1930 census got underway, their numbers were so great that the government felt it necessary to add a Mexican category to the census form. To this point, Mexicans and Latin Americans more generally had been enumerated as white. Now, however, they were to get their own racial designation, separating them from the white population. "It was the first racial category created for a non-Asian population since 1850 [and] it was the first racial category to apply to potentially white people with a view to confining them to a permanent, exclusive, and subordinate *status*."[40]

The census question was subsequently protested by U.S. citizens of Mexican descent, by a federation of Mexican American advocacy organizations, and by the Mexican government, which actively lobbied the U.S. State Department. It was dropped from the 1940 census, when Mexicans were again counted as white. The successful protest was another step toward democratizing the census; such democratization would become fully apparent in the aftermath of the civil rights era, which also led to a reversal of 1930s politics. Hispanics demanded their own census category in the 1960s, though one that characterized them as a language-ethnic group, not a race (see chapter 6).

The Social Science Contribution

The debate over immigration and its resolution in the restrictive laws of the 1920s can be viewed as the culmination of what Josiah Nott had urged on the nation eight decades earlier. Social science theory supported by racial counting would save the nation from impurities imported into its ancestral bloodline by its desire for cheap labor—slaves for the plantation economy, Asians for mining or railroad building, Mexicans for agricultural work, southern Europeans for factory jobs.

The social sciences were active in several ways. They documented group attributes at the center of the policy debates, often disagreeing about what the data confirmed. Economists disagreed on whether the foreign born were a drag on the economy; political scientists argued about whether they were fit for citizenship; sociologists debated whether they were drawn to crime; and psychologists disputed among themselves whether such people had lower IQs. Overall, however, the social science voices most prominent in the popular press, on the lecture circuit, and in congressional hearings tilted toward restriction.

In addition to contributing ideas compatible with the developing policy, some academics had specific expertise relevant to applying the census data underpinning that policy. The American Council of Learned Societies (ACLS) convened historians and genealogists who consulted with the Census Bureau, helping determine the numbers of various nationalities in the 1890 census records. Critics decried this work as tainted statistics, and ACLS itself admitted that the estimates were "far from final." But they sharply reduced quotas for the "wrong" whites, and provided favorable grounds for President Herbert Hoover to declare the national origin numbers official and "scientific."[41]

Conclusions

Counting by race in the decades that stretch from the 1840s to the 1920s had three characteristics. First, the census grew progressively more important as an instrument of governance. Doubtless this would have happened had there been no statistical races, but there were, and no one thought it should be otherwise. It is no surprise that racial statistics were used on behalf of repressive policies targeted to Africans and American Indians. And then that they were suitably adjusted to focus on national origin in order to deny rights to Asians and later, even more ambitiously, to restrict immigration. Racial statistics did not cause these policies, but without them policy would have been shaped differently, and in the important instance of quota-based immigration restriction, would have been impossible.

Second, census taking on its own cannot carry causal arguments very far, and causal arguments—what makes things the way they are? how will they change in response to policies?—are the stuff of which public policy is made. The census can count and describe and in the early nineteenth century this was adequate. The task then was recording raw numbers needed for reapportioning Congress. The policy reach of the census extended substantially when early race scientists discovered statistical races as a venue for testing hypotheses about group characteristics. The initial hypothesis—rates of insanity or racial feebleness—was never confirmed, but it was promulgated as statistical truth. A primitive version of empirical sociology moved into the policy realm well before sociology was a recognized academic discipline.

Third, an increasingly professionalized census bureau and an increasingly confident social science studying social causation had something of import to offer the policy process. What emerged in the late nineteenth century were the beginnings of practices and institutional arrangements that have now grown into a strong bond between social science and social policy making. Social policy emerges from conflicting interests and ideologies and from the institutional arrangements in which political compromises are reached and policies chosen. Somewhere in this mix findings and evidence produced by social science will be present, especially as they predict, explain, and evaluate the consequences of policies.

The strong bond is not happenstance. Science policy sets research priorities, allocates funds, and sponsors some lines of work more than others. This science policy emerges from multiple settings in and out of government. But science policy has one constant feature: it attends to the main problems of the day and expects science to contribute to their solution. At any given time the institutions in which science policy takes shape overlap with what is on the mind of society and its political leadership. This held in 1860 (the future of freed slaves) as it did in 1920 (the consequences of immigration) and again in the civil rights era, which will be discussed in chapter 6.

In the twenty-first century this symbiosis is so deeply entrenched in the practice of American politics that it is hardly noticed. Social science and social policy share a common starting point—the problems before the nation. Moreover, they share a large appetite for the quantitative dimension of those problems. Policy and science need data produced by the federal statistical system as well as administrative data incidental to government record keeping. The way in which race is measured shapes social policy and simultaneously shapes the perspectives that social science offers on those policies.

Our story reaches a turning point. So far I have described policy purposes that generally shaped statistics. The founders struck a policy compromise between nonslave and slave states, and needed a statistical race, or three-fifths of one, to implement it. Later in the nineteenth century, entrenched slave-owning interests worked to justify slavery in the face of a strengthening abolition movement. They wanted statistics on fitness for civic inclusion across four groups—slaves, free blacks, mulattoes, and whites. Later, anxieties about alien immigrants required internal and external boundaries, which were implemented with yet more imaginative ways to deploy statistical races, adding an Asian race, and then statistically distinguishing between "desirable" and "undesirable" Europeans.

The next two chapters tell a story of how preexisting statistics shaped policy more than being shaped by policy goals. In the case of civil rights this has a defensible logic. Racial justice is about undoing the damage wrought by historical practices that used statistics to protect slavery, create second-class citizens, and implement a racist immigration regime. It is fitting that those same statistics were put to the task of righting those wrongs. But what if the statistical races, by virtue of availability, are used to make policy that should not be about race at all. This can lead to illogical policy and harmful outcomes. Chapter 7 presents two cases illustrating this risk.

There is a key lesson to be taken from the next two chapters. The nation is better served if guided by statistics designed with policy purposes in mind rather than fitting policies to preexisting statistics. This lesson shapes the recommendations argued in chapter 11—decide on the nation's policy goals *and then* focus on the statistical measures needed to reach them.

PART III

When You Have a Hammer, Everything Looks Like a Nail

CHAPTER 6

RACIAL JUSTICE FINDS A POLICY TOOL

"YOU DO NOT TAKE A PERSON WHO, FOR YEARS, HAS BEEN HOBBLED BY CHAINS and liberate him, bring him up to the starting line of a race and then say, 'you are free to compete with all the others,' and still justly believe that you have been completely fair." With this sentence, famously delivered at Howard University's commencement on June 4, 1965, Lyndon Johnson put the weight of his presidency behind a radically new way to deal with racial injustice in America.[1] Before he reached this part of his speech Johnson had ticked off some stunning legal and policy achievements in civil rights: "We have seen the high court of the country declare that discrimination based on race was repugnant to the Constitution. . . . We have seen in 1957, and 1960, and again in 1964, the first civil rights legislation in this Nation in almost an entire century." Also soon to become law was the Voting Rights Act (1965), which would guarantee every American the right to vote.

But, insisted the president, these unprecedented, sweeping antidiscrimination laws were "not enough, not enough." Leveling the playing field could not make up for the "consequences of ancient brutality, past injustice, and present prejudice." It was not enough "just to open the gates of opportunity. All our citizens must have the ability to walk through those gates." Johnson was reaching for a new principle of racial justice, one that extended beyond legal protections and freedom from discrimination. He spoke of a "more profound stage" in the battle for civil rights. "We seek not freedom but opportunity. We seek not just legal equity but human ability, not just equality as a right and a theory but equality as a fact and equality as a result."

Equality as a result was soaring rhetoric, but how, specifically, was the government to guide the country toward achieving it? If Johnson did not directly address that question,[2] his speech rested on a quantitative logic that pointed to the policy tool eventually adopted. Johnson and his audience knew that antidiscrimination laws were inadequate because they knew deep and persisting racial inequalities existed in employment, education, income, housing, and health care. Johnson used statistics to point out the harsh fact that "too many—far too many—are losing ground every day."

Citing statistical disparity between race groups as proof of America's failure to establish racial justice was itself not new. But when the president of the United States made erasing those statistical disparities the grounds for a fresh approach to civil rights, he opened the door to race-conscious government action. The statistics showing that the black population was losing ground became a new policy tool under the catchall label of *statistical proportionality* and eventually also for supporting a new policy, known as *affirmative action*. A racial classification used since 1790 to enslave, segregate, deny and exclude on the sole basis of race was given the radical task of reversing injustice and undoing the damage.

In this chapter we will examine the complex story of how the availability of statistical races in the 1960s led to affirmative action policies in the 1970s.

Rejecting Color-Blind Policies: A Change of Mind on the Part of Civil Rights Leaders

In his Howard University speech, Johnson reached beyond the Constitution to justify a "new doctrine of race-conscious affirmative action." He did so by citing the history of past discrimination as the cause of current racial disparities.[3] Johnson saw clearly that this history did not target individuals as individuals, but targeted them *because* they belonged to a racial group. Using group-based solutions to undo group-based injustices invited a political fight over American liberalism—how to square race-based policy with the creed of liberalism.

Classical liberalism holds "that the individual—and not the family, community, or the state—is the singular unit of society, and that the purpose of societal arrangements is to allow the individual the freedom to fulfill his own purposes—by his labor to gain property, by exchange to satisfy his wants, by upward mobility to achieve a place commensurate with his talents."[4] A liberalism based on an abstracted individualism must, by definition, be color-blind.

Initially, civil rights leaders were hesitant about abandoning the liberal creed. The Reverend Martin Luther King Jr. had based his powerful appeals for justice on universalistic, Christian doctrine—preaching that color distinctions should give way to biblical truths that individuals are created equal. "The civil rights lobby, with its roots deep in Jewish philanthropy and in social movements, was extremely wary of such historically unpleasant notions as racial or ethnic quotas and job and admissions applications that required minority group identification."[5] For a brief moment in the early civil rights era, college and job applications prohibited sending in photographs or otherwise identifying one's race.

Senator Hubert Humphrey, who a year later became Johnson's vice president, vigorously promoted the 1964 Civil Rights Act. In defending its equal employment section (Title VII, on which more shortly), he insisted that "Title VII prohibits discrimination. In effect, it says that race, religion, and national origin are not to be used as the basis for hiring and firing. Title VII is designed to encourage hiring on the basis of ability and qualification, not race or religion."[6] Humphrey was defending the Civil Rights Act against congressional opponents who saw race-based policy lurking in the future. This would not happen, he promised. Nothing in the enforcement powers of Title VII could lead to "racial balancing." Humphrey believed what he claimed, as did many others. Civil rights activists at that moment shared the goal of a color-blind society.

At the time, only a few understood that individual-based solutions could not get the country past centuries of group-based discrimination. One who did, Whitney Young, argued in 1962 that only compensatory, preferential treatment could ensure jobs for blacks. Young was prescient in seeing that race statistics would be needed for "a decade of discrimination in favor of Negro youth" in order to undo the inequalities left by "300 years of deprivation." (He was overly optimistic in suggesting "a decade" as the time frame needed.) Young was criticized by other civil rights leaders, who worried that such thinking would be politically disastrous.[7] His critics were not wrong in this worry, as we will see later in this chapter and more fully in chapter 8, when we review what is called "new racism," based on resentment of policies that favor racial minorities.

In the same year that Young promoted proactive government policies, a militant civil rights group, the Congress of Racial Equality (CORE), approached preferential hiring for blacks via a different route. CORE did not try to change employment practices by changing government policy; instead, it urged blacks to take matters into their own hands—to boycott businesses that did not have black employees. The boycott would be lifted when the targeted business promised to hire blacks. "[T]alking in terms of 'compensatory' hiring," CORE was clear about its strategy: "We are approaching employers with the proposition that they have effectively excluded Negroes from their work force for a long time and that they now have a responsibility and obligation to make up for past sins."[8]

By the summer of 1963, there were sit-ins, picket lines, and boycotts accompanied by demands for racial quotas in hiring. As pressure mounted for government action, the liberal Democratic administration of then president John F. Kennedy resisted: "[W]e ought not to begin the quota system, not hard and fast quotas. We are too mixed, this society of ours, to begin to divide on the basis of race and color." Kennedy most certainly knew that such divisions were as old as the nation, for he continued: "I don't think we can undo the past. In fact, the past is going to be with us for a good many years. . . . We have to do the best we can now. That is what we are trying to do. I don't think quotas are a good idea . . . I think we'd get into a good deal of trouble."[9]

The president was unaware that in his administration statisticians were doing what statisticians do—dividing and counting the population on the basis of race. Nor could Kennedy have known that this counting exercise was preparing the way for the targets, timetables, and quotas that he was sure would get the country "into a good deal of trouble." Chaos theory tells us that small perturbations in complex nonlinear systems can produce large, unforeseen outcomes. American politics are complex; policy making is nonlinear. Sometimes all it takes is a small perturbation in how things are counted to tip policy in unexpected ways.

To understand how racial counting led to group-based preferential treatment,[10] we must first recall dramatic events that transformed Johnson's 1965 nod toward policies beyond standard antidiscrimination law into full blown affirmative action that arrived several years later.

Institutional Racism: Crises Lead to a Novel Idea

Though little remembered today, few presidential commissions rival the impact of the Kerner Commission in 1968, named after its chairman, Otto Kerner, governor of Illinois. Its report was published as a government document and, simultaneously, as an inexpensive paperback.[11] The paperback's first printing sold out in three days, and it was reprinted twenty times; nearly two million copies were in circulation within a few months. Long excerpts appeared in leading newspapers, and actor Marlon Brando read sections on a popular television show. Its most widely quoted passage, "Our nation is moving toward two societies, one black, one white—separate and unequal," gained mythic status. It was also the report's title.

It was an epidemic of race riots in the mid-1960s that had led President Johnson to appoint the Kerner Commission. The first of these riots erupted in the Harlem neighborhood of New York City in midsummer 1964. The precipitating event was the funeral of an African American shot by police, leading to accusations of police brutality. When the riot subsided four days later, local businesses had been trashed, 1 person had been killed by gunfire, 5 were wounded, and many more were injured, including 35 members of the police force; arrests numbered 185.[12] Ominously, civil rights leaders trying to pacify the rioters were greeted with shouts of "Uncle Tom!" The legendary African American leader Bayard Rustin—who a year earlier had organized a quarter of a million marchers in Washington, D.C., where on the steps of the Lincoln Memorial Dr. King's soaring rhetoric gave the world "I Have a Dream"—could not persuade a few hundred rioters to go home.

In that summer of 1964, there were race riots elsewhere in the region. In each instance the issues were local and the protests locally contained but national leaders took notice. President Johnson ordered the FBI to investigate, and the National Guard to prepare riot-control techniques. A year later, the alarm bell was louder—and the response more frantic. On a hot August day in the Watts area of South Los Angeles, a white policeman arrested a black man suspected of drunk driving. One thing led to another, and not until the National Guard arrived on the fourth day of rioting was violence brought under control. Watts had become a war zone. Nearly a thousand buildings were damaged or destroyed during the six days of rioting. Thirty-four people were killed and more than a thousand injured, "including 90 Los Angeles police officers, 136 firemen, 10 national guardsmen, 23 persons from other governmental agencies, and 773 civilians. 118 of the injuries resulted from gunshot wounds."[13] The nation anxiously took it in on national TV. They were witnessing "Burn, Baby, Burn" push aside "I Have a Dream."

One scholar estimates that there were 290 violent racial outbursts in the mid-1960s, resulting in approximately 40,000 arrests. He opines that "the level of open defiance of the established economic and political order was as great during this period as during any other in this country's history, save the Civil War."[14] The defiance on the streets was a profound rejection of color-blind principles, and assertions of black pride and demands for black power worried civil rights leaders. King felt he had no option but to disavow the black power slogan, fearful that it would isolate the black community.

This mid-1960s outburst of urban violence created a crisis in government. The immediate goal was to get unemployed blacks off the streets and into jobs, even if that entailed taking race into account. Anxious political and business leaders inched ever closer to affirmative action, especially in employment. A shift from color-blind policy to preferential hiring would certainly face political challenges. The attorney general at the time advised that programs "should not be devised for Negroes, as such, but for all disadvantaged persons." Though permissible to concentrate "in areas in which the beneficiaries would be predominantly Negro . . . it would be wiser as a political matter if the affirmative action programs were not labeled civil rights proposals, as such. . . ."[15] A few business leaders were cautiously moving in a similar direction. As summarized in a *U.S. News and World Report* article from that time, "The aim would be to ease discontent that has brought violence and destruction to many of America's big cities in recent summers."[16]

These were quiet efforts, still operating under the assumption that color-blind rationales were politically safer than race-based policy; thus the reference in the attorney general's memo to "all disadvantaged persons" despite the intent to concentrate in black neighborhoods. It was in this context that the Kerner Commission offered its advice to the country. If the urban race riots and the mood of crises in the country made clear that status quo approaches were no longer workable, what should replace them?

In retrospect it is clear that the Kerner Report was less important for its specific policy recommendations than for its novel argument, which changed how America understood racial discrimination. Discrimination did not primarily result from individual prejudice. It was embedded in how institutions worked—in home mortgage lending criteria more likely to help whites than blacks own their homes and in job tests more suited to the experiences of white than of black applicants. Drawing on testimony from leading social scientists,[17] the report introduced the novel idea of *unintentional* discrimination. This was discrimination that flowed not from a racially prejudiced employer but from how the labor market was organized. An employment officer could believe in equal opportunity but still administer qualification tests that penalized blacks. Though the term *institutional racism* did not appear in the report, the idea was implicit in how discrimination was discussed.[18]

The Kerner Report endorsed, if only barely, black employment quotas. It specifically recommended race-based hiring in police departments and at newspapers. A city police force, it reasoned, needed black police as an answer to charges of white police brutality. Similar reasoning was offered for recruiting black journalists: this was not to compensate for historic discrimination in the media; it was so the press could better explain urban conditions to the public. In its rationale for limited preferential hiring, the report anticipated what a decade later we label *diversity hiring*, eventually endorsed in Supreme Court rulings (as will be discussed in chapter 8). In the Kerner Report, preferential hiring was viewed as instrumentally relevant to a social good—forestalling urban violence or informing the public. Later, diversity hiring was seen as instrumental to having a workforce able to compete in the world market or to helping universities prepare future leaders.

President Johnson was forced from office before he could implement policy based on the innovative formulations found in the Kerner Report—especially the idea of unintentional discrimination. New policies came in with the next administration, that of Richard M. Nixon, who took office in 1969. Nixon, more than any of his recent White House predecessors—Franklin Delano Roosevelt, Harry S. Truman, Dwight D. Eisenhower, John F. Kennedy, or Lyndon Johnson—actually delivered an employment program that opened the labor market to African Americans. This program rested on statistics.

Quietly Counting: Bureaucracies Doing What Bureaucracies Do

In chapter 3, citing *Calculating People*,[19] I noted that the fascination with statistics in the early nineteenth century set the stage for the use of the census by race science. This was an early, tentative step toward a time when policy challenges would automatically be approached quantitatively. By the mid-twentieth century a culture of quantification had embedded itself firmly in the government. Government had at hand a huge supply of population statistics from the Census Bureau and other statistical agencies—on employment, health, education, housing, income, and much more. As a by-product of program administration, the government also had a supply of individual records that could be converted to statistical products—the Social Security Administration on earnings history; schools' records on educational attainment; the criminal justice system on arrests, trials, and imprisonment; among dozens of others.

The most abundant population characteristics in these statistics were (and still are) age, gender, and race. As I have emphasized, no census in American history failed to measure the racial composition of the nation. When large-scale government surveys began in the 1930s, initially to make economic policy, they always included race data. Epidemiology, defined as how often diseases appear in different groups, always used race as a relevant group. Race was a constant in administrative records kept by the government. It appeared on birth certificates and death certificates and in other government records sandwiched between these bookends of life—those on education, employment, marriage, military service, and Social Security.

We are not surprised that racial justice concerns—civil rights policy in the mid-twentieth century—would turn to the treasure trove of data being collected by the government. The brief moment when it was thought that color-blind policy could be fashioned was swept away by a government that had always put racial measurement at the center of its statistical system. In the history of the term *affirmative action*, from its earliest appearance in government documents in the 1930s to its arrival as explicit government policy in the 1970s, never was there a moment when the government said "let there be affirmative action" and let us now specify the statistical tools needed to implement it. The policy and its programmatic tool—statistical proportionality—were not planned. They evolved because the basic statistics were already available.

Recall again the policy path that led to a quota-based immigration policy in the 1920s. There were several decades of trial and error, advance and retreat, false starts and small victories, and eventually imperfect numbers being attached to very ambitious policy goals. The process was swept along by a sense of national crises—immigrants overwhelming the country (chapter 5). It was similar for race-based programs in the 1960s and '70s—trial and error; small steps taken for one reason adjusted to reach other goals, a process also swept along by the sense of a national crisis. In both cases technical issues and conceptual ambiguities were worked out with help from social science experts outside the government. In both cases the census played a leading role.

If there are similarities to these two quota stories there are also, at a more general level, similarities between racial counting and other counting exercises that permeate policy making. Near the surface of almost any policy issue from the last hundred years you will find that the policy options and their quantitative underpinnings evolved together—education reform, universal health coverage, and social security protection. A telling example is currently unfolding in criminal justice where scholars are asking how many innocent people are in jail. It is the nature of false convictions that they are difficult to count. But there will be advocacy for criminal justice reform if it can be shown to be as high as 3 to 5 percent, as has been estimated by social scientists[20]—though rejected by many lawyers and judges, who are professionally embarrassed by such a high rate.

It is not that what is uncounted is unavailable as a policy target. Congress immediately passed the Patriot Act after 9/11 without knowing how many trained terrorists there were in the country. It is a different point I emphasize: when there are relevant statistics, different policy options are available. This is readily confirmed by the case of racial counting and affirmative action.

An early hint of what was to evolve dates from 1961, when Kennedy issued an executive order known for its use of the term "affirmative action," though the phrase bore little resemblance to what it came to mean a decade later. For Kennedy it meant that an unfairly terminated employee should be reinstated and awarded back pay. Kennedy certainly did not have in mind special preference for minorities or any other form of reverse discrimination. Nor did civil rights leaders, who in 1961 were arguing for color-blind laws.

What was newly introduced by Kennedy was not his word choice but an effort to add the insight of enforcement to his order. Earlier presidents—Roosevelt, Truman, and Eisenhower—had also issued executive orders designed to move an antidiscrimination agenda forward but the emphasis had been on fair employment across government agencies and in businesses that received government contracts. Nothing much came of those efforts because a conservative Congress made certain that no enforcement mechanism was established. Kennedy knew this history. Looking anxiously over his shoulder at the powerful Southern Democrats in congressional leadership positions, he inched toward enforcement cautiously. As he proudly announced, "Through this vastly strengthened machinery, I have dedicated my administration to the cause of equal opportunity in employment by the government or its contractors."[21]

This "vastly strengthened machinery" was an interagency committee with few resources and limited staff. Interagency committees in the federal government are known as good for a press release but not much more. Kennedy's committee produced little in the way of employment opportunities for America's blacks. But it left a large bureaucratic footprint that, with the passage of time, grew in consequence.

Kennedy's executive order included an instruction to determine whether firms bidding on government contracts had in place special recruiting efforts to find suitable black workers. Historically the burden was on the job seeker to prove that he or she was not employed because of discrimination, something that could be claimed only after the fact. The new requirement shifted the burden to the person doing the hiring, the employer. Firms bidding on a government contract had to offer evidence that they would not discriminate.[22] Firms needed to show how many people with what skills would be hired to build a public hospital or fighter plane. The compliance reports mandated by the interagency committee required that these numbers differentiate by race. In short order, addressing racial statistics showing systematic discrimination began to replace individual complaints before the committee.

The committee was also expected to determine if employment practices in the federal government were free of racial discrimination. To do so, it wanted statistics on the race of those who applied for jobs, were hired, and were promoted. In 1961, however, under the influence of color-blind principles, government departments had stopped recording employees' race. When departments were asked by the committee to report on the racial composition of their workforce, the best they could offer were impressionistic estimates. The committee was impatient with such sketchy data, and pressed for more. By 1963, "federal agencies formally understood not only that they could once again identify employee records by race, but that they *must* systematically do so."[23]

The committee's work was consequential in yet another way. It, of course, had to design forms on which to record employment data. The earliest forms distinguished only between "Negroes" and "Other." This was quickly recognized as inadequate because in some labor markets other racial minorities were too numerous to be hidden under the "Other" label. The form was expanded to include "Oriental origin, American Indian, Mexican, Puerto Rican," and a general Spanish-speaking category.[24] There is nothing surprising here. The named groups generally tracked the 1960 census categories.

What might surprise the reader today, however, is that this definitional exercise that determined the minorities eligible for government program support was politically invisible. In a political moment of dramatic and very public civil rights agitation, marked by protest marches, sit-ins, and demonstrations, the committee and its forms went unnoticed with one exception. By the mid-1960s it was politically prudent for the government to recognize the growing importance of Latinos. A new statistical race had arrived, counted in detail, though in this case it was labeled an ethnicity.

We can see in this otherwise ineffectual interagency committee's insistence on quantification the outline of what was to come. The normal workings of bureaucracy, described as "administrative pragmatism,"[25] quietly put in place the tools that an affirmative action policy would later deploy: the designation of minority categories, forms for counting those groups, and the idea of comparing the numbers hired with the numbers in the available labor pool. The latter, of course, could be taken from census numbers.

As social scientists have endlessly emphasized, the race categories that gave political traction to affirmative action were undertheorized. The process unfolded with practically no discussion of "what were the necessary and sufficient conditions or qualities for minorityhood."[26] White ethnics—Poles, Lithuanians, and Italians, for instance—were never eligible for compensatory attention. No reason was ever given, despite the employment, housing, and education discrimination they had suffered earlier in the century. A few years later these white ethnics and their trade unions reacted angrily to the racially designed hiring targets and timetables, and in large numbers they shifted their political allegiances from the Democratic to the Republican Party. In this and in so many other ways, starting down the path of affirmative action in a largely unreflective manner cast a long political shadow over the nation. Chapter 8 returns to a number of unanticipated consequences from the casual way in which minority status was defined in the 1960s, but here the focus is on how these early bureaucratic choices became affirmative action a few years later.

Statistical Proportionality: Implementing an Employment Policy

The Civil Rights Act of 1964, especially its Title VII, which established the Equal Employment Opportunity Commission (EEOC), moved center stage in the mid-1960s. The EEOC took over from the similarly named interagency committee Kennedy had established. Title VII was the government's best hope of getting blacks off the streets and into jobs. Employed blacks, so political thinking went, would not riot. Title VII was clear on employment discrimination, setting forth "it shall be an unlawful employment for an employer to fail or refuse to hire or to discharge any individual, or otherwise discriminate against any individual [regarding terms of employment] because of such individual's race, color, religion, sex, or national origin." Initially this sweeping prohibition of employment discrimination was to be enforced with a small staff and a smaller budget.

This staff was tasked with determining whether specific employers were guilty of denying jobs to specific black applicants. Any applicant denied a job could file a complaint with the EEOC. Proving discriminatory intent was laborious, slow, difficult. Hiring and firing takes into account qualifications, business needs, employment performance, and other factors that can always be cited to explain why one person and not another got the job. In the best of circumstances, proving discrimination was a time-consuming task. The existing structure hardly offered the best of circumstances. Complaints flooded into the new EEOC; the backlog soon reached 10,000 cases. The commission could not hope to meet its legal mandate that every case be investigated and resolved in two months—two years was more like it.

Under intense pressure to perform, the EEOC decided to count, led by the same logic that had pushed its predecessor committee to count. It developed a form instructing employers to report on the racial composition of their labor force. The idea was simple enough. In areas with a substantial black labor pool, businesses that had few black employees must be discriminating. In the mid-1960s, the government confronted enterprises, and sometimes entire industries, with statistics demonstrating that they were underutilizing black workers in the local labor pool. "Notice was served: Employers—if they wanted to avoid such unpleasant encounters with the federal government—should hire percentages of qualified blacks that came near to their proportions in the population."[27]

Although it was discrimination against black Americans that motivated the Civil Rights Act of 1964, the counting exercise initiated by the EEOC picked up on the practice of its bureaucratic predecessor by listing the following groups: Negro, Spanish-American, American

Indian, and Oriental. Congress did not dictate or even discuss these categories—the commission staff chose them. In fact, Congress in writing Title VII was altogether silent on issues of counting and categories. It simply authorized its new agency "to make such technical studies as are appropriate to effectuate the purposes and policies of this title and to make the results of such studies available to the public." Only a few members of Congress seemed to take note that enforcing Title VII necessarily involved a minority classification scheme and an enumeration. In an interpretive memo; two senators wrote that record keeping would be "essential in Title VII because whether or not a certain action is discriminatory will turn on the motives of the respondent, which will usually be best evidenced by his pattern of conduct on similar occasions."[28]

At the time of the Civil Rights Act, approaches to racial justice were still focused on the complaint model. Minority job applicants who believed they had been discriminated against would file a complaint. The complaint would be investigated, and if determined to have merit, either voluntary compliance or legal action could remedy the situation. But this case-by-case work was simply no match for the pervasive, systematic discrimination in employment, housing, education, health care, and business. An individual-based effort was not going to turn the country around and it was not going to stop riots in America's cities.

The EEOC's first year reflected "not a grand design but rather an honest groping among the conflicts between nondiscrimination and affirmative remedy, color blindness and minority consciousness, individual complaint processing and pattern detection. . . ."[29] But this honest groping was to generate a revolution in how the nation would deal with racial inequality. The first step was to alter the basic understanding of discrimination by shifting attention from the prejudicial intent of the employer to the unfair results of long-standing, institutional practices.

The distinction between discriminatory *intent* and discriminatory *effects* came into focus. Whereas intent was individualized, *effects* were population based. To detect the latter required a picture of industry-wide patterns—a statistical portrait of the employment market. Of course, statistics on employment conditions dated from nineteenth-century social reform in areas from child labor to unsafe mines and factories. The bleak conditions revealed through those statistics were ammunition for reform movements. A century later, with quantification much advanced, a more sophisticated strategy was available. The challenge was to link statistics to a new way of thinking about racial fairness. This "would necessarily be based on some variation of a theory of proportional representation. That is, equal opportunity would be defined as, absent discrimination, an equal chance to represent one's group in the work force relative to the group's size."[30]

The new policy tool, then, was a statistical ratio. A ratio has a denominator and a numerator. The denominator was at hand because the Census Bureau and other federal statistical agencies counted by race. The EEOC knew how many blacks there were in the general population, or in a city or region, or in the workforce. From labor statistics there was information on overall size of broad occupation categories, such as school teachers or construction workers. If blacks were 12 percent of the general population but only 2 percent of construction workers, discrimination was indicated.

But these macroratios could not pinpoint which firms or businesses were discriminating. What was the racial distribution of textile workers in Georgia's mills or construction workers in Philadelphia? Even more detail would be necessary to identify a specific textile mill or construction firm. The more detailed numerator would have to be found elsewhere—perhaps in the record keeping so innocently launched by the EEOC? Congress did not intend the EEOC to exercise broad reporting powers, but in ways familiar to any student of regulatory agencies, the commission found a way to do what bureaucratic logic dictated.

By the middle of 1967, the EEOC had amassed an enormous amount of race (and gender) data at a level of detail that allowed targeted action. Precise data were available to compute ratios showing that blacks were nowhere represented in white-collar jobs proportionate to their numbers in the population. For example, "blacks in Kansas City were 11.2 percent of the population and only 2.1 percent of the white-collar work force; in Cleveland the corresponding figures were 13 percent and 3.2 percent."[31] These and similar ratios could be calculated for specific industries and even firms within industries. The conclusion was inescapable—in industry after industry and in every region of the country, employment was so massively skewed against blacks that systematic job discrimination could not be denied.

But by 1967 the Vietnam War had moved center stage in national politics. Antiwar demonstrations more than civil rights protests captured the headlines. The Democratic Party of Lyndon Johnson was weakened by its effort to sustain its ambitious Great Society initiatives while fighting a war. In the face of the souring national mood over the war, Johnson announced in March of 1968 that he would not stand for reelection that year. Less than a week later Martin Luther King was assassinated, and cities again erupted in race riots. Yet with the presidential election heating up, there was little space in the political agenda for renewed government action on racial discrimination.[32] Republican Party nominee Nixon, running on a law-and-order platform, won the presidency and took office in January 1969.

Affirmative Action: The Philadelphia Plan Inches Forward

It was early in Nixon's first term that statistical proportionality was adopted as a key policy tool for confronting racial discrimination.[33] As Arthur Fletcher, the most senior African American in the U.S. Labor Department, put it, "Affirmative action means that Government contractors must pledge themselves to establish goals and timetables for employing minority personnel. They must make an honest and good faith effort to hire a percentage or number of qualified workers. Percentages or numbers are used because industrial progress itself is measured in numerical standards."[34] Fletcher set out to rescue what was known as the Philadelphia Plan (so called because that was the city in which it was first to be applied). It had been set forth but never implemented in the Johnson administration.

The Philadelphia Plan took aim at construction firms bidding on contracts to build large government facilities—veteran's hospitals, interstate highways, weather stations, and military bases. This was a big target, nationally involving 225,000 contractors. Confronting discrimination in these contracting firms offered an enormous opportunity to move the country toward fair employment practices.[35]

A few years earlier, the Johnson administration had introduced what was known as a "manning table"—a form on which a firm planning to bid on a government contract had to prespecify the number of workers it would hire if it won the government contract—how many electricians, pipe fitters, or carpenters. Although the government requested that the manning table show how many workers were expected to be minorities, it could not require a given number of minority hires. That would have meant imposing racial quotas, which were prohibited by law. Eager contractors, however, knew that if they promised a significant number of minority hires they stood a better chance of being awarded the contract. An unacknowledged and informal quota system resulted, though not one the government mandated.

The Philadelphia Plan was an effort to put more enforcement power into this informal quota system. Under the plan the Department of Labor would be granted authority to negotiate with bidders the number of minorities they would hire *before* awarding a contract. Congressional reaction was angry and swift. Conservatives asserted that the plan violated the prohibition against preferential racial hiring. In the Johnson administration, the plan was shelved.

In the newly arrived Nixon administration, at the urging of Secretary of Labor George Schultz, the Philadelphia Plan got a fresh look. Schultz (later to become secretary of state) was a University of Chicago labor economist. In his view, racial discrimination was bad economics: the only good labor market was one that recruited and promoted the most qualified for any given job. If qualified workers were being disqualified because of their race (or gender) the labor market was not free to function as it should. As Nixon later characterized the Philadelphia Plan, "We would not fix quotas, but would require federal contractors to show 'affirmative action' to meet the goals of increasing minority employment."[36] Setting goals without quotas was the task Fletcher outlined in the quotation cited above. Fletcher introduced the clever idea that contractors could be asked to meet a target range rather than a specific number. Thus contractors would be setting their own quotas rather than having the government impose one.

The Labor Department held hearings in Philadelphia in the summer of 1969, following which Fletcher published an implementation memo that set target ranges. In Philadelphia, for example, the plumbing and pipe fitters union had more than two thousand members; twelve were black. Fletcher's implementation memo set a minority hiring target range for pipe fitters at 5 to 8 percent in the first year, to be increased annually until, in three years, the range would be 22 to 26 percent, nearly the level of blacks in Philadelphia's general labor force (30 percent).[37]

The language of targets and timetables notwithstanding, clearly this was preferential hiring verging on quotas. Conservatives in Congress again mobilized. In one hearing North Carolina senator Sam Ervin incredulously asked a Labor Department spokesman, "Do you contend that there has been discrimination in the past and that therefore you are going to practice discrimination in reverse in the future to overcome that past discrimination?"[38] There was much more congressional and bureaucratic wrangling to come, but when the dust settled and the Supreme Court ruled, an enforceable program of reverse discrimination had arrived.

It first arrived in the boilerplate language of a Federal Register note, which defined "underutilization" as "having fewer minorities in a particular job class than would reasonably be expected by their availability." In fact, by 1968 the EEOC had largely dropped the term *discrimination* in favor of *underutilization*, which "implied a norm of proportional representation" that resulted from hiring or promoting "fewer workers in a stipulated category than were available in the labor pool."[39]

Contractors who intended to bid on government contracts should take into account the "percentage of the minority work force as compared with the total work force in the immediate labor area." These ratios calculated, the contractor must then "specify goals and timetables" to "correct any identifiable deficiencies."[40] It was either that or don't do business with the federal government.

The pieces had finally come together to establish that groups as well as individuals had rights. Substantive and not just procedural equality mattered. Discrimination was not limited to the intent of an employer but could be statistically demonstrated as a result of institutional practices. In a pivotal employment discrimination case that introduced the disparate impact theory of discrimination,[41] a liberal Supreme Court reasoned that Title VII of the Civil Rights Act required the "removal of artificial, arbitrary, and unnecessary barriers to employment," and ruled against "practices that are fair in form, but discriminatory in operation."[42] With this ruling, even practices that unintentionally penalized minorities could lead to litigation. The numbers that proved "underutilization" pointed to the remedy—employment proportionate to a base number. The census and labor statistics provided the base number; record keeping by government agencies provided the numerator.

The inherent contradiction between color-blind principles and race-conscious policies was not set aside by the arrival of affirmative action. If anything, they intensified—a topic for chapter 8. Nevertheless, if it took reverse discrimination, preferential hiring, and even goals and timetables to attack racial injustice, it had become evident to many that there was no workable alternative.[43] After all, for more than a century preferential hiring and quotas had been used to keep minorities out of prestigious and better-paying jobs, out of America's universities, and out of positions of power and influence. The practice was old and had been in place for generations. African Americans "have been discriminated against because they were black, and for no other reason. . . . Under affirmative action, they are compensated not for being black but only because they were subject to unfair treatment at an earlier moment because they were black."[44]

When the administrative and regulatory agencies of the government turned to the policy tool of statistical proportionality among groups, they achieved results not available with a strategy based on individual complaints. This gave a new purpose to statistical races.

Affirmative action spread quickly. The forms used to implement the Philadelphia Plan listed Negro, Oriental, American Indian, and Spanish Surnamed Americans, the latter being defined as persons of Mexican, Puerto Rican, Cuban, or Spanish origin or ancestry, a listing slightly different from the one the EEOC was using.

Cubans did not appear on this list because of past discrimination. These recent émigrés from Cuba were prospering in Miami and voting Republican. Their political reward from a Republican administration was to be included among the groups that would benefit from preferential treatment. Their addition to the form, unremarked at the time, emphasizes again the casual way in which the government defined which racial groups merited affirmative action. Several years later the government got around to resolving the resulting discrepancies and anomalies.

The groups listed on the forms were the groups that could make claims as affirmative action spread from blacks to other minorities and then to women. The logic of statistical proportionality also expanded beyond employment and government contracting. It included housing, credit markets, business ownership, education, welfare programs, and voting.[45]

As affirmative action emerged in different government programs, the lack of standardization in the definition of racial minorities from one agency to another was confusing. The anomalies, such as the addition of Cubans on the Philadelphia Plan form, were mainly a nuisance, but to bureaucratic tidiness it made no sense to have one list of groups made eligible for jobs and a slightly different list for home mortgages.

OMB Directive 15: Time to Standardize America's Statistical Races

Sorting out a few anomalies across bureaucratic forms turned out to be more consequential than those involved might initially have imagined. First, it became evident that groups more easily counted, either for technical or political reasons, were going to come out winners in the affirmative action programs. With one exception, the determination of the winners and losers was largely left to bureaucratic players. Congress was then, and remains today, only too happy to avoid a public discussion of what defines race in American society. The exception was in how to define the Spanish-speaking population, an issue that did (and continues to) engage Congress and advocacy groups.

Second, the effort to standardize race classifications marked the moment when minorities found a political voice in determining who would be counted as a racial minority. There had been instances in America's past when a group in danger of being racialized fought to remove itself from the census—Jews being the most prominent example.[46] As noted in chapter 5, other European nationality groups had pressed to be included in the late nineteenth century. But affirmative action marked the first time in American history when *race* groups pressed to be included in the classification system. Of course, never before had statistical races been used for policies that rewarded rather than penalized.

The initial step in this democratization process occurred in an obscure OMB document issued in 1977 (briefly introduced in chapter 1). Now known as Directive 15 (as we will reference it), it was formally titled Race and Ethnic Standards for Federal Statistics and Administrative Reporting.[47] The directive standardized the categories for collecting and reporting race and ethnic data by federal agencies. Although without legal standing in the private sector, the federal categories became the de facto practice for businesses and universities. If a private firm had to report the racial composition of its work force or a publicly funded university the composition of its student body, it was easier to collect the data using the government's categories in the first place.

There was more at stake than bureaucratic tidiness. Directive 15 was the bridge between the nation's statistics and population groups that had historically experienced racial discrimination. The controlling formulation in all civil rights legislation, dating back to the executive orders of Presidents Roosevelt, Truman, Eisenhower, and Kennedy, was the injunction against discrimination on the basis of race, religion, color, or national origin, to which sex was added in the language of the 1964 Civil Rights Act.[48] The time-honored phrase—race, religion, color or national origin—merits close attention.

Race and Color. Because these terms have been used interchangeably, as we were conditioned to think by Linnaeus (see chapter 2), they have come to constitute one category, not two. Listing them both in the act, and in probably millions of government documents referencing the act, was redundant, another small indicator of the casual way in which the government has defined race.

Religion. Religion did not fit the logic of statistical proportionality. The interpretation of separation of church and state doctrine precluded a census question on religious beliefs or church membership, so there was no denominator to establish how much underrepresentation there was of Catholics or Jews. Also, there was the lingering concern among Jewish leaders that quotas were intrinsically dangerous, so that even to undo the damage of racism, they shied away from them. Despite pervasive discrimination against Jews and Catholics dating to the nineteenth century and reemerging in the post-9/11 period toward Muslims, religion was not a central feature in the civil rights era.

National Origin. Notwithstanding the central importance of national origin in setting immigration quotas in the 1920s, national origin did not become an operable category as affirmative action policy arrived, except with respect to Hispanics. Or, more correctly phrased, national origin did not become a category unless it was converted into race, as it was for Asian nationality groups. White ethnics, starting with the Irish before the Civil War and continuing with Italians, Poles, and others, had been denied professional jobs, pushed into segregated neighborhoods, and rejected by private universities. This discrimination lingered into the 1960s, indicated by the political debate over whether an Irish Catholic (John F. Kennedy) should even aspire to the White House. White ethnic resentment over government indifference to a century of discrimination eventually became organized opposition to affirmative action (as discussed in chapter 8).

The immediate task in the 1970s, then, was to bring clarification to how the generic term *race* was to be understood in affirmative action programs. This task was assigned to the interagency Ad Hoc Committee on Racial and Ethnic Definitions. The committee adopted the race categories in use by the Census Bureau: Asian and Pacific Islander, Black, American Indian, White, and Latino (the term *Hispanic* came later), but in a critical modification decided to treat Latinos as an ethnic rather than racial group. Less consequential, because the population was then very small, the committee moved South Asians from the White category, where the 1970 census had placed them, to the Asian category, thereby redrawing the boundary between Europe and Asia. There were so few subcontinent Indians in the country in 1977 that this change attracted little attention.

Directive 15's standardization of race categories influenced what subsequent policy and law accepted as protected minorities.[49] Several issues merit emphasis.

First is the government's candid admission that program goals and political considerations—not science—determined the specific categories. The race and ethnic classifications, said the government, "should not be interpreted as being scientific or anthropological in nature. . . . They have been developed in response to needs expressed by both the executive branch and the Congress."[50]

Second, because there was no agreed-upon science on which to base the classification, the directive offered no consistent rationale for its categories. For two groups, color is mentioned. Blacks, said the government, are persons with origins in any of Africa's "black racial groups." This definition gave emphasis to color and to continental origin. Similarly for the White category: white is a color (or the absence of color), but the directive also described whites as persons who come from any of the original peoples of Europe, North Africa, or the Middle East, here introducing national origin in the definition.

Descent is the key criterion for defining American Indians and Alaskan Natives, who are described as descendants of the original peoples of North America. The directive then adds another: anyone classified as an American Indian or Alaskan Native is expected to maintain a *cultural* identification through tribal affiliation or through recognition by others that they belonged to that group. Cultural identification is of course not a criterion for whether a person is black or white.

The Asian category references neither color nor culture. It is understood in the directive as a catchall racial home for groups more commonly described by nationality—Japanese, Korean, Chinese, and Hawaiian/Pacific Islander. The 1870 decision to racialize these nationality groups and to assemble them in one umbrella category was not questioned a century later.

Latinos (later adding the term Hispanics) are again treated differently. They are persons of "Mexican, Puerto Rican, Cuban, Central or South American or other Spanish culture or origin, regardless of race." Culture (subsequently including language), origin, and nationality are blended into an ethnic group, members of which also belong to one the four designated primary race groups.

The government sent a confused message with Directive 15. Depending on the circumstances, race could mean color, descent group, culture, tribal affiliation, or nationality. Paradoxically, the directive includes a nonrace—an ethnic group—for which race-sensitive policy is applied. Directive 15 made public and official how affirmative action should extend beyond black Americans. *People of color* became a commonly used term.

This broad construction of groups eligible for preferential treatment by the government had far-reaching political consequences. Obscured under the people-of-color construction were the unique circumstances of two unique groups: African Americans—a people who experienced two centuries of enslavement and then another century of apartheid and one-drop laws carried out under explicit constitutional authority; and American Indians, victims of genocidal wars and the forced removal from their homelands.

It does not make light of the discriminatory treatment of Asian workers or the exploitation of Mexican labor to say that the treatment of slaves and freed blacks and the total destruction of the Native American way of life occurred at a scale and over a time frame that could have justified policies that compensated for the African American and Native American experience differently from the discrimination toward Asians and Hispanics. Had policy been more differentiated, the history of affirmative action would have followed a different track.

The undifferentiated nature of the entitlement programs attached to the racial classification set the stage for the widely used people-of-color formulation that carried into the 1980s and '90s. This period witnessed a surge of new immigrants from Asia and Latin America, which greatly expanded the people characterized as protected minorities. This fueled political anger and resistance to affirmative action, and today clouds the nation's effort to deal with its immigrant population.

The final matter to emphasize about Directive 15 returns to a point made in chapter 2: the study of race is the study of principles and practices that render groups intelligible. The most pronounced and durable way to make groups intelligible is to classify and count them. It is easy to say that Directive 15 offered an incoherent rationale for its standardization of categories. It is difficult, however, to offer a more coherent rationale or an alternative set of categories. The nineteenth century tried to construct a classification based in biology. It failed. In a long and serious research in social anthropology, the twentieth century offered social construction as the process that creates races in America's social and political life. This research never proposed categories different from those it found in the statistical record. It seems social science no less than social policy depends on what the U.S. government decides to count as race groups.

Conclusions

Seventeen decades into racial counting by the government, what had been used to discriminate, segregate, and penalize was applied to antidiscrimination, integration, and benefits. Racial counting made a 180-degree course correction, unplanned, not even imagined as the civil rights era got underway. It happened incrementally. Statistical proportionality had an air of fairness about it. This, at least for a period, was compelling enough to counter the assumption that a post–civil rights America had to be color-blind.

From this point come a number of less encompassing but still important observations. Bureaucracies have jobs to do, and standard bureaucratic practice naturally draws agencies to measure the subjects of their concerns—in the 1960s, black unemployment. As the resulting statistics filtered through executive committees, then to congressional debates and press coverage, they were discovered by civil rights advocates. The pressure to make use of them increased. Targets and timetables were among those uses.

There were times in the development of these new policy instruments that forced a consideration of how best to count by race—Directive 15 was an important instance. However shallow it may appear to policy intellectuals some thirty-five years later, the directive gave the country something that worked well enough at the time. It provided an opportunity for any group with strong views to be heard. Hispanics made the most of this opportunity by becoming an ethnic group, thus avoiding being racialized without distancing themselves from the benefits that the classification made possible.[51]

That the government would listen to the racial groups being classified was new. It was quickly institutionalized in the racial advisory groups at the Census Bureau, which by the end of the century numbered five: Asian, Black, Hispanic, Native Hawaiian/Pacific Islander, and Native American. Later, when it came time to revise Directive 15 (see chapter 8), the racial advocacy groups testified in congressional hearings and public forums. Racial counting had been democratized, a development that has much to do with the complex situation in which we find ourselves today.

The remaining point to make about the lessons of racial counting underscores that governments make use of what is available. Had there been no statistical races at midcentury, civil rights policy could not have unfolded as it did. There could still have been marches, sermons, riots, commissions, hearings, committees, and court cases. There could still have been civil rights laws—perhaps exactly the ones that were passed. But there would not have been policies and programs shaped by the logic of statistical proportionality.

The account of civil rights in this chapter is highly selective and makes no assertion other than the quite narrow one that racial counting was available when programs were designed and, being available, it was used. It is this seemingly trivial observation that is driving the resurgence of political support for a color-blind America that would stop racial counting, as discussed in chapter 8. But first we take a detour—asking whether "being available and therefore used" presents instances of "being available and therefore misused."

CHAPTER 7

WHEN YOU HAVE A HAMMER: STATISTICAL RACES MISUSED

THE THREE-FIFTHS CLAUSE AND AFFIRMATIVE ACTION ILLUSTRATE HOW STATISTICAL races were put to policy purpose, in the first instance offering an example of how statistics were shaped in order to implement a policy and in the second instance offering an example of how policy was shaped to make use of available statistics. This chapter is about policies being shaped by the available statistics, but the two policy areas discussed here differ from affirmative action, which relied on the statistical races because the issue was racial injustice. In this chapter statistical races are misused because the policies to which they are applied are not really about race at all. The first example is known as the fair census controversy; the second considers the Human Genome Project.

The fair census controversy is about a technical issue—the census undercount—that had the statistical races at its center. On close inspection, however, we learn that it need not have been—*and would have been better had it not been*—about race at all. The ubiquity of race statistics poses a danger to policy making. When race statistics are readily available, policy can be inadvertently or inappropriately racialized. When you have a hammer, everything looks like a nail. Advocates for color-blindness justifiably warn of this.

The Human Genome Project, our second example, considers an issue altogether more consequential than the census undercount—*race-targeted medicine*, which hovers in the background of genomic medicine. If it develops, the odds are high that it will use the race classification at hand. It will revive the eighteenth-century insistence that the five Blumenbachian races are biologically real and can be put to work on a biochemistry project—different medical treatments for different races.

The Fair Census Controversy

Whether a particular statistical method can improve the census is not a trivial issue. It is, though, small scale compared to the three-fifths clause, the claim that freedom leads to insanity among blacks, quota-based immigration policy, or affirmative action. Small scale though it was, the issue did—if briefly—fully and sharply engage every branch and level of government, and was caught up in an intense partisan battle that spanned two decades. It soured sampling when linked to the decennial census, and as a result the Census Bureau has largely discontinued technical work on a statistical methodology successfully used in other countries to improve census accuracy.[1]

No census is a complete count of the population. President George Washington complained about the nation's first census. "One thing is certain," he insisted, "our real numbers will exceed, greatly, the official returns of them."[2] Every president since could offer the same complaint. Censuses are plagued by an undercount. Some people refuse to cooperate—asserting their right to privacy. Others don't want to bother and are shielded by unlisted phones or gated communities. People who live alone and who have few community ties can be missed, as can those who often travel. For those in the country illegally, fear of deportation motivates census avoidance (the fear is groundless; the census does not ask about legal status). Negligence on the part of census takers plays a role, though today quality control procedures identify and correct such problems quickly. Around the world census offices typically design special efforts to reach the hard to count.[3]

Throughout American census history an undercount was routinely assumed and anecdotally discussed. But statistical theory was insufficiently advanced to provide reliable estimates of its magnitude and distribution. There were no good answers to seemingly straightforward questions: How many people are missed? What are their characteristics? Where do they live?[4] A moment's reflection suggests why. There is only one census. To what, then, could it be compared to determine how complete it was? To assess census accuracy would require two population counts, allowing the results of one to check the other. Historically this would have been prohibitively expensive.

Then, in the 1940s, there was an unexpected opportunity to compare the census with an independent and accurate count of a major population group—men between the ages of twenty-one and thirty-five. These draft-eligible Americans were required to register for military service

Table 1. Percent net census undercount, 1940–1990*

Census Year	Percent Net Undercount
1940	5.4
1950	4.1
1960	3.1
1970	2.7
1980	1.2
1990	1.8

Note: *Based on a comparison of census results with a population estimate from demographic analysis. The net undercount is calculated by subtracting the estimated number of duplicates in the census from the estimated number of persons missed. One source of the comparatively low net undercount of 1980 is the large number of suspected duplicates in that census, which has the result of increasing the overcount and thus depressing the net undercount. Census-to-census comparisons are difficult because procedures, including how duplicates are removed, vary from one census to the next.

following the declaration of war after the Japanese attack on Pearl Harbor in 1941. Though hardly its intent, the universal military registration gave statisticians two independent estimates of young men—one based on the 1940 census and the second from the compulsory registration. Comparing these two numbers provided the first reliable measure of how many people, at least among young men, were missed in the census.

From this starting point a method to estimate the census undercount for both genders and all age groups was developed. Known as *demographic analysis*, it is in theory quite simple. It starts with a basic population number (taken from the prior census) and using vital statistics and other administrative records, updates it by adding every birth and every arriving immigrant and subtracting every death and every person who moves out of the country.[5]

The Census Bureau went to work on reducing the undercount, and was remarkably successful, as can be seen in Table 1.

It Is the Differential Undercount That Matters

Most of the benefits of a census are allocated not on the basis of absolute numbers but as proportionate shares of the total count. The most notable instance is each state's representation in the House of Representatives. The 435 positions are apportioned among the fifty states in relation to each state's share of the nation's total population.[6] Federal grants-in-aid in education, transportation, and health are also allocated on a proportionate share basis. The annual dollar amount of those

Table 2. Percent census undercount by Black/Non-Black: 1940–1990*

	1940	1950	1960	1970	1980	1990
Black	8.4	7.5	6.6	6.5	4.5	5.7
Non-Black	5.0	3.8	2.7	2.2	0.8	1.3
Difference	3.4	3.6	3.9	4.3	3.7	4.4

Note: *Based on demographic analysis.

grants-in-aid now exceeds $4 billion, which translates into millions of dollars for towns and communities across the country.

When benefits are preportionately allocated, politics fastens on the differential undercount. Differential simply means a nonrandom distribution of who is missed in the census. For example, if the same percentage is missed in every state, there is no differential undercount. Each state's share of the total population would be identical to its share if there were no undercount, and seats in Congress would be fairly allocated. But what if the percentage missed varies from one state to the next? The state with a higher percentage missed would get less than its fair share of federal funds and might even lose a seat in Congress.[7]

The differential undercount applies to groups as well as states. The census could miss a higher proportion of children than adults, or of men than women. More consequentially for the argument made in this chapter, the census could miss a higher percent of racial minorities than it does of whites. That, in fact, seemed to be the case. We saw above that young men counted by the mandatory military registration were more numerous than the 1940 census had counted. The country in the 1940s was, of course, racially segregated, and when young men showed up at the draft board they were recorded as white or black.

The population statisticians who compared the census with the draft records discovered that a higher share of young black men had been missed in the 1940 census than had young white men. The key notion of differential undercount entered census lore as a differential *racial* undercount. Table 2 shows that the magnitude of this differential undercount persisted despite the Census Bureau's success at reducing the undercount overall.

The Differential Undercount and the Politics of Racial Justice

The visionary social scientist Daniel Patrick Moynihan, then a Harvard University professor and one of the nation's leading urbanologists (and later a senator from New York), knew that the Census Bureau did a better job at counting blacks in 1960 than it had in 1950 or 1940. But he did not miss the troubling fact that the black/white gap had not narrowed over the same period. He organized the Conference on Social Statistics and the City. The published volume from that conference drew the obvious conclusion:

> When a group defined by racial or ethnic terms and concentrated in special political jurisdictions is significantly undercounted in relation to other groups, then individual members of that group are thereby deprived of the constitutional right to equal representation in the House of Representatives and, by inference, in other legislative bodies. That group is also deprived of its entitlement to partake in federal and other programs designed for areas and populations with its characteristics. In other words, miscounting the population could unconstitutionally deny minorities political representation or protection under the Voting Rights Act. It could also deny local jurisdictions grant funds from federal programs.[8]

Read this passage carefully. It starts "when a group defined by racial or ethnic terms," and concludes with racial minorities denied political representation. Because, in fact, the census *did* define groups racially, a technical problem in census taking, the undercount, suddenly and dramatically became politically treated as racial injustice. The Census Bureau came under enormous political pressure to fix the differential undercount.

Although demographic analysis could document the inequity in census numbers, that method could not fix it. Demographic analysis provides a national estimate of the undercount, but the inequity occurs at local levels—the very place where congressional districts are drawn and federal funds allocated. The census needed a more sophisticated statistical method if it was to fix the undercount problem.

Dual-system estimation was developed: first take the census, and then immediately follow it with a large sample survey. If correctly done, the sample survey offers a second population count that, when compared to the census, allows adjustment—block by block—that aligns the census with the "true" number of people in the country.[9] Starting in 1950 the method was steadily improved from one census to the next; though not until 1990 was the bureau confident that it could be applied to adjust the undercount.

Whether to adjust the undercount had by 1990 become the focus of an intense and nasty partisan battle. The initial salvo in 1980 was legal action from Democratic Party leaders who went to court to force the Census Bureau to adjust that decennial census, despite the bureau's position that the adjustment method was not reliable enough to apply. The court ruled in favor of the Census Bureau but instructed it to continue working on the methodology so it could be used in 1990.[10]

The politics did not let up. The electoral strength of the Democratic and Republican Parties was closely balanced; the margins in the Congress were close. Small changes in census numbers used to reapportion and draw electoral boundaries could determine party control of Congress. Sophisticated computer-assisted methods allowed the two parties to make fine-grained estimates of voter behavior census-block by census-block, and to use those estimates to draw districts favorable to their partisan interests. The Democratic Party, responsive to pressure from civil rights groups, believed that census adjustment of the undercount might produce more congressional districts favorable to Democratic candidates. For this reason, Republican Party strategists strongly resisted the adjustment method. Republicans demanded a traditional census, which works well in the white suburbs, where their support is concentrated.

In 1990 the Census Bureau's specialists were more confident of their methodology and decided to adjust the census apportionment counts. It was overruled by the Republican Secretary of Commerce (the bureau is a unit of the Commerce Department).[11] Census method had collided with partisan interests. Both sides framed their arguments in high-minded language. Democrats spoke of fairness, not partisan advantage. They insisted that the Census Bureau be allowed to apply whatever scientific methods it believed would improve census accuracy. Republicans cited the constitutional provision that an actual enumeration be taken as reason to reject any plan using sampling. Both sides found support among reputable statisticians.[12]

The technical challenge of producing an accurate count did not go away, and the Census Bureau continued to improve dual-system estimation. After the election of Bill Clinton, a Democrat, to the presidency in 1992, the bureau's technical work had more political protection. But partisan polarization reached new highs when the 1994 congressional elections brought to Congress a number of conservative Republicans deeply mistrustful of Clinton. The congressional election gave Republicans control of Congress, which they held during the years in which the 2000 census was being prepared.

Congressional Republicans who reviewed the census plans and appropriated funds were told that allowing the census to be adjusted would have a "negative effect in the partisan makeup of 24 Congressional seats, [and at the state level] 113 State Senate seats and 297 State House seats nationwide. . . ."[13] Charges of census tampering were in the air. The Congressional Black Caucus—all Democrats—took up the census as a leading civil rights issue, and they were often joined by Hispanic and Asian members of Congress. A leading civil rights coalition with 180 member organizations framed the issue, writing, "Because the accuracy of the census directly affects our nation's ability to ensure equal representation and equal access to important governmental resources for all Americans, ensuring a fair and accurate census must be regarded as one of the most significant civil rights and equal rights issues facing the country today."[14] When Democrats played the race card by accusing Republicans of derailing a fair count of minorities, Republicans answered by voting funds for efforts targeted at reducing the minority undercount: more money for community partnerships and promotional campaigns in minority neighborhoods. The Republican Congress, the Democratic president, numerous advocacy groups, and widespread media coverage turned the 2000 census into a debate about racial fairness.

But Was Race the Issue?

Yet, wait a minute. Households are not missed in the census because they are black or included because they are white. They are missed when the Census Bureau's address file has errors, when the household is made up of unrelated persons who are seldom at home, when there is a low sense of civic responsibility or an active distrust of the government, when occupants live in the community a short time, when English is not spoken, when community ties are not strong. *Race* was shorthand for many characteristics that themselves were not racial. The long, nasty, damaging partisan debate over census methodology need not have been about race at all. It was only because the U.S. government counts by race.

The first reasonable estimate of the differential undercount had a racial dimension simply because the draft system set up in 1941 recorded the race of every registrant. Birth and death records also record race. So when statisticians used these vital statistics in demographic analysis, they had a racial breakdown easily at hand. From that time on, the undercount was always discussed as if it were about race. Table 2, documenting the undercount by race, could not be constructed using, for example, a measure of social isolation or of linguistic barriers to completing a census form. They don't appear in the vital statistics on which demographic analysis is based.

Shifting to the statistical method of dual-system estimation continued the practice, again for reasons that were a by-product of other considerations. Dual-system estimation relies on census counts at the block level; these are available only from questions that are asked on the census short form.[15] Very few questions are asked on this form, which includes age, race, and Hispanic ethnicity. This information is required by the Voting Rights Act of 1965, which is administered using block-level data on the voting age population broken down by age, race, and ethnicity.

In 1990 and 2000, however, the short form also asked whether the home was rented or owned. The Voting Rights Act does not use this question. Why was it necessary to have block-level data on rental status but not, for example, on marital status, veterans status, or any of the other fifty or so variables on the census long form? Because the Census Bureau had determined that homeownership is a useful predictor of census coverage. The rental/ownership item correlates with census cooperation, and it was on the short form so that it could be used in dual-system estimation and census adjustment calculations. It is a far-fetched hypothetical, but if every young male registered for the draft had been asked not his race but if he came from a household that rented or owned, and if administrative records on rental and ownership status were accurate in 1941, the entire history of the census undercount could have turned on that variable rather than race.

In fact, there are many household characteristics that in principle might offer much better predictors of census coverage than does race: the language skills of household members, length of time in the country, education and income levels, marital status, or whether there are other family members living nearby.[16]

The Census Bureau recognizes this. In preparation for the 2010 census, the bureau identified the especially hard-to-count census tracts, using twelve characteristics.[17] Race was *not* one of characteristics. However, when the bureau reported to the public on the 2010 undercount, the press release emphasized the rate at which racial groups were missed, with the bureau taking credit for reducing the differential racial undercount. Race remained the lead story.[18]

I use the census adjustment issue to emphasize that, in the policy and political worlds, what is easily available is what is used—even if on close inspection it is poorly matched to the task at hand. In the 1960s what was available to the government—how many blacks there were in the labor pool and how many blacks got jobs—became the foundation of affirmative action policy, and this made sense. After all, affirmative action was a policy designed to end racial discrimination and improve employment of racial minorities. It was about race, as is the Voting Rights Act using block-level race data to challenge election boundaries that weaken minority voting power.

In the 1960s what was available to the Census Bureau—how many minorities were recorded in the nation's vital statistics and how many were counted in the census—became the foundation of an adjustment method to improve the decennial census. But, unlike affirmative action or voting rights, adjusting the census is not per se a race issue. If knowing that someone who rents or is unmarried or has no telephone is a better predictor of whether that person is counted, then that characteristic, not race, should be the center of a statistical procedure to improve the census.

Racializing the undercount was unfortunate, as was the partisan debate over sampling to improve the census more generally. It would have been better for the decennial census and for the quality of political debate in the nation had it not happened. But it did, and today it hampers progress toward census improvement. If the hammer-and-nail analogy applied only to a statistical method in census taking, it could be brushed aside as only marginally important in the big sweep of American politics.

If, however, it is relevant to an issue of much broader importance to America's views about its own people, then we might have second thoughts about leaving the hammer lying around.

The Human Genome Project and Race

The ancestors of modern humans who migrated from Africa's Rift Valley developed small genetic differences according to where the migratory streams settled, and for how long and how completely they were isolated from each other.[19] The earliest archaeological evidence of our genetic ancestors dates back about 160,000 years, and it clusters in a small area of eastern Africa. Over the next 25,000 years humans spread to southern and western Africa, then gradually down the Nile. Not until 90 thousand years ago was there a permanent settlement along the southern coast of the Arabian Peninsula. All non-African people are descended from this group.

Over the next ten to fifteen thousand years, humans made their way along the coast of the Indian Ocean, settling as far south as today's Indonesia and as far north as lower China. In today's terms, three race groups—Africans, Asians, and Pacific Islanders—were then identifiable. Following an ice age that dramatically lowered the world's population and temporarily disrupted migration, humans spread to Australia and up the western coast of today's China. Not until about 50,000 years ago was the Fertile Crescent settled; this also was the time when humans first crossed the Bosporus into today's Europe, creating the fourth of Johann Blumenbach's—and the Census Bureau's—five primary races. Another 25,000 years passed before humans reached northeast Eurasia, the departure point for crossing the Bering land bridge connecting Siberia to Alaska. The last ice age again interrupted migration, leaving a few isolated groups in North America. It was not until about 15,000 years ago that humans reached South America, and then gradually spread along the coasts and into some places in the interior of northern and southern America, adding the fifth (red) race to the world's population.[20]

Blumenbach's climate theory of race differences is based on the five continental descent groups that were formed during the 150,000 years it took for *Homo sapiens* to spread across the planet from their origins in Africa's Rift Valley. The basic conclusion of modern genetic science is that it is nonsense to think there are character traits such as inventiveness or indolence that can be traced to the genetic variation between one continental descent group and another. Evolutionary biologists and geneticists concur that the variations in humans that correlate with conventionally defined races or geographic descent groups are comparatively small, and in any case within-group variation is much greater than between-group variation.

However, contemporary genomic medical science has not yet reached consensus on whether paying attention to even these small differences between groups can advance medical treatment. This issue comes up because certain diseases are found more often in particular race or ethnic groups. Examples frequently cited include the prevalence of sickle-cell anemia among Africans and Tay-Sachs among Jews from northern Europe.

The founder effect in evolutionary biology explains why descent groups might vary in their susceptibility to particular diseases. Although the migratory flows sketched above started from a common gene pool, migration to East Asia led to a people isolated by culture and geography from those who migrated to Europe, and so forth. Because of inbreeding, random changes from one generation to the next, known as genetic drift, could produce genetic traits common in one region and absent in others. When a mutant gene led to a rare disease, the group reproducing in isolation from the rest of the human species would over multiple generations share that disease susceptibility more frequently than unexposed groups. For example, because of a sickle-cell mutation, Equatorial Africans and their descendants today have comparatively higher resistance to *falciparum malaria*, the type most likely to prove fatal and fairly common in tropical Africa. This particular mutation has a downside, however: the unusual formation of the red blood cells relevant to malaria resistance makes it harder for them to absorb oxygen, and this has some predictable negative effects. There are other such examples.[21]

Genetic clustering by descent group means that the human species "possesses what population geneticists call 'population structure': that is, certain DNA sequences are found at slightly higher frequencies in Africa, others in Asia, and so on. . . . These findings also mean that different groups of people might differ in subtle aspects of their biochemistry."[22] Given what is known about population genetics, population structure on a small fraction of the human genome is not surprising.

Geneticists have used computer programs to identify population clusters based only on genetic information. Although research on population clustering is in its infancy—and early findings will no doubt be modified—one research team found four clusters that map to the continental descent groups, or what today are taken to be four of the world's major race groups. In this study, research subjects, not knowing what descent group their genes had assigned them to, were asked their race using the census classification. Overwhelmingly the research subject's racial self-identification matched the population cluster that had been assigned by the computer program using only genetic information.[23]

It is understandable that the ability of science to map the human genome has accelerated the search for associations between diseases and gene expression. When those associations appear in one ancestry (race) group more frequently than another, medical science has reason to argue that knowing a patient's ancestry is diagnostically useful. For many health researchers and medical practitioners, not to use that diagnostic tool could retard health improvements and would be medically irresponsible. In this reasoning, if those population groups are conventionally labeled by race terms—Europeans, Africans, and the like—this does not lessen the usefulness of the diagnosis. Other scientists sharply disagree with this reasoning.

Those disagreeing do not question that genes are powerfully predictive of susceptibility to various diseases or that pharmacogenomics has great promise in the treatment of illness and improvement of health. However, they argue it is the genes that matter and *not* the race of the person carrying those genes.

Race categories found in the nation's statistical system were created for political and policy reasons that have nothing to do with medicine. In fact, genetic medicine loses efficiency by using race as shorthand. Even if certain race groups are more prone to particular diseases, not everyone of that race is susceptible and not everyone susceptible belongs to that race. Race-targeted drugs and medical treatment will necessarily and often miss the target; in technical terms, there will be false positives and false negatives.

While Waiting for Personalized Medicine, an Interim Strategy?

To these criticisms the answer is, "You might be right, but you aren't being practical." When geneticists have analyzed every person's individual genome and doctors can tailor person-specific treatment, the great promise of genomic-based personalized medicine will (perhaps) be realized. But the cost is enormous, even for the richest nations of the world.

Personalized medicine is not around the corner.[24] Race-targeted diagnostics and therapeutic intervention are accepted as a reasonable first step according to this argument—while medicine works toward personalized medicine. As a leading science journal quoted one geneticist, if individually tailored medical treatment is a distant promise, "the big question is the *interim strategy*: how to use ancestry now."[25]

It is this "interim strategy" that has many worried. Under the sponsorship of a private foundation, the Wellcome Trust, scientists from the United Kingdom offer a thoughtful reflection and warning on using ancestry (race) as an interim strategy as we wait the promise of genomic-based personalized medicine.[26]

The results of medical studies routinely report differences across racial groups. This comes as no surprise, nor does the fact that the differences are attributed to everything from prenatal care to lifestyle choices such as smoking, diet, and exercise, which vary from one group to the next. At issue is not whether differences in disease and health vary by race group, or whether environmental factors specific to experiences of race groups have explanatory power. It is a different question that has to be answered. Do statistical races as defined by the government work when scientific attention shifts from environmental to genomic explanations of disease susceptibility and optimal therapeutic treatment? This question motivated an investigation of how contemporary genetic and biomedical research in the United Kingdom makes use of race and ethnic census categories.

Biomedical scientists in Britain routinely apply a race classification in their research. The classification is not, however, constructed scientifically. It is borrowed from the UK census. Why? Because, report the biomedical scientists, these race categories were "felt to have proven practicability and portability—i.e., they had political legitimacy; they were acceptable to the public; they were easy to use; they permitted comparisons between studies; and they facilitated the translation of research findings into clinical practice."[27] The scientists who offered "political legitimacy" and "easy to use" as reasons for borrowing such a key variable as race from political sources are not altogether comfortable about it. It may be safe, they reason, to use the official categories for drawing samples or as descriptive variables. However, they acknowledge, "it seems unlikely that 'official' socio-political categories such as these [from the UK census] will be useful for identifying the underlying causes of any observed differences in disease susceptibility or therapeutic efficacy, because these categories can only ever offer crude proxies for the complex interplay of structural, socio-cultural and genetic factors involved."[28]

Moreover, points out the report, the official categories developed for the UK censuses "arose out of complex social and political debates about immigration, representation and equality, as well as from external and internal claims for separate group identities that continue to this day. As such, these categories are not fixed but have changed over time and are likely to continue to do so in response to shifts in emphasis within social and political arenas."[29] But what if medical scientists unfamiliar with this history adopt the categories as analytic variables? This can "prove problematic . . . due to their socio-political origins and inherent flexibility over time and place."[30] Genetic science operates on a time scale measured over millennia; census categories operate over a time frame measured in decades.

If the problems inherent in applying census categories in biomedical research were only scientific in nature, it could be assumed scientists would identify and correct these problems. But there is a much broader alarm to sound, and the report does so in its title: *Reviving "Racial Medicine"?* Could the use of census race categories in genetic research, because they are practical and because they have political legitimacy, bring a return of eighteenth-century racial medicine?

The report's authors are worried.[31] Applying the official categories in genetic research "runs the risk of 'geneticising' or 'biologising' such categories by treating them *as if* they reflected a reliable, valid and natural classification of discrete and biologically homogenous racial/ethnic groups."[32] It is this *as if* that poses the moral challenge to genetic medicine. If scientists can fall into the *as if* trap—can treat a census classification *as if* it is a truth of nature—is not the general public likely to come to the same conclusion? When you have a hammer, does not everything look like a nail?

The *As If* Risk in the United States

Not surprisingly, U.S. scientists have engaged similar issues to those debated in Great Britain. The match among the five races in the U.S. census with population clusters identified by evolutionary biologists and geneticists make it inevitable that there are worries about treating census races as genetically bounded population groups. That certain DNA structures appear at higher frequencies in different ancestry groups does "not mean that human races necessarily or even probably differ in profound ways," observes the biologist H. Allen Orr.[33] It does mean that subtle differences in biochemistry from one group to the next could, at the margins, be relevant to disease susceptibility or responsiveness to pharmacological treatments.

In a widely cited paper, Stanford University geneticist Neil Risch and colleagues argue this point. They claim "that from both an objective and scientific (genetic and epidemiologic) perspective there is great validity in racial/ethnic *self-categorizations*, both from the research and public policy points of view."[34] Risch and colleagues claim that people categorize themselves racially in genetically meaningful ways. After reviewing the major efforts by population geneticists to identify clusters, they conclude, "Effectively, these population genetic studies have recapitulated the classical definition of races based on continental ancestry—namely African, Caucasian (Europe and Middle East), Asian, Pacific Islander (for example, Australian, New Guinean and Melanesian), and Native American."[35] If these differences are cosmetic only, they will have no consequences for medical research. But, suggest the authors, they are not cosmetic; they are genetic, and therefore biological: "If biological is defined by susceptibility to, and the natural history of, a chronic disease, then again numerous studies over past decades have documented biological differences among the races. In this context, it is difficult to imagine that such differences are not meaningful."[36] It is, they note, irresponsible to ignore these differences in medical research:

> A "race-neutral" or "color-blind" approach to biomedical research is neither equitable nor advantageous, and would not lead to a reduction of disparities in disease risk or treatment efficacy between groups. Whether African Americans, Hispanics, Native Americans, Pacific Islanders or Asians respond equally to a particular drug is an empirical question that can only be addressed by studying these groups individually. Differences in treatment response or disease prevalence between racial/ethnic groups need to be studied carefully; naive inferences about genetic causation without evidence should be avoided. At the same time, gratuitous dismissal of a genetic interpretation without evidence for doing so is also unjustified.[37]

Elsewhere Risch is quoted as saying that ignoring race in gene studies will "lead to the disservice of those who are in the minority."[38]

His arguments are echoed by many in the biomedical community. The Nobelist Francis Collins, appointed as director of the National Institutes of Heath by President Barack Obama, is quick to say that race and ethnicity "are poorly defined terms that serve as flawed surrogates for multiple environmental and genetic factors in disease causation, including ancestral geographic origins, socioeconomic status, education and access to health care." Flawed though they may be, Collins is nevertheless endorsing the statistical races as surrogates for genetically based diseases: "it would be incorrect to say that genetics never has a role in health disparities." The bottom line is that "[w]e must continue to support efforts to define the nature of human variation across the world, focused primarily on medical goals."[39]

If many scientists are in agreement with Risch and Collins, many are not. Among the naysayers are most social scientists, but they are joined by major biologists and geneticists. Richard Lewontin, evolutionary biologist at Harvard, has for decades been an influential voice arguing that races as defined by government statistics are not biologically significant. He dismisses the importance of Risch's finding that genetic clustering and racial self-identification with the census categories correspond. The only way to cluster populations that match the continental ancestry groups is to use "a special class of non-functional DNA microsatellites. By selecting among microsatellites, it is possible to find a set that will cluster together African populations, European populations, and Asian populations, etc. These selected microsatellite DNA markers are not typical of genes, however, but have been chosen precisely because they are 'maximally informative' about group differences. Thus they tell us what we already knew about the differences between populations of the classical 'races' from skin color, face shape, and hair form."[40] For Lewontin, the clusters produced by microsatellites cannot lead to advances in medical science.

The population geneticist David Goldstein of University College London agrees. He argues that the best science occurs when patients are assigned to different groups based only on their DNA, not on racial self-identification. To understand the geographic pattern of human genetic variation, notes Goldstein, "you want the best representation you can find, and it is a technical question as to whether explicit genetic representation or racial labels are better. That's an argument we will have in the scientific literature, and Neil [Risch] will lose."[41]

Other scholars warn against the fallacy of misplaced concreteness that assumes that what is labeled a race "coincides with the obdurate character of the empirical world."[42] An example of misplaced concreteness is Risch and colleagues' assumption that the number of Americans who self-identified as being of more than one race in the 2000 census tells us something useful about the true number of multirace Americans. About the "mark one or more" option introduced in the 2000 census Risch and colleagues write, "According to these numbers, if mating were at random with respect to these racial categories, 42% of individuals would result from 'mixed' matings and hence derive from more than one race, as opposed to the 2.4% reported. These figures highlight the strong deviation from random mating in the US."[43]

Mating in the United States is, of course, not random. Whatever the true number of Americans with DNA traces from more than one race group, it is not 2.4 percent, no matter what is put down on a census form. Genetic admixture across the five eighteenth-century races is probably closer to 100 percent. For persuasive argument to this effect, see the work of Henry Louis Gates, Jr., who finds that "all African-Americans are genetically mixed, the only question is how much?"[44]

Risch and colleagues are extremely careful in how they handle genomic data. They are careless in their treatment of demographic data, especially self-reported race in the U.S. census. The "mark one or more" responses to the 2000 census are scientifically unreliable. Forty percent of those who gave multiple-race responses in 2000 answered differently to a follow-up survey conducted by the Census Bureau a year later. Of those who did identify as multirace in the follow-up survey, nearly half (45 percent) had declared they were in a specific race group a year earlier.[45] A genetic experiment based on data that unreliable would be discarded.

Of course, the census race categories can find their way into genomic medicine without relying on the self-reported data collected by the census itself. DNA is inherited; this implies ancestors and descendants. Descent groups have a "genomic geography." This phrase "refers to how, through the tools and practices of human genetics, bits of genomic sequence become associated with specific geographic locations, posited as the place of origin of people who possess these bits."[46]

Joan Fujimura and Ramya Rajagopalan offer a sobering account of the slippery slope from "genomic geography" to "biological races." Genomic geography, they observe, "is one thread between population, race, and 'genetic ancestry' that renders the three concepts difficult to untangle." Based on ethnographic research in the laboratories and professional meetings of genetic scientists, Fujimura and Rajagopalan conclude that the boundary between genetic ancestry and the government's "non-scientific" race classification is easily and frequently blurred.

Even scientists using an analytic technique specifically designed to avoid race categories are vulnerable to downstream translation by colleagues who confuse "clusters of genetically similar samples" with "samples with similar 'genetic history' or 'shared ancestry,'" and then take the latter to imply race or ethnicity. They are vulnerable even to the public relations efforts of their own universities, which "often use simplifying, provocative terms in press releases about their research results."[47]

It is beyond the scope of this chapter (and this author's competencies) to offer an informed view on whether statistical races, based on self-categorization or on technologies that create clusters based only on DNA, can be of worth in medical research. Genomic research is in its infancy; there is great uncertainly over the pace, scope, and validity of "race-targeted medicine." One thing we do know, however, is that in June 2005 the Food and Drug Administration licensed a heart drug, under the label BiDel, exclusively for use by black patients of African descent.[48] This generated an intense scientific and political debate; it is not yet clear how effective this drug is, or whether nonblack patients have been put at risk by targeting it as suitable only for black patients. Years into the very well funded and extremely active field of genomic medicine, it remains the only race-targeted medicine ever marketed.[49] For lack of sales, it is no longer produced.

Our focus, however, is not the future of race-targeted medicine; it is the risk associated with the blurry boundary between genomic medicine and the government-sanctioned statistical races. The National Institutes of Health (NIH) encourages "the inclusion of women and racial minorities in clinical research and requires that practitioners in clinical and basic biomedical research receiving federal funding report on the diversity of their research subjects," using the race and ethnic categories set forth by the Office of Management and Budget (OMB).[50] The NIH, however, does not require that the race categories be used in analysis. Fujimura and Rajagopalan report that the geneticists they interviewed do not interpret the NIH reporting requirement as an edict to use race in their research beyond including diverse subjects in field studies.

Other government initiatives, however, have had the effect of directly promoting the OMB categories in genomic research. A large international collaboration, launched in 2002 as the HapMap Project, brought together two prior efforts: the government sponsored Human Genome Project, with laboratories from around the world,[51] and the International SNP Consortium, whose members were large pharmaceutical companies.[52] The HapMap Project is tasked with cataloging common genetic variants in human beings, with the goal of locating patterns that frequently occur for persons having particular health risks. Four population groups were sampled for the HapMap Project: Americans of European ancestry, Nigerians, Japanese, and Chinese.[53] A plan to include a sample of Native Americans met resistance, and this project, then, represents only three race groups: European, African, and Asian.

The international collaborators involved in the HapMap Project include countries with widely different census racial classification systems, none of which match the American five races/one ethnicity structure. In setting up the project there was intense argument in the scientific community about the proper sample design. Some scientists promoted global grid sampling, which would ignore previous notions of who was related to whom and would not take into account national or continental boundaries as they exist today. The alternative was to recognize predefined ethnic, linguistic, racial populations as a guide to reproductive isolation.[54] This strategy is adopted in the HapMap sample.

Decisions about how to sample human populations for genomic research were at various critical steps influenced by the American government, especially by the NIH and the U.S. Food and Drug Administration. These agencies have different constituencies, medical and health researchers in the former case and drug companies conducting clinical trials in the latter. Both, however, apply the OMB recommended race classification that, of course, was constructed for the U.S. census and related population surveys.[55] America's statistical races have now migrated into international collaborations mapping the genome of the world's population.

Science is only a few decades into genomic medical research, and I again emphasize that much will shift as new discoveries are made. Yet also worth reemphasis, category systems have staying power in research and in policy.[56] That worldwide genomic research practices and clinical trial protocols are incorporating a basic racial classification system from the American census increases the stakes for the *as if* risk articulated in the UK report. There is the risk that census statistical races adapted in genetic research will be treated *as if* they were discrete, homogenous groups found in nature.

Why the *As If* Risk Matters

Despite the triumphs of the civil rights era, the public mind has not completely dismissed the thought that persistent racial differences in educational attainment or rates of criminal activity signal differences in aptitude and attitude that are, perhaps, biological. A dense academic book suggesting that enduring racial differences in genetically inheritable IQ help account for who fails and who succeeds in American education and employment markets reached the best-seller list in 1994.[57] One of its authors, a political scientist, has also offered an evolutionary and genetic explanation for elevated Jewish intelligence.[58] Genetic explanations for IQ are strongly denounced by other scholars, yet they retain some academic respectability.

More generally, Ann Morning has shown that racial essentialism remains very pronounced in what students are taught in high school and college.[59] Textbooks, for example, routinely present genetic explanations of diseases in terms of the familiar census race categories. The assumption that "race is biological" is certainly true across the biological sciences, but is also found in physical anthropology, world history, and often in the social sciences—with the only exception being social anthropology, where the emphasis is on races as socially constructed.

In this context, it seems plausible that race-targeted medicine could legitimate other biologically based arguments about racial differences, perhaps that the brain evolved faster in some races or that there are genetic predispositions to violence. Medical science does not take place in a social and political vacuum. When the U.S. Food and Drug Administration licenses a heart drug it sends a message to a much broader audience than to the doctor who prescribes it and the patient who takes it.[60] It is that broader audience and what it is prepared to hear, perhaps even wants to hear, that raises nonmedical questions about medical practices.

And the message does not come only from medicine. The lead article in a prestigious political science journal reports "a significant association" between genetic traits and voting behavior for African Americans, but not for Asians, American Indians, and nonwhite Hispanics. The authors offer a complicated genetic-based explanation, one that cautions against the conclusion that differential voter turnout across the race groups has a genetic base. The explanation does, however, include this passage: "a gene that is in linkage disequilibrium with a polymorphism of MAOA and occurs at a higher rate among African Americans predicts voter turnout."[61] There will be more such articles, always cautious, but still leaving an impression that racial genetic differences have predictive power for behaviors—voting, in this case—well beyond health issues.

"Race in America has always explained too much and too little," writes historian of science Evelyn Hammonds. "Yet, Americans are deeply attracted to and readily accept racial narratives—especially when they are produced by biology."[62] The arrival of genetic medicine can easily deepen and strengthen this narrative, as race-as-biology moves from disease incidence to intelligence to criminology to social violence. Genetic science may stop at disease incidence, but this will not prevent the political resurgence of a racial narrative that appropriates a scientific metaphor for seemingly analogous public policy questions.

Biology's Century

We might not worry so much were it not for the powerful way in which biology is reaching into our lives. It is now commonplace to say that what physics was to the twentieth century, biology will be for the twenty-first. As renowned physicist Freeman Dyson notes, "Biology is now bigger than physics, as measured by the size of budgets, by the size of the workforce, or by the output of major discoveries; and biology is likely to remain the biggest part of science through the twenty-first century. Biology is also more important than physics, as measured by its economic consequences, by its ethical implications, or by its effects on human welfare."[63] This prediction leads Dyson to an even more audacious claim, that "the domestication of biotechnology will dominate our lives during the next fifty years at least as much as the domestication of computers has dominated our lives during the previous fifty years."[64] By "domestication" he means, for example, the biological equivalent of a computer in every household, down to video and computer games for children, games that will be played with actual eggs and seeds. The winner of a science fair might "be the kid whose egg hatches the cutest dinosaur."[65] Even if this image is far-fetched (it might not be), it is certain that we are entering an age of greatly increased attention to biology and genes.

It is no small matter to ask, Is this not an exceptionally risky time to adopt race as an interim strategy on the road to personalized genomic medicine, an interim strategy that *only* makes sense if race is presented as biologically real? Perhaps medicine will reach its goal of individually tailored diagnostics and health treatments, and will then set aside its interim strategy. Even if this occurs within a few decades (very unlikely),[66] having used biological race as an organizing principle in the interim will leave a sizable imprint in public consciousness. It is a judgment call whether the expected benefits of reporting research and, if indicated, targeting treatments to race groups outweigh the danger that political interests and social processes unrelated to medicine will latch onto the "new proof" that race is biological. I believe that danger is real, despite reassurances by the biomedical community.

Risch and his colleagues, among many others, have provided a carefully argued scientific rationale for "identifying genetic differences between races and ethnic groups," emphasizing what can be learned about disease susceptibility or variation in drug response. They recognize that "[g]reat abuse has occurred in the past with notions of 'genetic superiority' of one particular group over another." Reflecting views held by the vast majority of scientists engaged in genomic research, Risch and colleagues insist that the "notion of superiority is not scientific, only political, and can only be used for political purposes."[67]

It is, of course, these *political purposes* that are worrying. In the 1930s, reputable geneticists were tragically naive in failing to understand the political purposes to which eugenics was being applied in Adolf Hitler's Germany.[68] I intend no direct analogy to the current adoption of the race classification by modern genomic science. But history confirms time and again that science has few defenses against the political appropriation of its results. Among the eugenicists were many who expected that their field of study would never be used to justify genocide. It was. Among the physicists who developed the atom bomb were many who expected that it would never be dropped on civilians. It was—twice.

Reputable geneticists today insist that their science does not imply racial inferiority. But they are mistaken if they think that others will forgo the racist ammunition they are providing. Hanna Arendt taught us that the Enlightenment did not banish radical evil. Concentration camps, she wrote, must cause "social scientists and historical scholars to reconsider their hitherto unquestioned fundamental preconceptions regarding the course of the world and human behavior."[69] A political rebirth of scientific racism is not out of the question. We hear echoes of it in how the

French speak of the Roma, the Dutch speak of Muslims, the Germans of the Turks, and here in the United States of undocumentred migrants—four countries proud of their racial tolerance but in some quarters now given to xenophobic and racist assertions about the foreign born.

I am not predicting a resurgence of racist political doctrine. I am claiming that it is naive to assume that it cannot happen. If it does re-emerge, in whatever guise, the creation of race-targeted medicine will not be an innocent bystander. It certainly will not be so if racial terms are superimposed on continentally mapped genetic variation and this becomes a commonly accepted global vocabulary via genomic research. In this context, what are we to make of the government in the voice of the OMB, telling the country that its official census categories "should not be interpreted as having anthropological or scientific origins" and that they are a "product of US political and social history"?[70] The status of this social constructionist assumption is not so clear if the government, in the voice of NIH research or its protocols for drug trials, is also saying that the census classification is being used by genomic researchers because they have "documented biological differences among the races."[71]

The voices insisting that race is socially constructed will find themselves defending what will be dismissed as "politically correct science" against arguments from the "real science of biomedicine." If it comes to this, if it is "my science is better because I give African Americans a drug that will protect them against heart attack," the OMB's assertion that the census's race statistics have no scientific basis gets lost in the noise.

I conclude this chapter by returning to its title. The census undercount never was a nail, but it was treated *as if* it were. That's the problem when a hammer is the tool at hand. Real damage was done, though at a scale that can be shrugged off.

If the hammer-and-nail aphorism is even slightly applicable in the case of genomic medicine, the damage will not be easily shrugged off.

PART IV

The Statistical Races under Pressure, and a Fresh Rationale

CHAPTER 8

PRESSURES MOUNT

THE PROSPECTS ARE NEGLIGIBLE THAT THE DANGER OF MISUSING RACIAL STAtistics outlined in chapter 7 will by itself end race counting in the U.S. Census. Other pressures, however, might. In this chapter we consider three:

- Multirace as a census option, driven by multiculturalism and identity politics.
- The gravitational pull of the diversity agenda and its relation to racial statistics.
- Political pressure for color-blind statistics.

Offical recognition of multiraciality, the legal endorsement of diversity programs, and color-blind political pressures are, in their respective ways, seriously intentioned, complex social and political developments. In this chapter the importance of these developments is reduced to simple questions: What does each portend for racial counting? Will any of them hasten an end to America's statistical races or, unexpectedly, give them new purposes and extend their policy importance deeper into the twenty-first century?

On initial inspection, multiracialism and diversity appear to strengthen the mission of race statistics, while pressures for color-blind statistics are an unambiguous challenge to the entire project. Closer examination reveals a more subtle play of forces. Multiracial recognition lies in a self-esteem rationale, which challenges the racial justice rationale that gave momentum to statistical races in the last half century. The diversity agenda, also linked to self-esteem and recognition rationales, produces in law and in practice results that render race statistics difficult to use. The color-blind pressures reflect a widespread public unease toward most policy uses of statistical races, leading to demands that the government get out of the business of racial measurement.

These three interlinked pressures have created political space for reconsideration of whether the nation needs racial and ethnic statistics at all, and if the answer is yes, whether those now being produced meet current policy needs. To understand America's statistical races in light of the political space in which they now operate requires attention to a broad sociological argument briefly noted earlier (see p. 11). Statistics create as well as reflect reality. They can be designed to serve prescriptive purposes that go beyond their conventional descriptive tasks. It is easy—but a mistake—to overstate this point, especially with respect to the realities of race. Nearly anything about race in America, from racial discrimination to racial pride, has a reality independent of whether it is statistically measured. It is also easy—and also a mistake—to understate the point. How a society thinks about race is necessarily linked to its racial vocabulary and how it experiences race is necessarily linked to its racial policies. This vocabulary and these policies are embedded in what the state and its scientific backing present as our statistical races. This point bears on the next topic, and is more fully developed in chapter 11.

Identity Politics Adds an Expressive Purpose to Census Taking

When in 1977 the government resolved a few inconsistencies in how race was being counted from one agency to another and issued OMB's Directive 15, it could assume that racial classification was now cleaned up for the purposes at hand. The hot political issue was not, after all, *why* or *who* to measure, but *how* the statistics were to be used. Had the politics been different, had they focused on *what a race is*, and *who belongs to which race*, the relatively quiet bureaucratic resolution that standardized racial definitions would have been impossible. That it was possible confirms that America at the time was comfortable with its racial classification. (The appendix describes cases in three other countries where racial justice policies are being debated in the absence of such agreement.)

Less than two decades passed before this comfort gave way to a political debate that raised an old issue, one now refashioned on the eve of the twenty-first century: where to assign people who straddle the boundaries of a limited and rigidly fixed taxonomy? The nineteenth-century Mulatto category was an early but ultimately flawed effort to answer the question.

The issue of fixed racial boundaries again reached the political agenda late in the twentieth century, with much more at stake. The issue was given life by the swirling debates around multiculturalism and by the emergence of identity politics. Measurement decisions could no longer be contained in little-noticed bureaucracies and backroom legislative wrangling. Issues of whom to measure, and why, now belonged to the world of aggressive advocacy, congressional hearings, public debate, party politics, and media coverage. Those issues will not again return to the quieter times that gave us Directive 15 in 1977.

Substance as well as process changed at this time. Revised standards for racial classification were announced in 1997, timed to allow for their use in the 2000 census.[1] There were two changes. One dealt with fixed boundaries, and we will examine that shortly. The other was whether there are five or four primary races. Recall that in chapter 2 Linnaeus's classification listed four races, but that of Blumenbach a few years later added a fifth race by separating Pacific Islanders from the Asian race. In modern times it was a senator from a Pacific Island, Hawaii, who gets credit for a 2000 census in America that finally confirmed the five-race taxonomy.

Adding the Brown, Fifth Race: Native Hawaiians/Pacific Islanders

Senator Daniel K. Akaka, the first senator of Native Hawaiian ancestry, for years maintained that Native Hawaiians and Pacific Islanders were misclassified by their placement in the Asian category. In influential congressional testimony, Akaka offered two points. One, based in civil rights reasoning, argued that Native Hawaiians and Pacific Islanders had lower incomes, fewer educational opportunities, and less access to health care compared to the larger Asian population. He urged that these disparities be separately tabulated, and that government programs be targeted accordingly.

Akaka then added that the "current classification by the Federal Government denies us our identity as indigenous peoples."[2] Akaka prevailed. The OMB, persuaded by both the disparity and the identity rationale, accepted that Native Hawaiians/Pacific Islanders would henceforth be treated as a primary race group rather than a subgroup of the Asian population. With little fanfare, the government added brown to the black, red, white, and yellow groups already fixed in the classification.

More consequential for our purposes is Akaka's reference to being denied "*our identity* as an indigenous people." Pride in identity is central to the second major change made in preparation for the 2000 census.

CHAPTER 8

"Mark One or More"

Signaling a turning point in census history, the 2000 race question allowed multiple answers to the census question. "What is this person's race?" was followed by the instruction, "*Mark one or more boxes*" (see fig. 1).

Racial classification is a political exercise in reducing social complexity. Reduction inevitably produces instances that don't fit the categories. Multiracial Americans have been around a very long time. Census designers know this, as evidenced in the politically misguided but statistically reasonable effort to count mulattoes in the nineteenth century. By the early twentieth century, eugenics and doctrines of racial purity pushed aside counting mixed races in favor of the one-drop rule assigning anyone with a trace of African ancestry to the black race. The one-drop rule was applied in the Jim Crow South to prevent marriage across the color line, and then made its way from state legislature to state legislature, reaching much of the country. Not until the 1960s was it legally erased, taking with it the prohibition of interracial marriage.[3]

Discarding one-drop thinking opened up political space for a multirace movement. It emerged in the 1980s, framed not as a civil rights issue but in concert with a multicultural movement stimulated by the immigrant wave of the period (as will be discussed in chapter 9). Immigration in large numbers put under question a late-nineteenth-century metaphor—the melting pot. This metaphor held that beliefs and habits brought to America by Italians, Poles, and Slavs would fade as immigrants were assimilated into the superior mainstream culture. The mainstream was, of course, Anglo and Protestant. Less melting took place than metaphorical writing assumed. Jews and Catholics stayed Jewish and Catholic; Poles and Italians claimed hyphenated identities. The idea of the "hyphenated American" took hold. First proposed by Jewish intellectuals in the 1920s,[4] it was then adopted by groups long in the country—"Mexican-Americans," "Irish-Americans," "African-Americans"—and retained its attractiveness to those arriving in great number a half century later: "Korean-Americans," "Arab-Americans," and so on. Today we encounter the term *multicultural* more often than melting pot, and speak of ethnic diversity as well as assimilation.

It was in the context of immigrant-driven multiculturalism that the movement to recognize multiraciality in the census gained political traction. Demographic trends were part of the picture. Biracial marriage was on the rise. At 1.3 percent in 1980, by 2000 it reached nearly 5 percent.[5] The OMB was receptive to changes in the census race question if they would better match population realities. The Census Bureau took note that states were adding a multirace option on school records, employment applications, and birth and death certificates.[6] Congress was alerted to these stirrings. Republican Congressman Newt Gingrich, elected to the powerful position of Speaker of the House in 1994, advocated for a multiracial option on the census questionnaire, arguing that "America is too big and too diverse to categorize each and every one of us into four rigid racial categories. [The census should] . . . stop forcing Americans into inaccurate categories aimed at building divisive subgroups and allow them the option of selecting the category "multiracial," which I believe will be an important step toward transcending racial division and reflecting the melting pot which is America."[7]

An activist in Gingrich's congressional district had a few years earlier initiated an effort to change census practice. In 1996, Susan Graham, the white mother of a biracial child and cofounder of Project RACE (Reclassify All Children Equally), testified in Congress: "I'm not a scholar, attorney, or lawmaker. I'm just a mother . . . and whether I like it or not, I realize that self-esteem is directly tied to accurate racial identity . . . my child has been white on the U.S. census, black at school, and multiracial at home, all at the same time."[8]

Civil rights organizations rejected this self-esteem rationale, noting that a multirace option dilutes minority numbers and sets back the cause of racial justice. The National Association for the Advancement of Colored People (NAACP) testified that the "creation of a multiracial classification might disaggregate the apparent numbers of members of discrete minority groups, diluting benefits to which they are entitled as a protected class under civil rights laws and under the Constitution itself." The testimony insisted that the basic purpose of the race classification is "the enforcement of civil rights laws." Its categories were not called on "to provide vehicles for self-identification."[9] In a show of racial solidarity, Asian and Hispanic advocacy groups joined the protest.

Self-identification, however, was exactly what multiracial advocates wanted. For them the issue was social recognition, not social justice. If there was a conflict between those agendas, so be it. The Association of Multiethnic Americans was explicit, commenting, "We want choice in the matter of who we are, just like any other community. We are not saying that we are a solution to civil rights laws or civil rights injustices of the past." [It is ironic that] "our people are being asked to correct by virtue of how we define ourselves all of the past injustices [toward] other groups of people."[10] In this testimony official statistics are a proper site for personal choice, and of expression of one's identity. This is generally summarized as the expressive or, in some analysis, the aspirational function of a census.[11] A stodgy data collection bureau had become an agent of deconstruction.[12]

Reflecting the fading urgency of civil rights concerns so compelling forty years earlier, the multiple-race argument prevailed. A revision of

OMB Directive 15 was announced in the October 30, 1997, *Federal Register*. This revision introduced the "mark one or more" option, thereby allowing mixed racial heritage to be taken into account. With five primary races now established, the "mark one or more" census instruction allows for 63 racial possibilities and, of course, 126 ethnoracial options when race is tabulated in conjunction with the Hispanic/non-Hispanic distinction.[13]

Adding an Expressive Rationale to the Census

I wrote above that the "mark one or more" option exerts pressure on our current classification. This is not because the statistics had important political or policy consequences. To begin with, only 2.4 percent of the population used the option when it was made available in the 2000 census. Although the low rate of multiple-race identifiers has since doubled, the rate remains too low to upset most uses to which race data are put. In fact, the government took action to minimize the policy importance of the multiracial statistics. In enforcing nondiscriminatory laws, the Department of Justice assigns multiple-race responses to a single race category, favoring plaintiffs who claim discriminatory treatment. If a black contractor sues a city council for awarding a building contract to a white firm, the Department of Justice calculates statistics relevant to the case by adding to the city's black population all those who in the census were counted as black and some other race—usually white. This practice, devised in the last year of the Clinton presidency, was left intact by the next two presidents, Bush and Obama. Race statistics continue to map disparities—health, education, employment, incarceration, and the like—much as they had prior to the multiple-race option. Changing the census race question *without* altering its policy uses was something new in census history.

Seen from a less policy-focused perspective, the multiple-race change is anything but trivial. In adding an expressive rationale to the census race question the "mark one or more" option calls into question the standard justification the government offers for asking What Is Your Race?—the emphasis on statutory and administrative purposes. The Census Bureau explains that statistics on race are needed "to assess fairness in employment practices, meet legislative redistricting requirements by knowing the racial make-up of the voting age population, learn who may not be receiving medical services, determine disparities in health and environmental risks" and other purposes of this kind. The bureau lists ten key executive agencies that require race data.[14]

Although the bureau's reasons for the race question make no mention of self-esteem or recognition, public discussion of the "mark one or more" option focuses on its expressive rather than racial justice function.

In accepting the legitimacy of expressive rationales, the government has quietly given a new and very twenty-first-century reason for asking Americans what their race is. In chapter 11 we return to this feature of the census, and there justify changes in the race question *because* it has expressive consequences. We will examine why a change in the census that upends conventional thinking about race *does not* upend current policy uses. This is a guide to further and more ambitious reform of the nation's race statistics.

The Fast-Growing "Some Other" Race

A significant anomaly appeared on the 2000 and the 2010 census forms. Since 1930 the census has included a "some other race" option at the end of the race question (see fig. 1). The historical record is not too clear about the reasoning, but it is generally accepted that the "some other race" option was a way to capture mixed-race responses. If that was still its purpose in 2000, it was, of course, redundant. The "mark one or more" option eliminated the need for the "some other" line.

In fact, the "some other" option had been left there inadvertently. When this was realized after the 2000 census, the Census Bureau tried to make the statistically sound decision to remove it from future census questionnaires. This decision ran afoul of a demographic fact, one with powerful political significance. More than fifteen million Americans used the "some other race" line in 2000; 97 percent of them were Hispanic, primarily Mexican and Central American. About half of the entire Hispanic population in the United States asserted that they did not fit into the standard classification. This group—the fastest growing race group in America—was inventing for itself a "new" race, called "other" in the statistics but widely understood as Mexican American/Central American. The "some other" option remained on the 2010 census form; nineteen million Americans used it, 97 percent again being Hispanics.

The Census Bureau is now in the awkward position of providing counts from the Hispanic/non-Hispanic question for legal and administrative use, and also reporting Hispanic counts from the "some other race" line. These counts allow a large and politically significant group to express a clearly important self-identity, and to boast that it is America's largest minority.

The multiple-race option and the "some other" option in the race question open the door for additional expressive demands on the census. How soon and in what numbers others may try to walk through the door is not our question here; it is the fact that the door has been opened that matters. For more than a half century racial justice has been the powerful justification for counting America's races. The newly asserted expressive rationale veers off in a different direction.

The Diversity Agenda, Spreading Rapidly

When it was introduced as government policy in the 1970s affirmative action was politically resisted by many Americans. For them, using race to undo racism made no sense.

By the 1990s opposition to race-sensitive affirmative action coalesced around several themes, as cogently summarized in a memo prepared for a White House task force appointed by President Clinton soon after he took office, "The long-standing arguments against race-based affirmative action are basically these: (1) that it unfairly discriminates against innocent whites because of their race; (2) that it compromises many good meritocratic standards; (3) that it benefits many groups and individuals that are not sufficiently disadvantaged; (4) that it stigmatizes its purported beneficiaries; and (5) that using race to distribute benefits deepens racial divisions and entrenches racial ways of thinking, instead of moving us toward a more colorblind and united society." The same memo set out the justification for affirmative action. It is "a corrective for the continuing effects of *past* discrimination" as well as "a prophylactic against *future* acts of discrimination." The memo then added a rationale that was only tangentially related to past or future discrimination. Affirmative action was viewed as a way to "to promote diversity, provide role models," and, notably, to "develop competitive advantages in a demographically changing labor market."[15]

The Supreme Court Rules against Quotas, but in Favor of Diversity

Diversity as an extension of—or, depending upon who does the interpreting, an alternative to—affirmative action entered public consciousness in a landmark Supreme Court ruling in 1978. This case was brought by Allan Bakke, a rejected applicant to the medical school at the University of California–Davis, who claimed that the university had denied his application because of his white race, violating his rights under the equal protection clause of the Fourteenth Amendment. His case rested on the argument that slots had been reserved for less-qualified nonwhite candidates, and that this amounted to a race-based quota system. The Supreme Court agreed that quotas were unconstitutional, but on other grounds upheld the university's decision.

Writing for the majority, Justice Lewis Powell noted that "racial and ethnic classifications of any sort are inherently suspect and call for the most exacting judicial scrutiny," but "the goal of achieving a diverse student body is sufficiently compelling to justify consideration of race in admission decisions under some circumstances."[16]

A diverse student body was, in 1978, a novel idea, but soon universities began to cite it as reason for seeking minority students. A quarter of a century after the case, the Supreme Court reaffirmed the social value of diversity, and in the process extended diversity rationales beyond higher education to the business world and to the military.

Diversity came before the court again in 2003 when the University of Michigan Law School was sued for considering race, among other factors, in deciding whom to admit. A narrow court majority (five to four) ruled in the university's favor. Taking account of race furthered "a compelling interest in obtaining the educational benefits that flow from a diverse student body," wrote Justice Sandra Day O'Connor in the majority opinion. "In order to cultivate a set of leaders with legitimacy in the eyes of the citizenry, it is necessary that the path to leadership be visibly open to talented and qualified individuals of every race and ethnicity."[17] A record number of organizations, representing education, labor, corporations, and the military, filed friend-of-the-court briefs endorsing the benefits of diversity.

The wording of the Supreme Court decision indicated that these briefs mattered. The court first said, "Enrolling a 'critical mass' of minority students simply to assure some specified percentage of a particular group merely because of its race or ethnic origin would be patently unconstitutional." The Law School noted, however, that it

> defines its critical mass concept by reference to the substantial, important, and laudable educational benefits that diversity is designed to produce, including cross-racial understanding and the breaking down of racial stereotypes. The Law School's claim is further bolstered by numerous expert studies and reports showing that such diversity promotes learning outcomes and better prepares students for an increasingly diverse workforce, for society, and for the legal profession. Major American businesses have made clear that the skills needed in today's increasingly global marketplace can only be developed through exposure to widely diverse people, cultures, ideas, and viewpoints. High-ranking retired officers and civilian military leaders assert that a highly qualified, racially diverse officer corps is essential to national security.[18]

This wording confirmed that diversity is relevant to achieving significant social goals, giving legal sanction to what was already an explosion of diversity initiatives. By 2000, the websites of American universities and corporations, in the hundreds if not thousands, offer homage to diversity. Some examples:

Harvard University: Diversity "develops the kind of understanding that can only come when we are willing to test our ideas and arguments in the company of people with very different perspectives."

The University of Texas: Diversity "prepares educated, productive citizens who can meet the rigorous challenges of an increasingly diverse society and an ever-changing global community."

Exxon-Mobil: "By hiring people from diverse cultures and with diverse backgrounds and experiences we gain essential local knowledge and the breadth of perspective necessary for achieving our business objectives."

DuPont: "When employees offer their own diverse insights and cultural sensitivities, they open new customer bases and market opportunities."

Type "diversity colleges universities" into a search engine, and in a half second nearly thirty million sites become available; type "diversity business corporations" and the number jumps to forty-five million. The language of diversity swept across higher education and America's business sector at a speed and scope difficult to grasp, and with instrumental justification.

Of course, instrumental justifications for affirmative action are not entirely new. Decades earlier the Kerner Commission urged preferential hiring of black police and journalists, less to compensate for racial exclusion than to control and explain urban violence (see p. 86). This instrumental reasoning found its way into many arguments on behalf of accelerated minority hiring in the 1960s, when urban riots were much in the news.

But something was new by the time of the Michigan case—a very much broadened definition of who is to be included under the label of diversity. It seems as if corporations and universities are in competition to separately list the widest possible number of groups eligible. Procter & Gamble lists *race*, *sex*, *age*, *cultural heritage*, *personal background*, and *sexual orientation*. General Motors includes those traits, and then adds *education level*, *family status*, *language*, *military status*, *physical abilities*, and *union representation*.

Universities are equally expansive, as is rather dramatically illustrated in this Diversity Policy Statement posted by the City University of New York, which reads,

It is the policy of the Board of Trustees of the City University of New York (CUNY) and constituent colleges and units of CUNY to recruit, employ, retain, and promote employees and to admit and provide services to students without regard to age, alienage, citizenship, creed, color, disability, gender identity, genetic predisposition or carrier status, legally registered domestic partnership status, marital status, military or veteran status, national or ethnic origin, race, religion, sex, sexual orientation or status as a victim of domestic violence.[19]

The statement goes on to add as "protected classes" all those appearing in the census race and ethnic classification, as well as women, and then, in an only-in-New York moment, added yet one more category—Italian Americans.

This enlarged understanding of diversity was anticipated years earlier in the *Bakke* case. Justice Powell clearly expected diversity to apply to more than race and ethnicity. He complimented Harvard University on its diversity effort, because it gave "some attention to distribution among many types and categories of students" including "the number of blacks, or of musicians, football players, physicists or Californians to be admitted in a given year."[20] Football players, musicians, Californians! Powell gave judicial endorsement to a notion of diversity far broader than the affirmative action focus of redressing historic wrongs visited on racial minorities.

In time, even critics of affirmative action made use of diversity rhetoric, now insisting that universities are insufficiently diverse in their intellectual and ideological makeup. These critics challenge the preponderance of left-leaning academics in universities. The webpage of the Students for Academic Freedom, for example, directs its readers to research indicating that Democrats outnumber Republicans fifteen to one in the social sciences and seven to one in elite law and journalism faculties. Under the banner "You can't get a good education if they're telling you half the story," this group issued an Academic Bill of Rights advocating intellectual and ideological diversity in higher education.[21]

Interesting as all this is, my purpose is not to assess the many claims made about diversity or to document how quickly and extensively it spread across the institutions of American society. My task is much narrower. What does diversity as a social goal imply about asking Americans their race? The rise of instrumental affirmative action rooted in the diversity rationale poses an unfamiliar challenge to racial counting.

A racial justice rationale for affirmative action led to statistical proportionality. Instrumental affirmative action is (thus far) not about statistics at all. In its arguments before the Supreme Court, the University of Michigan emphasized the importance of "critical mass." When pressed to state how many of a particular group represented critical mass, the school sidestepped the question. To have cited a number would have opened the university to the charge that it had an unconstitutional quota for racial minorities.

Given the broadened definition of diversity noted above, it is not surprising that statistical proportionality fades from the picture. What statistical system is robust enough to balance "race, ethnicity, culture, social class, national origin, gender, age, religious beliefs, sexual orientation, mental ability, and physical ability,"[22] to say nothing of the combinations across these many characteristics? If one adds to this list intellectual, political, and ideological diversity, the possibility of measurement approaches zero.

Diversity—You Can't Measure It, but You Know It When You See It

This measurement challenge is unlikely to be resolved with a crisp definition of diversity. Diversity found its way onto America's political agenda as a code word to protect affirmative action for racial minorities when quotas were ruled unconstitutional. From this starting place it spread widely, though never with an agreed-upon meaning. I commented in chapter 6 that very little theory lay behind the selection of the initial list of protected minorities in affirmative action programs. There is even less theory underpinning the term *diversity*. It echoes "you know it when you see it," a phrase famously introduced into American jurisprudence when the Supreme Court found pornography hard to define, let alone measure.[23]

The application form for Visiting Fellows at the Russell Sage Foundation, one of the nation's oldest and most sophisticated social science institutions, illustrates the lack of definitional precision. Russell Sage starts with a long list; diversity includes: "race, color, religion, gender and/or gender identity, pregnancy or parental status, marital or domestic partner status, national origin, ancestry, age, sexual orientation, disability or medical condition, veteran status, or any other characteristic protected by law." Obviously, to meet its diversity goals, the foundation needs to know into which of these categories its applicants fall. But in trying to assess the extent to which its applicant pool matches this array of traits, it invites responses not readily converted to statistical proportionality. Having defined diversity broadly, the application form then instructs: "The Russell Sage Foundation values diversity in its class of Visiting Scholars and in the broader social science community. At your option, please tell us anything that would be useful for us to know regarding your racial, ethnic, cultural, or other background."[24] It is particularly telling that this foundation, which has published hundreds of major books that heavily rely on government race statistics, asks such a vague and open-ended question that produces responses not convertible to statistical proportionality.[25]

This general retreat from numbers in implementing diversity goals does not in itself mark the end of racial statistics. It does separate those statistics from one arena in which they have been heavily applied since the 1970s—statistical proportionality in university admissions and in employment practices. In this way, diversity is similar to—and, of course, interacts with—multiculturalism and identity politics. Both of these developments gained momentum in what is labeled the *post-civil rights era*.

Together with the third development of interest, a color-blind initiative, they open up new political space to freshly examine the two fundamental questions: Why does the government ask What Is Your Race? Are the resulting statistics adequate to the governing challenges of the twenty-first century?

Color-Blind Politics and the Dilemma of Recognition

The Civil Rights Act led to policies that relied on race statistics to proactively remedy past wrongs. This provoked a political reaction. Affirmative action is zero-sum. Minorities benefit but at a cost to whites who might otherwise have been awarded a coveted university admission or a contract to renovate city hall. In the same years that identity politics and diversity rhetoric confused the rationale for race statistics, a more direct political challenge to the project of racial statistics was mounted. The census should be color-blind. In large part the goal was to dismantle affirmative action. Without the census race question there is no ready measure of statistical proportionality or disparate impact. But this does not tell the whole story. Even if affirmative action is ended, color-blind advocacy will remain. It is also motivated by concern that insistent racial counting divides us as a people, and postpones the dream of a postracial society. This second critique is taken up later in this chapter, where we discuss the dilemma of recognition.

The Color-Blind Idea in American Jurisprudence

The Fourteenth Amendment to the Constitution, passed in the immediate aftermath of the Civil War, overturned an earlier Supreme Court ruling that denied citizenship to black Americans. The Fourteenth Amendment required every state to provide equal protection under the law to all people under its jurisdiction. This equal protection clause was frequently challenged as defenders of white racial privilege looked for loopholes. They were famously successful when the Supreme Court ruled that "separate but equal" was not prohibited by the equal protection clause.[26] *Plessy v. Ferguson* (1896) entrenched the Jim Crow racial order deep into the twentieth century.

Although the court majority endorsed "separate but equal," a vigorous minority dissent was mounted by Justice John Harlan. He saw that separate but equal would not be equal in practice but would send black Americans to poor schools, low-paying jobs, second-class transportation, and marginal, segregated housing. His dissent penned these famous words: "Our constitution is color-blind, and neither knows nor tolerates classes among citizens."

Color-blind law and policy was, for Harlan, a way to undo practices that penalized one race and rewarded another. A half century later, Thurgood Marshall, the great African American civil rights lawyer who was soon to reach the Supreme Court, began his legal practice in agreement with Harlan, noting that "classifications and distinctions based on race or color have no moral or legal validity in our society. They are contrary to our constitution. . . ."[27] Two years later he reprised his position, stating, "Racial criteria are irrational, irrelevant, odious to our way of life."[28] Marshall was using a color-blind argument to assert that the Fourteenth Amendment should be cited to put a stop to a legally protected racial hierarchy.

Not until the 1950s did the federal government begin to dismantle what in fact was a legally sanctioned racial hierarchy in employment, education, transportation, health care, and housing. Racial equality did not then suddenly arrive. Making discrimination illegal could not by itself change inequalities and injustices that had become deeply embedded in the institutions of society. To challenge institutional racism, government intervention was necessary, and this intervention could hardly be color-blind. Marshall, by then a Supreme Court justice, saw this clearly: "It is because of a legacy of unequal treatment that we now must permit the institutions of this society to give consideration to race in making decisions about who will hold the positions of influence, affluence, and prestige in America."[29]

But if Marshall found the color-blind terminology a barrier to the Supreme Court overcoming the consequences of historic discrimination, conservatives on the court used it to challenge race-sensitive affirmative action. Ian Haney Lopez calls this reactionary color-blindness, defined as a legal strategy to protect rather than dismantle America's racial hierarchy.[30] There is truth to Haney Lopez's argument, but color-blind politics can involve more than this reactionary strategy. It is possible to advocate color-blind law and a color-blind census with the hope that this will lead to a nonracist society.

The legal reasoning employed by challenges to affirmative action rests on a simple premise: policy based on a racial classification is morally objectionable irrespective of its purpose. Justice Clarence Thomas argues that "there is a moral [and] constitutional equivalence between laws designed to subjugate a race and those that distribute benefits on the basis of race in order to foster some current notion of equality. . . . In each instance, it is racial discrimination, plain and simple."[31] The equivalence principle is not in itself a conservative or liberal position, though argued with the certainty Thomas gives to it, it does assume that slavery, Jim Crow apartheid, the forced relocation of American Indians from their homelands, and the internment of Japanese Americans are morally equivalent to setting aside funds for minority businesses or university efforts to recruit minority applicants. It is clear that color-blind arguments have reentered jurisprudence to buttress a conservative challenge to race-sensitive social justice policies.

In a Supreme Court case shortly after the *Bakke* decision, Justice Potter Stewart dissented from majority opinion. First quoting the phrase made famous by *Plessy v. Ferguson*—"Our constitution is color-blind, and neither knows nor tolerates classes among citizens"—Stewart continued: "I think today's decision is wrong for the same reason that *Plessy* was wrong."[32] This "dissent marks the first judicial commitment in a Supreme Court case to an anticlassification interpretation of the Constitution itself."[33]

A decade later, the minority opinion had become the majority view of the court. In a case challenging a minority set-aside program in Richmond, Virginia, the court ignored the statistical record demonstrating a nearly complete lack of minority access to city construction contracts. In the opinion of Justice Antonin Scalia, "To accept Richmond's claim that past societal discrimination alone can serve as the basis for rigid racial preferences would be to open the door to competing claims for 'remedial relief' for every disadvantaged group. The dream of a Nation of equal citizens in a society where race is irrelevant to personal opportunity and achievement would be lost in a mosaic of shifting preferences based on inherently unmeasurable claims of past wrongs."[34] To his argument that past wrongs are "inherently unmeasurable" Scalia added that the tendency "to classify and judge men and women on the basis of their country of origin or the color of their skin" can itself "be fatal to the nation."[35]

The court did not stop there. Two years later it ruled on a jury exclusion case in which the prosecutor had used peremptory challenges to disqualify all bilingual speakers by making the argument that they already understood Spanish and would not rely on the English translation of the court interpreter, which was the official text on the case. Their disqualification superficially had nothing to do with the potential jurors' race, only with their language competencies. The court upheld this practice, reasoning that disqualification was not based on race.[36]

This ruling disconnects race completely from anything remotely related to lived experience. By this logic, there is no justification "for the government's use of racial classifications, since by definitional fiat race lacks all social relevance.[37]

Color-Blind Arguments in the Political Arena

In 2003 the voters of California turned down a ballot proposition that, if passed, would have prohibited the state from using racial classification in most of its business. Though soundly defeated, more than three million California voters did agree that the "state and local governments [should] be prohibited from classifying any person by race, ethnicity, color or national origin."[38] As the supporters of the measure made clear, the intent was to take the first step toward a color-blind society. In the text accompanying the proposition, "classifying" was "defined as separating, sorting, or organizing persons or personal data."[39] This proposition owed its place on the California ballot to the American Civil Rights Coalition, an organization funded and led by Ward Connerly, a conservative African American businessman.

Connerly had been successful in an earlier effort to amend the California state constitution, effectively ending affirmative action in public education, contracting, and employment.[40] This proposition easily passed. There were similar successes in Washington (1998), Michigan (2006), and Nebraska (2008).

National opinion polls indicate substantial public opposition toward collecting race statistics. A poll in 2000, which overlapped the period when the 2000 census was being widely promoted, reports that nearly two-thirds of the public said that boxes indicating race should not appear on government forms.[41] A more recent poll, in 2007, has the public agreeing that efforts should be made to improve conditions for minorities, but not, said two-thirds, through preferential treatment.[42] Minorities typically offer more support than do whites for such programs, but in this survey, about one-third of the minority respondents opposed preferential treatment.[43]

This quick sketch of how color-blind arguments fare in the legal and political arena indicates substantial opposition to affirmative action in particular and racial counting more generally. To the degree that opposition to affirmative action and preferential treatment is the primary political good motivating advocates for a color-blind society, this advocacy fades as affirmative action is progressively weakened. To some extent this has happened.

The Dilemma of Recognition

By the mid-twentieth century, most Americans accepted that if racial inequalities were traceable to state-sponsored or state-tolerated discrimination, social justice in a liberal democracy requires corrective action. The public consensus broke down over what was a reasonable corrective action. Is it reasonable to use "race" to undo "racism"? Chief Justice John Roberts thinks not: "The way to stop discrimination on the basis of race is to stop discriminating on the basis of race."[44] He speaks for many thoughtful Americans who worry that race-targeted remedies put at risk political principles honoring universalism and individualism. Carried too far, policies that reward on the basis of group membership create divisive politics. Republican Congressman Gingrich was quoted earlier urging that the census "stop forcing Americans into inaccurate categories aimed at building divisive subgroups."

"The dilemma of recognition" is a phrase capturing what is at stake. The phrase describes a dilemma that emerges when liberal governments pursue group-based redistributional policies by giving official recognition to the targeted or protected groups. This accentuates racial and ethnic distinctions that liberal universalistic policies are expected to eliminate. Especially problematic is how official recognition seems to invite political mobilization of race, ethnic, religion, or language groups, or whatever serves as the basis for group-targeted redistribution. Might targeted redistributions thought necessary to reduce group inequality instead "promote ethnic conflict, create vested interests in group distinctions, diminish public support for redistribution, and thus defeat their own purpose"?[45]

To its supporters, affirmative action is a great American success story, as confirmed by the rapid movement of African Americans into the highest reaches of government and corporate America, and the steady broadening of the civil rights agenda to other racial minorities, with especially notable success for Asians. It is difficult to weigh the various factors that explain the remarkable transformation in American life starting in the mid-1960s, but explicit, government-backed affirmative action can certainly be credited for helping to create a more racially equal and socially just society.

Yet affirmative action was, from the beginning, resisted. Opponents framed it as just "another group interest" with minorities lined up to capture government benefits. Quotas were described as a new form of racial discrimination. The primary justification for affirmative action—undoing the nation's legacy of racism—was weakened when the definition of protected groups expanded to include recent immigrants who, of course, were not victims of three centuries of slavery, genocide, contract labor, and systematic, state-sanctioned discrimination.

The disparate-impact doctrine further complicated matters. As described in chapter 6, employment and education discrimination was found to be more than the prejudicial behavior of employers or university admission offices. Discrimination could be discovered statistically in the impersonal workings of institutions. Statistically described groups were the victims of discrimination, and remedies were group-based. But how can a nation founded on individual rights accept affirmative action for selected groups?[46] The law was clear when discrimination was targeted at an individual because of his or her race. It was contested when targeted to a group defined racially—and statistically.

In the course of time, statistical proportionality (as a policy tool) and institutionalism racism (as its target) were challenged. Affirmative action—understood as quotas, timetables, numerical targets, or reserved places—has been significantly weakened as racial justice policy. Further weakening the 1970s formulation is the way in which new issues have crowded into the political space previously reserved for racial justice claims: diversity, multiculturalism, and identity politics. A clear example was the failure of the NAACP and its allies to prevail when, in opposing the multiple-race option, the racial justice rationale was insufficiently persuasive.

The weakening of affirmative action policy has left a bad aftertaste. Those who aggressively support proactive law and policy feel abandoned. They point to continuing injustices and inequalities as reason to maintain the policy. Opponents, though pleased to see the gradual shrinking of affirmative action, remain aggrieved by what they see as an injustice visited on whites for the sins of their ancestors. They resent the processes that have allowed recent immigrants to claim the status of protected minority, and to be advancing at the expense of whites.

A senator from Virginia, James Webb, voiced this resentment in a 2010 *Wall Street Journal* editorial. Government programs "allow recently arrived immigrants to move ahead of similarly situated whites whose families have been in the country for generations." He faults affirmative action for moving "away from remediation and toward discrimination, this time against whites." The government should not be picking winners but "enabling opportunity for all." It can do so by ensuring that "artificial distinctions such as race do not determine outcomes." He asserts that white America is itself diverse, with some whites faring no better that racial minorities. The editorial "strains to find the logic that could lump [whites] together for the purpose of public policy." The logic, of course, is the census category of "white" that has no further breakdown.[47]

The editorial captures the widespread resentment toward race-targeted policies that ignore deserving low-income whites in the rural South while rewarding undeserving nonwhites, such as students from prosperous Korean or Japanese families getting into elite universities. The Tea Party movement that became an anti-Obama political force in 2010 was partly fueled by this resentment. Its appeal was captured in another newspaper editorial appearing a few weeks after Webb wrote.

Gregory Rodriguez, a liberal, Hispanic *Los Angeles Times* columnist, wrote that with minorities soon to be half of the American population, whites feel that the playing field has tilted against them. This is generating white racial anxiety, which, Rodriguez argues, "will be the most significant and potentially dangerous socio-demographic trend of the coming decade. The combination of changing demographics and symbolic political victories on the part of nonwhites will inspire in whites a greater racial consciousness, a growing sense of beleaguerment and louder calls to end affirmative action or to be included in it."[48] Extending affirmation action to immigrants has "upset the political calculus" that made it viable in the first place. Rodriguez concludes that the country had better find a less divisive way to reduce inequalities and injustices.

An increasing number of commentators see as a worrying trend what is described by scholars as a "new racism." This racism differs from nineteenth-century beliefs that blacks, being biologically inferior, have no place in America's civic life. The new racism is based on white resentment that "blacks do not try hard enough to overcome the difficulties they face and that take what they have not earned."[49] Affirmative action is un-American, and any who benefit from it prefer special favors and government handouts to the virtues of hard work and self-discipline. Nearly nine of ten white Americans oppose what they view as preferential treatment for minorities.[50] Their "racism" is resentment of minorities who fail to embrace the basic American values of individualism and meritocracy.

The resentful whites do not see themselves as racist, largely because they reject that disparities between race groups are caused by discrimination. They point to substantial accomplishments by Asians, Hispanics, and blacks who work hard and play by the rules as evidence that discrimination is no longer an issue in American society. If some members of some minorities remain uneducated or cannot hold down a job, that is evidence of cultural choices. Sometimes labeled *laissez-faire racism*, inequalities are "not the deliberate products of racial discrimination. They are outcomes of a free-market, race-neutral state apparatus and the freely taken actions of African Americans themselves."[51]

Why should "freely taken actions" by minorities lead to tax-supported subsidies? Resentment at this is not only an American phenomenon. The Netherlands, famous for a racial tolerance that led to aggressive multicultural policies in the 1970s and '80s, is today being described very differently. The European Commission writes about the Netherlands' "worrying polarization between majority and minority communities" and "racist and xenophobic discourse in politics," as well as an "integration deficit."[52] In a few years, the Netherlands' ethnic policies shifted from directing funds to minority cultural groups and protecting their cultural heritage to insisting that they rapidly assimilate or find someplace else to live. The Netherlands, once "Europe's most explicitly multiculturalist regime," has now retreated from that political agenda "with a vengeance."[53]

This retreat "illustrates the risks of unchecked institutionalization" of ethnic statistics. The Netherlands' statistical system was assembled on behalf of redistributive policies to improve ethnic relations—especially benefiting persons of Antillean, Moroccan, and Turkish descent. But the statistics acquired a political momentum beyond their immediate technical application. They ceased to be a tool designed to cope with an exceptional circumstance. Strong anti-immigrant sentiments in Dutch society fed on "an elaborate system of ethnic categories."[54] The ethnic recognition facilitated by the categories "create vested interests in group identities, cause groups and claims to proliferate, accentuate group boundaries, and promote segregation rather than cohesion."[55]

Statistical races in America long predate the civil rights policies that adapted them to the purposes of racial justice. But they were bureaucratically standardized in 1977 specifically to recognize protected minorities and facilitate redistributive policies that, in the eyes of many, have deepened rather than ended racism. America is not immune to the dilemma of recognition, nor to the corrosive political discourse that accompanies it.

The United States and the Netherlands share something else. In both countries, the initial turn to race and ethnic statistics in the 1960s and '70s was in part responsive to social unrest and urban violence. In the U.S. case, steps to move young black men into the labor market were promoted as a way to get them off the streets. In the midst of a crisis, this instrumental use of affirmative action was persuasive to whites who were otherwise skeptical about group benefits. The crises passed, but by then the statistically supported policies had become institutionalized, and it is this institutionalization that is so strongly disliked by Americans who earlier had accepted proactive steps as a temporary measure needed to manage civil strife.

The renewed interest in a color-blind statistical system is a response to the dilemma of recognition. Color-blind advocacy embraces a narrative that Americans across the political spectrum take pride in repeating. The nation of immigrants, so the narrative goes, has made diversity itself the source of national unity. George Washington noted that America "is open . . . to the oppressed and persecuted of all Nations and Religions . . . [who] would be assimilated to our customs, measures and laws: in a word, soon become one people." Ralph Waldo Emerson wrote of America as an "asylum of all nations" that would forge a fresh identity "as vigorous as the Europe which came out of the smelting pot of the Dark Ages." Outside observers repeat the praise. James Bryce, Great Britain's ambassador to the United States on the eve of World War I, was struck by "the amazing solvent power which American institutions, habits, and ideas exercise upon newcomers of all races . . . quickly dissolving and assimilating the foreign bodies that are poured into her mass." More recently Margaret Thatcher opined, "No other nation has so successfully combined people of different races and nations within a single culture."[56] Listen to most American politicians and soon you will find them either harking back or looking forward to, as in the Gingrich quote earlier in this chapter, "transcending racial division and reflecting the melting pot which is America." Overlooked in this continuing praise of the "melting pot" was its exclusion of non-Europeans. The phrase itself dates to 1782, when a French American described America as a place where "individuals of all nations are *melted* into a new race of men."[57] This writer's "new race of men" had in mind the English, Scotch, Irish, French, Dutch, Germans, and Swedes. Neither he nor his readers imagined it as a new race to which the black African or the American Indian could belong. Even when the phrase was resurrected in the early twentieth century, it was the Polish Jews and Italian Catholics who were now to "melt" into the mainstream. Not yet was the country ready for African slave descendants, Asians, or Mexicans as full citizens.

That time has come—rhetorically, if not yet completely in practice. Refitting the melting pot metaphor for the twenty-first-century is about including non-Europeans. The racial divisions Gingrich would like us to transcend are those demarcated in the American census. It is in this context that color-blind advocates make a strong case for getting rid of racial classification altogether. Why do we need to divide the country into race groups if our grand national project is, this time around, truly inclusive? The final three chapters offer answers.

Conclusions

This chapter has reviewed three challenges to policies that have relied on statistical races. One challenge is the claim that the census race classification should serve expressive purposes, not just administrative or political ones. Another is the marginalization of racial measurement if affirmative action and racial justice arguments are displaced by a diversity agenda linked to instrumental goals much broader than righting historic wrongs. The third is the political concern that counting by race and the policies attached to it feed a new racism, and are a barrier to national unity.

Whatever may be the merits of these challenges, and each will be considered further in later chapters, collectively they open up political space for fresh thinking about an official racial classification scheme anchored in eighteenth-century thinking. More specifically they require us to ask whether we need our statistical races at all. My answer is "yes," but ones reengineered for twenty-first century policy tasks. The next chapter outlines these tasks, answering the "why" question. Chapter 10, a technical detour, provides needed detail about what we have and therefore what we should change. The final chapter turns more explicitly to "what" we should change to. It ends with a strategy that can bring about the change.

CHAPTER 9

THE PROBLEM OF THE TWENTY-FIRST CENTURY IS THE PROBLEM OF THE COLOR LINE AS IT INTERSECTS THE NATIVITY LINE

"THE PROBLEM OF THE TWENTIETH CENTURY IS THE PROBLEM OF THE COLOR-line."[1] This sentence, famously and presciently penned in 1903 by political intellectual W.E.B. Du Bois, merits revisiting as we ask why, more than a century later, America still collects race statistics. The color line described by Du Bois was white racism directed at African Americans, reflected in legally imposed segregation in social practice and in public sentiment. Du Bois, the first African American to earn a Harvard doctorate, voiced a powerful racial equality argument through his writings and his political activism. His initial color line, the white/black divide, was subsequently expanded to critique European imperialism, not just over the black race but in colonizing the yellow, brown, and red races. Du Bois anticipated what later in the twentieth century was the color line between whites and all people of color—on the one side of the line, white privileges, and on the other, inferior education, employment, housing, and health for everyone not white.

But that was the twentieth century. What use is the color line terminology in twenty-first-century America—now multiracial, diverse, even, for some, postracial? Is there a color line? If so, who is on what side? Scholars do not give one answer; they spread their answers across several possibilities. I briefly summarize them here, and return to them in this and following chapters.

Some scholars emphasize the coming disappearance of the color line altogether. Du Bois was right about the twentieth century but not a guide to the twenty-first. America is well on its way to becoming post-racial, a result not of color-blind referenda or legal decrees but occurring naturally in a society transformed by immigration and increasingly comfortable with biracial marriage, multiculturalism, and ethic diversity. *Beyond the Color Line* is illustrative of analysis giving evidence and argument that America is on a path to a postracial future; indeed, it is already in reach as is indicated by the election of a multiracial president.[2]

Other scholars are skeptical. America is far from "beyond the color line." If the skeptics are of one mind about the persistence of America's color line, they are of several minds about where that color line is being drawn in the twenty-first century .

One line of reasoning remains true to the Du Bois formulation. The color line still separates the white from the nonwhite, with the later being all people of color, including recent immigrants from Asia and the Pacific Islands, from Latin America and Africa. Not so, declare other scholars. They, too, see a bright color line, but one drawn between the black and the nonblack. In this reasoning Asian Americans and many Hispanics are escaping a racial minority status, much as the white-ethnic Irish, Italian, and Polish did in the first half of the twentieth century. These scholars invoke "everyone but the black" to describe a steady racial blending in American society, but one leaving out the African American (and in some treatments, also the American Indian).

Other scholars believe that binary models over-simplify America's racial order. Eduardo Bonilla-Silva proposes a more complex model based on a racial re-sorting into three categories.[3] One category—labeled "augmented whites"—includes the European whites and the assimilated white Hispanics, the assimilated American Indians, and multiracial who are more "white" than not.

Another category—labeled "collective blacks"—includes African Americans as commonly understood, but also recent African immigrants, darker Hispanics, American Indians on the reservations, and the darker and less economically successful Asians such as the Hmong and Laotians.

The third category—labeled "honorary whites"—includes Americans whose ancestry is northern Africa and the Middle East; most of the multiracial population and their offspring; light-skinned Hispanics from Cuba, Colombia, or Chile; Asian Indians, and model minority Asian Americans, especially those originally from China, Japan, and Korea. Herbert Gans, a close observer of race relations, is among those who at one time saw black/nonblack as the likely color line but, taking into account the steady growth of biracial marriage, now believes the racial hierarchy is better described with the tripartite model.[4]

Scholars may differ on whether the color line is what it has always been, persists but in a very twenty-first century version, or is fading into a postracial future, but they agree on one critical issue: immigration is hugely important. It is impossible to assess the staying power of the color line without attention to the line separating the native born from the foreign born. As shorthand, I label this the *nativity line*. The nativity line is hardly fresh to the twenty-first century; it is as old as—often the same as—the color line.

The Nativity Line

Of course American Indians are the original native-born population in what became the United States. When their ancestors arrived, fifteen thousand years ago, they were the first *Homo sapiens* in the land mass now labeled the Americas. This indigenous population lived here undisturbed until two foregn groups arrived—the Europeans eager to claim a new land and their enslaved Africans. Each of these groups reproduced and became "native born" in short order. They were soon joined by a steady stream of other immigrants, the latter welcomed proportionately to how closely they resembled the original white settlers.

Consider this remarkable passage written by Benjamin Franklin in 1751: "[W]hy should the Palatine Boors [Germans] be suffered to swarm into our Settlements, and by herding together establish their Language and Manners to the Exclusion of ours? Why should Pennsylvania, founded by the English, become a colony of *Aliens*, who will shortly be so numerous as to Germanize us instead of us Anglifying them, and will never adopt our Language or Customs, any more than they can acquire our Complexion."[5]

There are familiar anxieties in this passage. The foreign born are *alien* even in the colonial era, despite the colonies having themselves been established by foreigners who immediately set about removing the real native born. The foreign born are too attached to their language and culture and are hesitant to adopt Anglo customs. Third, they are threatening: if too many they will take over. Finally, Franklin marks them as phenotypically different from the native born, being of a complexion that elsewhere in his essay is labeled "swarthy." In 1751, in this passage, the color line and the nativity line were merged.

More than two and a half centuries have passed since Franklin laid out the case against the foreign born. But in every particular his fears echo down to the present. A widely cited and well-regarded book, alarmingly titled *The Disuniting of America*, concludes: "A cult of ethnicity has arisen among both non-Anglo whites and among nonwhite minorities to denounce the idea of a melting pot, to challenge the concept of 'one people,' and to protect, promote, and perpetuate separate ethnic and racial communities."[6]

Even more alarmist is Samuel Huntington,[7] describing an insular Mexican American culture as an "invasion of over 1 million Mexican civilians . . . comparable [to an armed invasion] . . . and Americans should react against it with comparable vigor."[8] This flow of Hispanic immigrants "threatens to divide the United States into two peoples, two cultures, and two languages." Mexicans are not accepting American customs, he writes, "but forming instead their own political and linguistic enclaves" and "rejecting the Anglo-Protestant values that built the American dream." Mexican American population growth promotes cultural consolidation, leading them "to glory in the differences between their culture and the U.S. culture." In a multicultural society, a consumer economy, and a democracy, "numbers are power," and numbers are what Hispanics aspire to.[9]

A companion argument, presented aggressively by one-time presidential candidate, Patrick Buchanan, views the "endless migration from Mexico north, the Hispanicization of the American Southwest, and dual citizenship for all Mexican-Americans" as a deliberate strategy to merge the United States and Mexico. This "Aztlan Strategy" will "erase the border." The strategic goals are to "[g]row the influence, through Mexican-Americans, over how America disposes of her wealth and power. Gradually circumscribe the sovereignty of the United States. Lastly, economic and political merger of the nations in a bi-national union. And in the nuptial agreement, a commitment to share the wealth and power. Stated bluntly, the Aztlan Strategy entails the end of a sovereign, self-sufficient, independent republic, the passing away of the American nation. They are coming to conquer us."[10]

Hovering over these passages (and the thousands of essays, books, editorials, and blogs of similar sentiment) are Franklin's four anxieties: the foreign born are alien; they hold to their own culture and are growing in number; they are threatening and could "win," destroying the nation in the process; and they are nonwhite. In the 250 years separating Franklin's swarthy Germans from Buchanan's alien Mexicans, other foreign born were similarly described, feared, and racialized. The Irish, Chinese, Japanese, Italians, Jews, and Polish, to name the most prominent, were doubly alien. They were foreign; they were nonwhite, at least for a time.

A great responsibility of the nation's social statistics is untangling the messy, fluid, overlapping issues that separate by color and by place of birth. In making this argument, I argue that today's statistical races do not meet this responsibility.

America's New Demography

When the statistical races were fixed by OMB's Directive 15 nearly nine of every ten Americans was enumerated as white. Today that percentage is closer to six of every ten. As the proportion of whites in America's population shrinks, the Asians (starting from a low base) have increased fivefold and the Hispanics (starting from a higher base) have nearly quadrupled (see table 3).

There is no sensible way to talk about the recent racial transformation of America without attention to immigration. If Americanness is defined by the ratio of native born to foreign born, the country in the 1960s was more American than at any point in its entire history: the ratio in 1960 was 19 native born for every 1 foreign born, a ratio not seen since the earliest European settlers were heavily outnumbered by the native population. Today that ratio is half that, closer to 8 to 1. Add the second generation—children of the foreign born—and the ratio drops to 4 to 1. This is an enormous change, expressing itself in every facet of life. If in 1960 you might be surprised to find a foreign-born American in the drugstore, the classroom, or waiting in line for the movie, in most of the country today you would be surprised if you *failed* to find a one. It's likely that at least one in four readers of this book is foreign born or a second-generation American.

The change in racial composition over the last half century, including the possible upending of white numerical dominance, and the changing ratio of native born to foreign born is, of course, one not two transformations. Immigration has changed America, at least demographically, in ways unanticipated when the OMB decided in 1977 that the country had four primary races and one ethnicity, and designed a statistical system to represent that reality.

If the population change in the four decades between 1970 and 2010 is already striking, what is forecast for the next four decades is more so. The Census Bureau estimates that in 2050, only four censuses from now,

Table 3. Percentage of the American population in the census race and ethnic categories, 1970 and 2010

Races	1970	2010
White	87.5	64.0
Black	11.1	12.6
Asian/Pacific Islander	0.9	5.0
American Indian	0.5	0.9
Hispanic (of any race)	4.5	16.3

America's white population will shrink to about half (52.5 percent) of the total. The Asians/Pacific Islanders will increase to one in ten (10.3 percent) and Hispanics will number more than a fifth of the population (22 percent).[11] The African American share will slightly increase, to one in six (15.7 percent) and American Indians will remain in the 1 to 2 percent range.

Of course these projections are only as firm as the meanings attached to the standard race categories. If the color line puts white Hispanics and high-achieving Asians on the white side, the projected reduction in the white proportion disappears. Figure 2 announces that in 2011 newborn whites were fewer than newborn minorities, signally a trend not likely to reverse itself *if* the category "white" continues to exclude the white Hispanic or light-skinned multirace baby. But this figure and the public commentary it heralds are seriously misleading if the color line shifts—creating the three-category model with its "assimilated whites" and "honorary whites."

As the nation experiences this uncertain transformation, can statistical races fixed a half century ago tell us what we need to know? That is doubtful, for three reasons. First, the familiar racial justice agenda has

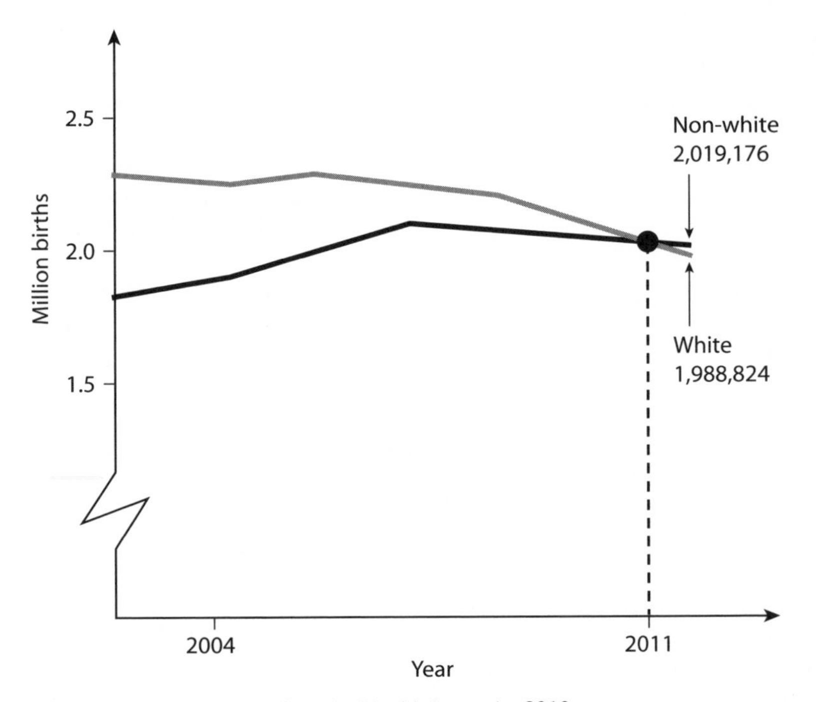

Figure 2. Minority births outnumbered white births on the 2010 census.

to be rethought, and remeasured, given some very new dynamics in employment, education, health, and housing. To cite one example: today the fastest growing, wealthiest, and best-educated race in America is Asian—whose median income at approximately $75,000 easily tops that of the whites ($62,000.), and is nearly double that of African Americans ($38,000).[12] The educational achievement of Asians explains this income success. More than half have graduated from college, compared to less than a third of whites and a fifth of African Americans.[13]

Second, the nation lacks an effective measurement strategy for understanding how today's foreign born and their children are "becoming American"—are integrating linguistically, culturally, politically, and economically. Our ability to track today's pathways to Americanization is seriously hampered by shortcomings in our national statistics.

Third, will the color line shift? This is largely a matter of attitudes, how will Egyptians, Bahamians, or biracial Americans see themselves and how will whites see them? For example, will professionally successful high-tech scientists born in India, but schooled at MIT or Stanford and living with their families in all-white suburbs, be viewed by their coworkers and their neighbors as white or as the census views them—as Asian?[14] Gans offers this possible future: "If the processes that turned the Italian, Hebrew and other Eastern European races of the 1880–1924 immigration into White ethnics after the end of World War II repeat themselves, many Latinos and Asians at least will be perceived and counted by Whites as Whites before mid century."[15] But of course there is no "counted as Whites" in any meaningful sense of that phrase unless the census race categories change. It is the census form that will determine what category will include Latinos and Asians at midcentury.

In the 1970s, civil rights policies focused on the color line and ignored the nativity line. This was deliberate. "Government agencies, employers, civil rights organizations and the immigrant rights bar" were anxious to avoid connecting immigration and racial justice policies. A political coalition between "the antipreference groups and the immigration restrictions" was described in some circles as the ultimate nightmare of affirmative action.[16] To understand this complicated interaction of the color line and the nativity line we take a deeper look at immigration reform in the civil rights period.

Immigration Reform in 1965

Chapter 5 reviewed why and how immigration was abruptly closed in the mid-1920s, by means of a quota system excluding all immigrants except the few still arriving from ancestral Anglo-Protestant Europe. The quota system worked as designed. It stopped immigration. It worked in other unanticipated ways: it provided four decades of breathing room for the successful integration of southern European Catholics and eastern European Jews. The nation that elected a Catholic to the White House in 1960 gradually accepted the idea that America could be less Anglo-Protestant and the Republic would not crumble. The nation that gradually opened higher education to deserving Jewish applicants found its universities to be the better for it. The early twentieth-century nativity line faded in importance.

Because fertility rates were at a level guaranteeing steady population growth there was no reason in the 1930s or '40s to revisit the restrictive immigration laws on the books. In the 1950s, two issues returned immigration to the policy agenda, both related to World War II: humanitarian concern for the displaced peoples of European allies, and the related search for a propaganda victory against a new threat, the Cold War enemy of communist Russia. Attempts in the 1950s to reform immigration law were resisted. It required more than a decade of political work before Congress finally abolished the old quota system. In 1965, amendments to the Immigration and Nationality Act replaced quotas with three principles: unlimited family reunion, occupational skills, and sanctuary for refugees fleeing communism.

Senator Ted Kennedy, younger brother of the first Catholic president and an impassioned supporter of immigration reform, spoke reassuringly on the floor of the Senate: "our cities will not be flooded with a million immigrants annually. Under the proposed bill, the present level of immigration remains substantially the same . . . the ethnic mix of this country will not be upset. . . . Contrary to the charges in some quarters [the bill] will not inundate America with immigrants from any one country or area, or the most populated and deprived nations of Africa and Asia."[17]

Kennedy was wildly wrong. Immigration numbers grew steadily across the 1970s, '80s, and '90s. By 2000, twenty-three million new immigrants had arrived, from the Caribbean, Mexico, and Central America (nearly half) and from Asia (nearly a third), with the remaining mostly from Russia, eastern Europe, and the Middle East. It was primarily family reunification that led to this explosion. The sociological explanation was (and still is) chain migration, through which new arrivals allow more brothers and sisters and nephews and nieces to migrate. The foreign born in the United States reached an all-time absolute high of nearly thirty-eight million in 2008, approximately one in eight of America's population.[18] The children of the foreign born are another 8 percent, resulting in a population that is 20 percent first- or second-generation American.

As noted above, immigration radically altered the racial and ethnic makeup of America. The Census Bureau reports that in 2023, only a decade from when I write this paragraph, more than half of the children in the country will be racial minorities.[19]

Demographic transformation through immigration is America's oldest story. It has always posed the question: What constitutes Americanness? The nineteenth-century alarm was whether Asians were destroying the American way of life. Later in the century and well into the twentieth, the Ku Klux Klan conflated race and religion with its virulent anti-Jewish (eastern European) and anti-Catholic (southern European) xenophobia. Muted echoes reverberate in today's immigration debates, often focused on Muslims, heightened by post-9/11 fears, and on whether to grant amnesty to the undocumented.[20]

To better understand the demographic transformation underway I outline, in summary fashion, four general issues. Each is an example showing that the color line and the nativity line, jointly considered, cannot be adequately grasped through the prism of today's statistical races, and why this limits the nation's policy options.

Anxiety about Insular Cultures

There are tensions at the cultural, economic, and political boundaries between the native born and the growing numbers of immigrants and their second-generation children. TV, radio talk shows, the press, and thousands of blogs dedicate their energies to explaining how America is changing, sometimes in celebration and sometimes in alarm. Novels and movies by the hundreds tell the stories of the new Americans, asking again and again what it means to be a nation of immigrants.

Once there was a simple answer. There was a mainstream; it was WASP (white, Anglo-Saxon, Protestant). Successive immigrant waves would melt into this mainstream, or at least those immigrants from Europe would. This narrative, though popular enough to leave echoes today, was inaccurate, not least because it had no place for nonwhite immigrants and, of course, no intent to include the American Indian and the African American.

The "mainstream" terminology notwithstanding, the melting process always had a reciprocal character, as commonly illustrated by noting that the celebration of Christmas, including the iconic Christmas tree and Christmas carols, is a present from the Germans who so worried Benjamin Franklin. Cuisines, music, art, and fashion borrow liberally across cultural and linguistic boundaries. Even hyphenation itself illustrates how the outsider transforms the mainstream. "Jewish-Americans" were held back by quota systems in higher education and the professions for more than a half century and used hyphenation to fight this discrimination while retaining their Jewishness. In paving the way for other groups to insist that Americanness did not have to come at the expense of discarding ethnic or religious identities, Jews successfully challenged the Anglo-Protestant mainstream to make room for other religious practices and cultural beliefs.[21]

The mainstream/melting-pot narrative once in vogue is now so redefined as to bear little relation to its earlier version. More familiar today is the narrative that religions, ethnicities, races, and nationality groups can retain their different cultures and yet coexist as Americans. Though the term *multiculturalism* is often used in this context, the phrase *composite culture* describes America's historic success at integrating successive waves of immigrants. Composite culture is defined as "the mixed, hybrid character of the ensemble of cultural practices and beliefs that has evolved in the United States since the colonial period."[22] In this view of America, cultural assimilation can occur "on a large scale to members of a group even as the group itself remains a highly visible point of reference on the social landscape."[23]

I noted earlier in this chapter that not all observers are sanguine about this version of assimilation. Skeptics such as Huntington cite statistics indicating less assimilation and more social fracturing than is healthy for a democracy. Skeptics explain these developments by insisting that Mexican Americans are willfully choosing cultural isolation. In sharp disagreement, other scholars argue that what is taken to be self-chosen cultural isolation is the unwillingness of whites in power to allow millions of Americans access to the voting booth or employment or housing.

This mingling of race prejudice with the exclusion of foreigners is not new to American politics. In the late nineteenth century, Anglo-Protestants routinely treated Italians, Irish, Poles, Jews, and Slovaks as race groups with alien habits, languages, cultures, and religions. They were unwelcome in white neighborhoods, discriminated against in the employment market and universities, and expected to "stay in their place." The attempt to keep more of these alien races from coming to America led to the contortions of the quota system described in chapter 5. The nation now looks back on that period with disbelief, knowing that nineteenth-century immigrants proved themselves American in every way imaginable—as soldiers, inventors, entertainers, scholars, entrepreneurs, politicians, citizens—knowing that they married Anglo-Protestants and produced successful children no less American than the immigrant English who sailed on the *Mayflower*. Today the Supreme Court is composed entirely of justices who are from either Catholic or Jewish backgrounds. We know the story; we know it to be a success story.

But we cannot assume that the gradual erasure of racialized European immigrants in the twentieth century predicts what is happening today. The southern and eastern European immigrants were, after all, white, and by the 1930s the nativity line was not an issue for their children, who were duly recorded in the census as native-born white citizens. Today's immigrants are not arriving from ancestral Europe but in great numbers from Asia, Africa, the Caribbean, and Central America. The question is whether the country has sufficiently shed its racist past that no racial barriers will impede their efforts to "become American."[24] If what is described as insularity results from discrimination and forced segregation, the policies needed will resemble those ending the Jim Crow racial order and the separate-but-equal doctrine that kept African Americans segregated and American Indians on reservations. Completely different policies will be called for if in fact there is an attempt to create a way of life separate from and in defiance of American values, a deliberate disuniting of the country.

One domain—employment opportunities—offers strong evidence of racially constructed barriers to assimilation. Poorly paid and onerous jobs such as meatpacking, fruit picking, and making beds in hotels recruit immigrants who have a good "work ethic"—who make no demands about workers' rights and offer no complaints about long hours or dangerous and dirty work conditions.[25] These workers are recruited by referral rather than by job postings, as compliant workers find others like themselves at no expense to the employer. If the available labor pool includes a large number of undocumented workers, referral recruitment is often the only way to locate labor that will work for less than the minimum wage: "employers perceive certain employees to have abilities or competence for a particular job or organization that others do not have *because of their race*."[26]

To create a vulnerable workforce based on racial recruitment specifically focused on recent immigrants is an obvious target for antidiscriminatory policy—but only if the phenomenon is well documented.[27] The only chance of doing so is for advocates to present a compelling statistical record of its magnitude and consequences.

Racialization of selected jobs also occurs at higher levels of the employment market. Businesses want to match the ethnic or racial characteristics of the marketing staff with the racial groups targeted in the marketing effort.[28] Universities practice a version of this, seldom recruiting white professors to head up African American studies programs or Hispanic institutes. Museums search out black curators for their African art collections and Asian curators for their Asian art collections. Although racialization of job categories toward the top of the employment ladder legitimates occupational specialization by race, it is unlikely to invite policy attention. It fits with diversity goals attractive to corporations and universities, and diversity hiring does (as of this writing) have legal protection.

This brief look at racialized labor markets illustrates why statistics are needed before accepting claims about "the disuniting of America" or the "Mexican invasion." These claims, if true, call into question whether assimilation will work in the twenty-first-century as it did in the twentieth. To address such claims requires that we know who is learning English, graduating from high school, going to college, finding decent jobs, starting families, buying homes, serving in the military, voting, seeking citizenship, and otherwise "becoming American."

The Importance of the Second Generation

Any effort to understand how the color line and the nativity line intersect, and any study of the insular culture hypothesis, must have reliable information about second-generation Americans—defined as children with at least one foreign-born parent. Readers might be surprised that the census does not provide data on the second generation (how to correct that is discussed in the next two chapters). It did in early decades, but stopped in 1970.

If we briefly turn from census data to a privately funded study that did collect second-generation data we find powerful evidence of how important those data are to understanding the dynamics of immigrant assimilation.[29] This study, *Inheriting the City*, could frame issues critical to the country's future because it was not based only on census data, though, unlike census data, it was time and place limited. What it tells us about the immigrant experience in New York in about 2000, the nation should also know about cities across the country and across several decades. For this deeper and broader understanding we need reengineered national statistics.

Inheriting the City focuses on eight nationality groups: three native-born groups (white Americans, African Americans, and Puerto Ricans) and five foreign-born groups (Dominicans, Russian Jews, West Indians, South Americans, and Chinese). Simply listing these nationality groups already signals two key matters. First, the focus is on nationality groups and not on the statistical races. This allows comparison within and not just between the census race groups: white Americans compared to white Russian Jews; Puerto Ricans compared to West Indians. Second, it allows simultaneous attention to the color line and the nativity line because it includes native-born whites, blacks, and Hispanics and foreign-born whites, blacks, and Hispanics.

The study constructed three immigrant groups: (1) the first generation, or born abroad; (2) the "1.5" generation, defined as foreign born but mostly schooled in America; and (3) the second generation, born in the United States but with at least one foreign-born parent. Across the country *one-fourth* of all Americans under the age of eighteen today are either in the 1.5 or second generation. As the authors convincingly argue, these Americans "will define how today's immigrant groups become tomorrow's American ethnic groups [and will] define the character of American social, cultural, and political life."[30]

These young people "see themselves as very 'American' compared to their immigrant parents and yet still feel—and seem—very much like foreigners compared to the children of natives."[31] In New York, and every large American city, the color line and the nativity are present. For example, the foreign born and their children who could be mistaken as African Americans, "such as West Indians or dark-skinned Latinos, have experiences unlike those of other nonwhite groups. They face more systematic and authoritative racial boundaries than do Asians and light-skinned Latinos."[32] English language acquisition, success in school, and employment opportunities of the dark-skinned immigrant is regulated by American race relations; that of the lighter-skinned much less so.

How different groups succeed is clearly illustrated by findings on educational attainment: "Dominicans and South Americans are doing better than Puerto Ricans, West Indians are doing better than African-Americans, Russian Jews are doing better than native whites, and the Chinese are doing better than everyone."[33] These findings—for the nationality groups studied, in New York and at the end of the twentieth century—are striking. Whether the children of the foreign born are succeeding is in part a result of values instilled by their parents. The New York study finds that many are children of exceptional parents. "Although parents have measurable characteristics that put their children at risk—low education, low incomes, poor language skills, and so on—they have unmeasured characteristics" (a work ethic and belief in education) that are advantageous for their children.[34] But the study also reports that these children have benefited from civil rights and diversity policies, which have accelerated language acquisition, educational achievement, and employment opportunities for nonwhite immigrants.[35]

In addition, the ethos of multiculturalism has protected today's children of immigrants from the "torn between two worlds" that faced children of nineteenth-century immigrants, sometimes leading them to change their names and reject their parents. Today's second generation does "not have to choose whether being foreign or being American is 'better.' They can draw on both cultures."[36] An example: although it is the American norm to leave home at eighteen, some of the second generation are finding it economically advantageous to live with their parents until their midtwenties, using the money saved to continue their education. Others remain in enclave employment markets not as a refusal to assimilate but as a strategic choice that leads to career success.

It would be a hopeful message if the findings from New York and the reasons for them prevailed in every major city in the country. Obviously the groups studied would change and the difficulty of negotiating the color line and/or the nativity line will vary regionally, but if the broad pattern demonstrated in New York were repeated elsewhere the debate about whether immigrants are assimilating and how to accelerate that assimilation would shift dramatically and positively.

This very brief summary of an ambitious and complex study tells us that there is no "single, predominant outcome . . . such as assimilation or racialized exclusion; instead, it is the diversity within groups of patterns of incorporation into American society that needs recognition today."[37] The study identifies policies that facilitate assimilation, but designing and targeting these policies is hampered by inadequate statistics—especially statistics limited to broad race groups and lacking second-generation data.

The successful socioeconomic and political assimilation of white ethnics between the 1920s and 1970s made America what it is today. Many things contributed to this assimilation—among them an investment in urban public schools, unionization, expansion of occupational opportunities, and declines in residential segregation.[38] The parallel policies relevant to assimilation of today's new Americans are being actively debated, drawing as best they can on statistics ill-suited to the task. That can be changed.

Everyone Except the Blacks

One possible future for the color line is black/nonblack, as noted above. A recent study concludes that America in the twenty-first century appears to be moving in that direction.[39] The study asks whether diversity brought about by immigration is weakening America's racial boundaries? The aswer is "yes," up to a point. The color line separating whites from Asians and Latinos (except for undocumented Mexican-Americans) is weakening and even disappearing in areas of the country where diversity is much advanced. This is evident in proud assertions of multiraciality, in the increase of biracial marriages, and in the acceptance by white Americans of educationally and economically successful Asians and Latinos.[40] This is not the whole story. Greater demographic diversity across America is having less impact on the line separating blacks from everyone else.

It is this "except for the blacks" that paints a mixed picture. With important exceptions, the twenty-first century nativity line seems to be following the twentieth-century pattern—steadily weakening as the second generation learns English, moves into the labor force, intermarries with whites, and generally "Americanizes." But if this does turn out to be a twenty-first century story (and it is much too early to be confident that it will), it may not work to the benefit of African Americans, for whom the long history of a legally imposed color line has left a deep legacy of cumulative disadvantage.

Cumulative disadvantage describes how the effects of discrimination outlive discrimination itself. African American parents forced to attend impoverished, segregated schools in the early decades of the twentieth century did not acquire learning habits they passed along to their children. These children, though not themselves suffering explicit discrimination, are still educationally disadvantaged in ways that are then passed along to their children. African American grandparents growing up in a discriminatory real estate market did not build a wealth asset from homeownership; there is no reserve to help pay college tuition for their grandchildren a half century later.[41] The legacy of slavery and persistent discrimination in the Jim Crow era led to the weak economic position of African Americans today, even if they are not penalized because of their blackness.

If additional studies find that blurring the color line does not extend to African Americans, cumulative disadvantage will certainly be a major explanation. Understanding this will bolster countless initiatives trying to undo the legacy of racism. Across America, in business and work life, schools and universities, churches and community organizations, there are active efforts to reduce racial inequalities. Hospitals hire nurses and doctors sensitive to the cultural practices and beliefs that influence how groups differ in the health care they seek and in their response to treatment. Universities offer special mentoring and academic counseling to African Americans at risk of dropping out because their high school experiences did not prepare them for the challenges of higher education. Businesses sponsor employment fairs in African American neighborhoods to expand their applicant pool. Community organizations and churches sponsor after-school reading classes funded by philanthropy.

These private-sector efforts share with government policies a dependence on estimates of the scope and location of racial disparities. Those estimates, of course, largely derive from census and census-influenced measurements—that is, on race statistics increasingly out of touch with the sources and consequences of disparities that result from the nativity line as well as the color line. When we turn in chapter 11 to fixing those statistics, I will emphasize the need for better measures of cumulative disadvantage than currently available. These statistics should, for example, distinguish between African American slave descendants, on the one hand, and recent immigrants from West Africa or the Bahamas, on the other. A color line based on cumulative disadvantage affects the slave descendants but not the immigrant. If there is a discriminatory nativity line, however, it has little to do with the former and everything to do with the latter. Failure to sort this out leads to ineffective policy responses.

Is America a Postracial Society?

Though widely debated, there is little agreement on the question posed in the heading of this section. There is not even agreement on what "postracial" means. Lawrence Bobo lists three ways in which the term is used: understanding America's racial order from the perspective that blacks are victims is losing its salience; the dichotomous formulation—white/nonwhite—is not informative in an era of mixed ethnoracial identities; the young, especially, are eager to move beyond the disabling racial divides of the past.[42]

Debates about the postracial society often turn on whether the glass is viewed as half-empty or half-full. The half-empty view cites readily available statistics documenting the persistence of debilitating conditions afflicting American Indians and African Americans, burdened by cumulative disadvantages inherited from genocide, displacement, slavery, and apartheid; by statistics showing that both native-born and recently immigrated Hispanics face major obstacles in education and employment markets; and, by statistics indicating that the remarkable advance of Asians in recent decades is not shared evenly across all Asian nationalities.

These facts can be recognized, and yet still we celebrate the distance traveled since the civil rights turning point a half century ago. Supporting the half-full reasoning is the upward mobility for a growing number of African Americans, bringing them to prominent positions in professions, politics, the military, universities, and the business world. Although these success stories are not proportionate to their numbers in the general population, they are more than token. It is not just an African American story. Large numbers of native-born Asians and Hispanics are in the process of closing the white/nonwhite gaps in education, employment, and income. Recently arrived African immigrants and their children are doing better than the average African American. If these minorities, including dark-skinned persons, are overcoming racial barriers, blackness itself is not an insurmountable barrier. And there are strong signals that intercultural and interracial barriers are weakening.[43] Trends in interracial marriage all point in one direction: up.[44]

A useful way to reformulate postracial terminology is to ask how much of what aspects of life are determined by race? In a classic essay, the historian John Hope Franklin described the life of enslaved Americans. "They were permitted no independence of thought," he wrote; "no opportunity to improve their minds or their talents or to worship freely, no right to marry and enjoy the conventional family relationships, no right to own or dispose of property, and no protection against miscarriages of justice or cruel and unreasonable punishment. . . . A separate world for them had been established by law and custom. Its dimensions and the conduct of its inhabitants were determined by those living in a quite different world."[45] Slavery was a life in which race determined everything.

A postracial society would mean the opposite. The conditions of life determined by a person's race shrink to very little about anything—or at least anything that is not freely chosen. In describing its ancestry question, the Census Bureau notes that "a response of 'Irish' might reflect total involvement in an 'Irish' community or only a memory of ancestors several generations removed." Perhaps a postracial society arrives when the Census Bureau writes that "a response of 'Black' might reflect total involvement in a 'Black' community or only a memory of ancestors several generations removed."

This is the spirit in which David Hollinger describes a postethnic society as one that allows "individuals to devote as much—or as little—of their energies as they [wish] to their community of descent."[46] President Obama, sitting in the Oval Office, says as much: "I think now young people growing up realize, you know what, being African American can mean a whole range of things. There's a whole bunch of possibilities out there for how you want to live your life, what values you want to express, who you choose to interact with."[47]

This chapter has shown that the nation needs race statistics to address the four issues reviewed: anxieties about insular immigrant cultures; challenges that affect second-generation immigrants; continuing anti-black racism and long-term effects of cumulative disadvantage; debates about a postracial America. A color line or nativity line that unfairly advantages some groups and disadvantages others is a blight on American society. The blight is only worsened if the lines are mutually reinforcing, as they often have been in American history. The nation has a moral responsibility to erase them. Public policy will not be the only instrument for doing so, but it cannot be absent. Modern democracies rely on accurate statistics to identify policy challenges, to design and implement appropriate policy interventions, and to then evaluate whether the interventions are working as intended. The statistical races as we know them are not up to these tasks.

Conclusions

America's racial statistics were designed for a different era, and to address urgent public issues facing the country. Not all of those issues have been resolved—the legacy of cumulative disadvantage prominent among them. New statistics have to be alert to unfinished business. But they also have to be designed around the new business of America, which means policies that will facilitate assimilating millions of recently arrived Americans and their second-generation children, policies attuned to the diversity agenda, policies that welcome the benefits of multiculturalism but avoid its traps, and policies erasing the lines separating this race from that one or separating the person born here from the person born there.

The biggest impediments to new statistical measures are the measures already in place. There is tremendous inertia in statistical practice. The next chapter describes exactly what that inertia is sustaining. Based on this detailed examination the final chapter makes recommendations. The inertia can be overcome if recommended changes meet two tests: technical feasibility and political acceptability.

PART V

What We Have Is Not What We Need

CHAPTER 10

WHERE ARE WE EXACTLY?

I APPROACH THIS AND CHAPTER 11 WITH THE MINDSET OF AN ADVOCATE, NOT an academic. Leaving behind the historical and sociological approach of previous chapters, now I focus on how the census can deliver a new kind of data on race. When advocates target a government policy or practice they want changed, they research it thoroughly. Change may require no more than a few words or a number in a regulation—the definition of syrup or the denominator used to calculate the price of sugar cane used to calculate subsidy payments. Advocates know the major gatekeepers in the key agencies and in Congress who have to be persuaded to advance their cause. They use arguments that will motivate allies, and tactics that anticipate and preempt opposition. Advocates focus on such matters because they want to deliver; they are paid to win. I also want to win.

I am familiar with the political and technical considerations relevant to changing a census question, especially one as visible and consequential as the race and Hispanic questions. This chapter describes some of those considerations, particularly those pertinent to what is technically feasible, that is, what the Census Bureau can effectively and efficiently administer. The chapter also considers some of what is politically important, but more of that appears in chapter 11—where specific recommendations are made and a broad multidecade strategy is outlined.

This chapter starts with the key bureaucratic players, and then turns to specific census questions.

CHAPTER 10

The Office of Management and Budget

The Office of Management and Budget (OMB), particularly its Office of Statistical Policy, is responsible for statistical classifications—that is, for creating a common language and practice across all government agencies. The OMB's Directive 15 was necessary because government departments used different race and ethnicity categories and this was complicating the administration of civil rights legislation. The OMB issues standards. It has no authority to tell any part of the government, including the Census Bureau, that it must collect race or ethnic statistics. It defines what to collect *if* the Census Bureau does collect such data—and not just the Census Bureau but any other statistical program or any agency that maintains administrative records. Hispanic/non-Hispanic and the five primary races are a *minimum* core set of categories. The Census Bureau could not ask a three-category race question without first getting OMB permission. It can ask for more detail, as it does for Hispanics, Asians, Pacific Islanders, and American Indians—but not for whites or African-Americans. These more detailed data must be subcategories of the primary groupings.

The OMB is, of course, subject to law and legislation, but in the specifics of race and ethnic classification the Supreme Court and the U.S. Congress have had little to say. The Supreme Court has never made a ruling that specifies what racial categories should be in the census. It is not likely to. It might (see the anticlassification cases mentioned in chapter 8) rule against the whole project of collecting race statistics, though it is much more likely that it will continue to rule on particular uses of the data—in affirmative action programs, for instance—than the classification itself. The Congress seldom considered specific race categories. The only group mentioned in legislation is Hispanic, where the law says that Hispanic must be included *if* the government collects race and ethnic statistics. There were many fewer Hispanics when that law was passed; it is inconceivable today that Hispanic would be left out of any ethnoracial classification and thus the law requiring it is superfluous.

The OMB and the Census Bureau are the two key actors. The discussion that follows and the recommendations in chapter 11 keep this firmly in mind. The specific questions I endorse for the 2020 census were tested in 2010. I would have preferred different wording to these questions (and discuss why in chapter 11). I am certain, however, that a question as authorized by the OMB and as tested in the decennial environment is much more likely to be adopted than anything I, or anyone, might recommend, no matter how compelling the reasons.

The Decennial Census Questions

From 1790 to 1960 there was one set of census questions asked of every household in the country, and this could properly be referenced as the "decennial census questionnaire." Starting in 1960, the decennial census adopted a two-form design: the "short form" (fewer than ten questions) sent to every household, and the "long form" sent to a sample of approximately one in six households. The long form included the questions asked on the short-form and then about fifty more questions on population characteristics such as occupation, marital status, educational attainment, household income, military service, and so on, as well as housing characteristics such as number of rooms, amount of mortgage or rent payments, and the like. From 1960 through 2000, there were modest changes in the questions asked from one census to the next. Of most interest to us here were changes to the race and ethnic question, extensively described in previous chapters. The 2000 census was the last time the "short form" and "long form" design was used. After 2000, the Census Bureau replaced what had been the long form with the American Community Survey (ACS).

The American Community Survey

The technicalities of the American Community Survey (ACS) are important,[1] and are described on the Census Bureau website. We will focus only on two issues that relate directly to my recommendations for collecting different race statistics for the future.

1. The ACS is based on a sample, as the long form had been. But the ACS differs in being administered on a continuous basis—approximately 250,000 households every month, or three million households every year. The information from one year of the ACS sample provides statistical estimates for all levels of geography—states, metropolitan areas, counties, cities, and rural areas for jurisdictions or areas of at least 65,000 people. The ACS design, however, allows for aggregation across five years of data, making a cumulative sample of approximately fifteen million households. This cumulative sample allows estimates of population and housing characteristics at a level of geographic detail similar to what the long form had provided once a decade. With respect to timeliness of information, the ACS is a significant improvement over the long from it has now replaced. It provides annual estimates for any area of 65,000 people and larger, and when aggregated

across five years provides estimates for areas with as few as several thousand people.

2. The major differences between the decennial census and the ACS is that the latter asks many more questions and offers slightly less geographic specificity. For example, while the decennial census can, in principle, tell us how many Hispanics live on a given census block of a few hundred people, the ACS can give that statistic only at the block-group level, averaging fifteen hundred people. However, race data taken from the decennial census form can only be analyzed jointly with the few other variables that appear on that form: age, gender, household composition, and whether the residence is owned or a rental unit. Race data taken from the ACS can be analyzed jointly with many more variables, including income, education, language, occupation, and—important to our purposes—immigration status.

Before considering the consequences of the differences between the decennial form and the ACS form, I emphasize that it is common to speak of "census data" even when referring to surveys that the Census Bureau takes other than the decennial census and the ACS. The largest survey is conducted on a monthly basis for the Bureau of Labor Statistics. This extensive study, the Current Population Survey, provides the nation's critical unemployment trends and related statistics. The Census Bureau collects data from other economic surveys, from a survey of governments (state and local), and on many other topics in partnership with federal statistical agencies, including the National Center for Health Statistics, the National Center for Education Statistics, and so forth. That is, there are many more sources of "census data" than the basic decennial census itself and the ACS. What is most important for our purposes is that the OMB ensures that the questions asked about race and ethnicity are as similar as is technically feasible across all government surveys and administrative records.

The 2010 Decennial Census Questions

The most important questions for our discussion have been the Hispanic and the race questions on the decennial census form, which in 2010 assigned each of the 308,745,538 American residents as Hispanic or non-Hispanic. The respondent is told that Hispanic origins are not races, and the respondent is expected to answer both a question about Hispanic origin and one about race. Figure 3 shows the Hispanic question as it appeared on the 2010 decennial census and on the ACS form.

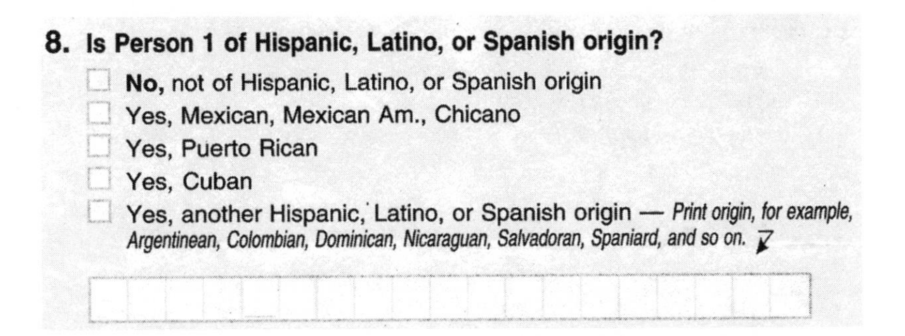

8. Is Person 1 of Hispanic, Latino, or Spanish origin?

- ☐ **No,** not of Hispanic, Latino, or Spanish origin
- ☐ Yes, Mexican, Mexican Am., Chicano
- ☐ Yes, Puerto Rican
- ☐ Yes, Cuban
- ☐ Yes, another Hispanic, Latino, or Spanish origin — *Print origin, for example, Argentinean, Colombian, Dominican, Nicaraguan, Salvadoran, Spaniard, and so on.*

Figure 3. The existing Hispanic question.

This question does not use the terms *ethnic* or *ethnicity*, even though the government documentation describes it as an ethnic question. In fact, by its choice of named check boxes and the "for example" list, Americans might assume that the question is a national origin question. The *only* way respondents can declare that they are of Hispanic, Latino, or Spanish origin is by choosing or writing in a nationality. Although Mexican American or Chicano can be interpreted as "ethnicities," they are presented as interchangeable with Mexican, which, of course, is a national origin.

The question immediately following is about race (see fig. 4).

In contrast to the Hispanic question, this question makes no specific reference to origin but instead uses the term *race* four times. Two of the races, White and Black, allow for no further breakdown. The American Indian/Alaska Native does not require, but does encourage, the respondent to list a tribe. The Asian question is designed to allow aggregation into two separate race groups: Asian and Native Hawaiian/Pacific Islander. The question does not make this clear. In fact, the Asian and the Native Hawaiian/Pacific Islander races in the census occur only when respondents select a nationality. In so doing, according to the stem of the question, they are saying that they belong to the Korean race or Pakistani race. This, of course, conflates nationality with race.

The "some other race" option allows for any number of additional races to be identified. If respondents enter, for example, German or Kenyan, the Census Bureau will allocate them, respectively, to the White or Black race. In practice, more than nine of ten persons who use the "some other race" line are Hispanics, thereby asserting a claim to a racial identity other than White, Black, Native American, Pacific Islander, or Asian. In the 2010 census, approximately nineteen million Mexican and Central Americans ignored the Census Bureau's

9. What is Person 1's race? *Mark* ✗ *one or more boxes.*

☐ White
☐ Black, African Am., or Negro
☐ American Indian or Alaska Native — *Print name of enrolled or principal tribe.*

☐ Asian Indian
☐ Chinese
☐ Filipino
☐ Other Asian — *Print race, for example, Hmong, Laotian, Thai, Pakistani, Cambodian, and so on.*

☐ Japanese
☐ Korean
☐ Vietnamese

☐ Native Hawaiian
☐ Guamanian or Chamorro
☐ Samoan
☐ Other Pacific Islander — *Print race, for example, Fijian, Tongan, and so on.*

☐ Some other race — *Print race.*

Figure 4. The existing race question.

instruction that they select a primary race, instead using only the "some other race" option.[2]

At different points in prior chapters I emphasized that the census race question is not based on a coherent definition of race, and that it mixes categories based on color with categories based on ancestry or national origin. The specifics of the question now make this clear. This is not a criticism of the OMB or the Census Bureau, which certainly have the technical capacity to design a less confusing question. It is a reflection of social reality and national history. As quoted in chapter 1, the Census Bureau "has no choice but to rely on incoherent categories if it hopes to measure race in the United States" because, Haney Lopez continues, "race arises out of (fundamentally irrational) social practices."[3]

Ancestry and Foreign Birth

Two additional questions asked on the American Community Survey, but *not* on the decennial census, are central to the discussion in chapter 11: an ancestry and an immigration question.

The ACS ancestry question is:

> What is this person's ancestry or ethnic origin?
> For Example: Italian, Jamaican, African Am., Cambodian, Cape Verdean, Norwegian, Dominican, French Canadian, Haitian, Korean, Lebanese, Polish, Nigerian, Mexican, Taiwanese, Ukrainian, and so on.

The reader may reasonably ask if this question is redundant with the race question. The race question, after all, tracks broad population groups that align with the original continental migratory flows out of the Rift Valley of eastern Africa; the five inhabited continents—Africa, the Americas, Asia, Europe, and the Pacific Islands—are sometimes understood, as they were by Blumenbach (see chapter 2), to be places of descent groups or ancestries broadly understood. Today, however, common usage treats ancestry on a much smaller scale, interchangeable with ethnicity or national origin as suggested by the question: What is this person's ancestry or ethnic origin? The Census Bureau emphasizes this narrow interpretation of ancestry: "Ancestry refers to a person's ethnic origin or descent, 'roots,' or heritage, or the place of birth of the person or the person's parents or ancestors before their arrival in the United States. Some ethnic identities, such as 'German' or 'Jamaican' can be traced to geographic areas outside the United States, while other ethnicities such as 'Pennsylvania Dutch' or 'Cajun' evolved in the United States."[4]

The bureau's explanation of ancestry is further elaborated in a revealing way: "The intent of the ancestry question is not to measure the degree of attachment the respondent had to a particular ethnicity. For example, a response of 'Irish' might reflect total involvement in an 'Irish' community or only a memory of ancestors several generations removed. A person's ancestry is not necessarily the same as his or her place of birth, i.e., not all people of German ancestry were born in Germany (in fact, most weren't)."[5] It is not possible for the census to measure strength of attachment to an ancestry, or to give it a very precise definition. Even the distinction between the term *ancestry* and the term *ethnicity* is hard to specify, though the United Nations, based on its survey of censuses around the world, makes an attempt. The UN concludes that in census taking, the word *ancestry* generally conveys an historical or geographic context, while *ethnicity* indicates self-perceived notion of group membership.[6] The U.S. census, however, sends a strong signal that ancestry means national origin. Of the sixteen examples listed on the ACS form starting with Italian, fourteen are nationalities; one is a subnationality—French Canadian. Then there is African American, which of course is elsewhere in the census considered a race, and neither a nationality nor ethnicity.

On initial inspection the ancestry question appears to be relevant to our understanding of race and ethnicity in America. As currently asked, however, it has severe problems, especially in suggesting that African American is an "ancestry or ethnic origin." Not surprisingly, a very large number of Americans do indicate African American as their ancestry, making this group, at about 9 percent, the third largest self-declared ancestry group in the United States—fewer only than those of German ancestry (15.2 percent) and Irish ancestry (10.8 percent).[7] But, of course, the African American has also been asked to indicate a race, though in that question African American is linked to a color, black or Negro (from *niger,* the Latin word for black).[8] *Eleven million more* African Americans appear in the statistics based on the race question than those based on the ancestry question.[9] This is a huge statistical discrepancy. Race, ancestry, ethnicity, and national origin are statistically mixed up in ways impossible to disentangle, and, depending on the term used, provide very different population numbers.

Discrepancies appear in the Asian statistics as well, where, not surprisingly, we find that very few claim Asian as their ancestry, but large numbers use the ancestry question to record their national origin. Responding to the ancestry question, 2.2 million claim Chinese, 1.2 million Korean, 1.1 million Japanese, and smaller but still significant numbers claim Taiwanese, Vietnamese, Laotian, and other nationality groups.[10] In the many instances where there is a discrepancy between the race numbers and the ancestry numbers, the Census Bureau tells us to rely on the former as "the official source of data."[11] Race trumps ancestry in the nation's statistics.

The Census Bureau can be casual about the ancestry question because it has no program purpose; nor is it used in any policy. Margo Anderson, the preeminent historian of the census, writes that the ancestry question displaced a parental place-of-birth question in the 1980 census because "pressure from white ethnics in the mid 1970s were objecting to the new emphasis on race and Hispanic ethnicity. White ethnics wanted the census to show how many 'ethnic' Germans or Poles or Italians, etc. there were, which, given their length of time in America, no longer showed up in the place of birth data."[12] The parental place-of-birth question should be returned to the census, for important purposes discussed in chapter 11. If necessary for space reasons, the ancestry can easily be dropped.

At present the immigration questions on the ACS are limited to these:

Where was this person born?
When did this person come to live in the United States?

The nation knows who is foreign born, but not who the children (the second generation) of the foreign born are. This is a major gap in our statistics, as discussed in the previous chapter and again in the next one. (There is a second generation question on selected Current Population Survey forms, but the CPS is very limited in information it collects compared to the American Community Survey.)

Does the Census Form Send a Signal to the American Population?

On the decennial census form, the Hispanic and race questions take up a lot of space. It may seem odd to point this out. But ask yourself, on what population characteristics does the government need statistical information as it formulates, implements, evaluates, changes, or even cancels various public policies? It needs statistics on a very large number of characteristics that are not on the decennial form: health, education, marital status, employment, homeownership. The form is far and away the most visible public projection of the government's need for statistics. In a census year, the form itself is widely displayed in promotional material. It is the signaling power of the census form that motivates my recommendation in chapter 11 to change when and where the government asks us to state our race. I will urge that a race question *not* appear on the decennial census form.

To justify this recommendation I emphasize that the fundamental, constitutionally mandated task of the census is to count every American once, only once, and in the right place. What is needed for this purpose are the number of people in the household, the address of the household, and such additional questions as allow the Census Bureau to determine if the information given is accurate. Race and ethnicity are *not* needed for this constitutionally mandated task. Yet simply inspecting the form leads to the conclusion that the government wants to know more about my ethnicity and race than anything else, including things I might think to be more important: am I healthy? a veteran? married? employed? Those questions are left to the ACS and other surveys. In this way, the census sends a message. It is reasonable to ask whether this is the message we want sent, an issue taken up in chapter 11, where I will recommend that the race and ethnic questions not be asked in the decennial census but be asked, differently, on the ACS and other government surveys. Several of those reasons are technical, and are discussed under the next four headings.

Small-Area Statistics

The most important difference between decennial census statistics and ACS statistics is that the former provides statistics down to the block level, though of course *only* for the very few population characteristics that appear on the decennial form. The major use of small-area racial statistics occurs when population shifts lead to redrawing of congressional districts, state legislative boundaries, and local political jurisdictions.[13]

Under the provisions of the 1965 Voting Rights Act, all or some parts of sixteen states are required to submit newly drawn districts to a preclearance review. These are states, mostly in the South, that historically had kept blacks from voting. Preclearance is designed to prevent boundaries that dilute the voting strength of minorities. This happens in one of two ways: by creating districts that pack as many minorities as feasible into as few districts as possible in order to limit how many of a racial group will be elected to a legislature; or, by spreading racial minorities across as many districts as possible so that everywhere they remain a voting minority.[14]

A significant advantage to litigating the Voting Rights Act with statistics from the ACE, and not the decennial census, is the ability to include income, education, and language and how these characteristics interact with race in voting behavior—and in any efforts to minimize the voting strength of America's minorities. In voting rights litigation there is growing interest in using characteristics such as income or education to buttress arguments of voter discrimination. The ACS is the only source of useful statistics because it allows for the combination of race with income or education.

As a practical matter, if the census produces an official redistricting file based on the ACS, the level of geographic detail available is what will be used in the redistricting process by state and local governments. It is no easier to hide discriminatory intent by moving block clusters than by moving individual blocks. Discrimination cases will be litigated using the same data the redistricters used. Nothing is lost and much is gained by dropping the ethnic and race questions from the decennial census form.

Contradictory Statistics

A second reason is the elimination of contradictory statistics. There are discrepancies between the race counts produced in the decennial census and the ACS—for example, there were approximately nine million people identifying as belonging to two or more races in the 2010 census, but less than seven million in the reports from the ACS a year earlier. There are technical explanations for discrepancies from one survey to another, but even if satisfactorily explained they greatly complicate scientific analysis and policy application, and lead to public confusion.

Deliberately Introduced Error

Redistricting has become increasingly precise. Political parties collect detailed information from various sources about political party registration, campaign donations, prior voting behavior, and such predictive characteristics as income, education, and, of course, race. An important database in this process comes from the decennial census, when it reports information at the level of census blocks. In redistricting, blocks are moved from one district to another in order to secure partisan advantage.

There is, however, a little-understood problem with race and ethnic data at the block level. The Census Bureau deliberately introduces errors. To protect privacy, the data are scrambled so that no particular individual can be identified.[15] A block that has a few Hispanic women will not be reported that way. Some of the Hispanic women might become Hispanic men or black women. On another block, Hispanic men become Hispanic women and black women become Hispanic women. When these blocks are aggregated to block clusters or census tracts, holding many more people than individual blocks, the correct number of Hispanic women, black men, and black women is reported. The level of aggregation needed in this correction process depends on the specificity of identifiable characteristics at various levels, and is produced by an algorithm that is itself protected by privacy and confidentiality policy. It is not the details that are relevant here; it is the fact that error is deliberately introduced into small-area racial statistics in order to protect privacy. The need to introduce error should be a compelling reason to remove the race question from the decennial form.

Administrative Data and the Decennial Census

To reduce the costs of the decennial census without impairing its accuracy, the Census Bureau is actively investigating whether administrative data can be used to help count households that, for one reason or another, are difficult to include in the basic census count. (See the discussion of the hard to count in chapter 7.) This requires that characteristics on the census form can be derived from administrative record sources such as social security, school enrollment, and the like. For gender, age, address, and homeownership, this is relatively straightforward. For race and ethnicity it is not. Administrative records vary widely in how they record races and ethnicities. A humorous example was shared by Katherine Wallman, chief statistician at the OMB.[16] She was asked to complete a medical form with two items, labeled as follows: "RACE—Hispanic, Non-Hispanic, Unknown" and "ETHNICITY—White, Black, Asian,

Chinese [plus a few other Asian groups], Native Hawaiian/Pacific Islander, Vietnamese, American Indian, Other." (Her e-mail concluded, "I kid you not.") The Census Bureau's otherwise extremely important effort to use administrative data will confront serious problems in matching race and ethnic characteristics. This problem disappears if the ACS is used as the national source of race and ethnic data, and only age and gender are on the decennial form, items much easier to match to administrative records.

Conclusion

The several points made in this brief technical detour are critical to the recommendations to which we now turn. One key recommendation is to ask about race and national origin only on surveys—especially the American Community Survey—because this allows jointly considering income, education, and immigrant status when formulating policy relevant to the color line and the nativity line. A second stresses the importance of giving greater weight to "national origin" than is currently the case in our understanding of and policies toward group disparities and toward the assimilation of the foreign born and their children. The third is to add a second-generation question, so the nation can understand assimilation much better than it does now.

CHAPTER 11

GETTING FROM WHERE WE ARE TO WHERE WE NEED TO BE

AT NO TIME IN AMERICAN HISTORY HAVE RACIAL STATISTICS BEEN AS PERVASIVE as they are today. And at no time have they been viewed so uneasily. Americans think it is important to understand why major racial inequalities remain despite civil rights protections. They believe it is important to know if children of recent immigrants are learning English and doing well at school. Yet many of these same Americans want government to stop asking about race and ethnicity.

The Supreme Court signaled this ambivalence when it concluded that the nation may still take race into account—but for a limited time. In 2003, the court ruled that universities could consider race in admission practices, but, wrote Justice Sandra Day O'Connor, "the Court expects that 25 years from now, the use of racial preferences will no longer be necessary. . . ."[1]

Are we on schedule to retire racial preferences in 2028? According to another Supreme Court justice, perhaps not. In 2009, a nominee for the Supreme Court, Sonia Sotomayor, was asked in her Senate confirmation hearing if race should be a policy criterion. She replied, "It is firmly my hope, as it was expressed by Justice O'Connor, that in 25 years, race in our society won't be needed to be considered in any situation."[2] Of course, if steady progress were being made, Sotomayor would have answered, "in 19 years." No one expected that answer, or even remarked that six years had passed since the twenty-five-year goal had been voiced. Justice O'Connor and, later Justice Sotomayor, were not proposing a real target date; they were metaphorically saying that sooner or later, we will stop this sorting and counting the American people by race.

Neither the court, the Congress, nor a majority of the voting public is willing to embrace color-blind doctrine. There is still a color line; there is still a nativity line and policy cannot be blind to these facts. Why, then, the uneasiness? Because the race statistics we have today are not the ones we needed. The country needs a fresh start.

Fresh starts in politics are difficult and rare. Political constituencies and commercial interests are invested in current practices. And there is the sheer weight of bureaucratic inertia. Even a messy history does not cancel out these inertial forces. Today's statistical races were pieced together from a long-discarded science of racial superiority; from practices and policies that for the better part of our history excluded, penalized, and damaged; from more recent practices and policies intent on undoing that damage; from successive waves of immigrants seen through the lens of race; from biological to anthropological to psychological constructions; from fixed race categories to boundary blurring.

It is not surprising that today's statistical races are a messy assemblage; but neither is it surprising that they are difficult to discard. If not discarded, they can be changed, bearing in mind that change is not an overnight project; it is a long-haul effort, to be measured in decades, and implemented incrementally. Change is also driven by the fact that race statistics do more than describe reality; they shape and even constitute it.

The Power of Statistics to Constitute Racial Realities

Statistics are normally thought of as holding up a mirror to society and reflecting what is out there—that is, as descriptive. But statistics create as well as reflect. Benedict Anderson, writing of European colonial powers imprinting their rule on colonized peoples, describes how powerful nations categorized and counted their subjects in order to rule them, and why those subjects gradually took on the identities imprinted on them by colonial census taking.[3] The French sociologist Pierre Bourdieu, in his influential *Identity and Representation*, fully elaborates the argument.[4] Struggles over ethnic identity (a term Bourdeau uses interchangeably with racial identity) are "struggles over classifications, struggles over the monopoly of the power to make people see and believe, to get them to know and recognize, to impose the legitimate definition of the divisions of the social world and, thereby, to *make and unmake groups*."[5]

Bourdieu writes that the power of statistical categories to move from descriptive to constitutive is proportional to the authority of agencies creating those categories. In modern societies statistics are products of the state, in all its power and majesty. When they are also products of science, as they were in the eighteenth century, their authority is substantially enhanced. Even if science doesn't create categories but borrows them from the state and then continually references them in analyzing social conditions, it adds its authority to that of the state (the point stressed in chapter 7). If the state and science use racial terminology, so will the media, schools, businesses, churches, and every authoritative voice in society. How citizens see themselves can only with difficulty escape the way in which the state, science, and other powerful entities portray them. Color lines or nativity lines exist in folk culture, but they gain strength when the state and science declare them to be real—and the census is a declaration.

Creating a New Racial Order

Creating a New Racial Order is the title of a recent book by Jennifer Hochschild, Vesla Weaver, and Traci Burch, who, citing their colleague Brenna Powell, define racial order as "the widely understood and accepted system of beliefs, laws, and practices that organize relationships among groups defined as races or ethnicities."[6]

Applying this definition to the twentieth century they identify two racial orders: first the rigidly segregated racial order known as Jim Crow, and then, secondly, a civil rights racial order. The first extended from 1880 through the mid-1960s. It positioned whites as superior and minorities as inferior. "The federal government and many states reinforced that group positioning by prohibiting actions such as interracial marriage, Asian immigration and citizenship, and non-Anglo voting. Government mandated segregation was pervasive. . . . Whites were seldom challenged and almost never with impunity."

But gradually white superiority was challenged. By 1970 the Jim Crow racial order "had been destroyed . . . through the combination of Supreme Court decisions, the civil rights movement, the 1965 Hart-Celler amendments to the Immigration and Nationality Act, and the Great Society. . . ."[7]

With the early-twentieth-century racist racial order destroyed, a new civil rights racial order based on principles of social justice and racial inclusion was created. A partial listing of the changes include "a rise in immigration, Blacks' assertion of pride and dignity, Whites' rejection of racial superiority (at least in public), a slow opening of schools, jobs, and suburbs to people previously excluded, and a shift in government policy from promoting segregation and hierarchy and restricting interracial unions to promoting (at least officially) integration and equality and allowing interracial unions."[8] According to Hochschild et al., this civil rights order is coming to an end. The racial order replacing it is based on multiracialism, demographic diversity, identity politics, and related issues reviewed in chapter 8.

I hold that the ending of one racial order and the beginning of another cannot be explained except by analyzing how the statistical races fit in. Consider more carefully how the racial order is characterized: the "relationships among groups defined as races or ethnicities."[9] Who or what does the defining is by definition a constituent feature of the racial order, for that order cannot exist independent of the races and ethnicities being defined. Defining makes and unmakes groups, divides and stratifies them—that is, it determines the relationships among them.[10]

Chapter 6 made clear that although the Jim Crow and civil rights racial orders, though differing radically in their goals, had in common a racial classification that—guess what!—had as its primary categories "Caucasian, African, Asian (often termed Mongoloid), and American Indian. Regardless of any mixture in his or her ancestry, each person had only one race, fixed at birth."[11] Readers can hardly be surprised. These races and their fixed nature is the story of the twentieth century *because* these were the statistical races constituting the Jim Crow racial order, constituting the policies that ended that order, and constituting the civil rights racial order replacing it. The great transformation from racial exclusion to racial inclusion notwithstanding, the twentieth century kept intact the statistical races that emerged from the turmoil of the prior century. Will they be kept intact in this century?

A racial order has five components, among them:

an authoritative typology of the society's racial categories
classification of individuals within those categories
permissions or prohibitions created and controlled by the state[12]

This list is a different way of saying what I have argued in this book. From the 1790 census to the present an authoritative census typology put people in categories used to permit and prohibit based on laws and policies created by the state. *Creating a New Racial Order* describes what is happening now:

the meaning of or elements encompassed by the term "race" are unclear . . .
people differ on the number of or boundaries around races . . .
racial identity might be fluid or idiosyncratic . . .
classifications may cross conventional boundaries . . .
the emergence of implicit or explicit new rules for new, smaller groups . . .[13]

These phrases make no reference to the present-day statistical races, but elsewhere the authors say that what would signal the arrival of the new racial order is "abandonment of the [census] racial classification."[14]

This is a critical point: though replacing Jim Crow with civil rights needed to keep intact the same racial classification, replacing the civil rights order needs to abandon that classification. What will be put in its place? One option is the color-blind route: let the racial order sort itself out without an authoritative taxonomy and statistics on people in its categories. France presents a current example, statistically ignoring its color line though trying, with limited success, to manage its nativity line with a French/non-French, citizen/noncitizen, statistical taxonomy. (See the appendix for a discussion of the French case.) Excepting the remote possibility that the U.S. Supreme Court makes an anticlassification, color-blind ruling (see p. 143), the French model is not in America's near future.

What, then, is that future? I strongly agree with the analysis behind the "abandonment of the racial classification" sought by the authors of *Creating a New Racial Order*. If the census remains structured in terms of the demography, politics, and policies of the mid-twentieth century, it will impede or even preclude the transformation normatively endorsed by Hochschild et al. If, as I argue above, racial statistics are a constituent feature of a racial order, the demographic and attitudinal dynamics identified in *Creating a New Racal Order* will express themselves through and be widely recognized in society *only if* the government produces a statistical representation of them.

The 2000 census presents a clear example. It rejected the principle, in place since the mulatto category was dropped by the census, that everyone belongs to one and only one fixed race. In doing so biracial marriages and biracial children were made visible and given legitimacy by the census, inviting a vibrant public conversation about multiraciality—reflected in pop culture, fashion, the media, and much more. A social practice that for three centuries had been disallowed, disowned, discredited, and discouraged was officially recognized, and despite lingering resentment among conservative whites, it will never be denied again. The "mark one or more" census option is a turning point.[15] Hochschild et al. note that what was socially prohibited is now permitted, and what is permitted is more readily and comfortably practiced "as multiracism becomes more common in definitions of a race, more people will identify as multiracial."[16]

The final argument of this book leads to specific recommendations for recasting the old racial measurement into a form conducive to—and in harmony with a new racial order. It proceeds in two steps: first I review the nativity line and the color line, bearing in mind the power of statistics to gradually create a certain type of reality; in conclusion, I detail recommendations that will introduce incremental but substantially critical change in the census.

The Nativity Line in the Twenty-first Century

Two statistical deficiencies hamper a national understanding of America's nativity line. Immigration statistics are insufficiently detailed. Second, they miss the second generation. The first is not a new idea. The foreword of a census publication on immigrants nearly a century ago complains that "little significant study of the foreign born can be made until they are divided into more homogeneous groups by classifying them according to the country or district of birth." This quote reappears in a contemporary essay tellingly titled "Studies of the New Immigration: The Dangers of Pan-ethnic Classifications."[17] The dangers are failures by policymakers concerned with matters such as human capital formation or family characteristics that are "obfuscated under the pan-ethnic classification of 'Latino.'"[18]

The obfuscation is compounded by the absence of sound information on the children of the foreign born, the second generation. America may be a "nation of immigrants," but it has inadequate statistics on the specific foreign born nationality groups and the pace at which they and their children are being integrated into the society. To understand these processes, the nation's statistical system is of little help, as "the second generation statistically disappears into increasingly problematic racial categories."[19]

We are forced to piece together explanations as best we can from privately funded surveys and research projects. One example was discussed in chapter 9, where we saw that a New York study revealed immigration dynamics that in the absence of such studies are hidden from view and thus from attention by policymakers.

Here I note other examples, keeping in mind the two deficiencies of census statistics: insufficient detail on different groups and inadequate second-generation data. The private funded Pew Hispanic Center reports that the majority of Hispanics surveyed prefer to self-identify by their family's country of origin rather than the umbrella Hispanic census designation.[20] Without that detail it is difficult to determine how young Hispanics "navigate the intricate, often porous borders between the two cultures they inhabit—American and Latin American." On the one hand, "Young Latinos are satisfied with their lives, optimistic about their futures and place a high value on education, hard work and career success." On the other hand, "they are much more likely than other American youths to drop out of school and to become teenage parents. They are more likely than white and Asian youths to live in poverty. And they have high levels of exposure to gangs."[21]

Or, consider recent immigrants from Africa, now approximately 7 percent of the U.S. immigrant population, and a proportion sure to grow.

Africa will add a billion people to its population by 2050.[22] That is a huge supply of potential immigrants. Already annual immigration to the United States from African countries is greater than immigration from India or China. African immigrants are well educated, and their children are excelling in American schools. But our understanding of how, where, and why this is happening is piecemeal at best. In the census, second-generation African immigrant children disappear into the black race category. They may share a color with descendants of enslaved blacks, but little else. What is not shared is, however, invisible to our statistics.

The Asian statistical race is equally problematic. In the aggregate, Asians have clearly overcome the legacy of discrimination. Based on its own survey, the Pew Research Center describes Asian Americans "as the highest-income, best-educated and fastest-growing racial group in the United States. They are more satisfied than the general public with their lives, finances and the direction of the country, and they place more value than other Americans do on marriage, parenthood, hard work and career success."[23] Asians' rate of immigration now outpaces that of Hispanics.[24]

Within the Asian category, however, all is not equal: "Asian Americans trace their roots to any of dozens of countries in the Far East, Southeast Asia and the Indian subcontinent. Each country of origin subgroup has its own unique history, culture, language, religious beliefs, economic and demographic traits, social and political values, and *pathways into America*."[25] It is understanding the "pathways into America" that requires statistics on different Asian nationalities and their children. For example, Chinese, Koreans, and Japanese are much more likely to graduate from college than Vietnamese, Cambodians, Hmong, and Laotians.[26] It is the former who are labeled the "model minority"; the latter are lagging in the indicators of assimilation.

The New York City study reviewed earlier (see p. 162) and the Pew Surveys noted here uncover assimilation patterns not evident in census data. But, of course, Puerto Ricans or Russian Jews in New York are a sliver of a much larger assimilation picture. What is going on in Los Angeles, where the distinctions that matter are among the second-generation Chinese, Korean, Cambodian, Hmong, and multiethnic groups such as Chinese-Vietnamese or Japanese-Europeans? What is going on in the Southwest, with its mixture of Hispanic nationalities? Only the government—especially via the American Community Survey—can provide detailed statistics on a regular basis at the level of group and geographic detail needed.

Assimilation can fail, leading to a xenophobic politics, a disillusioned and angry second generation, and heightened fears in white enclaves about the incursion of nonwhite "non-Americans." Or it can succeed, leading to cultural, economic, and political achievements similar to those produced by the successful assimilation of white ethnics in the twentieth century. More likely, there will be a mixed pattern. Some nonwhite population groups are assimilating into an America broadly understood as multiracial. But not every group is learning English, graduating from high school, naturalizing, finding a job, and buying a home at the same rate. There are second- and even third-generation Americans being left behind, perhaps being racialized in the process. The scope and distribution of this disparity determines what kind of America is in store for us.

Realistic policy and law—on school conditions, job training, language acquisition, and homeownership—can tilt the country away from failure and toward success. Accurate statistics cannot in themselves assure the right kind of policy and law, but the five statistical races plus the catchall Hispanic category hide variation, and are a poor basis on which to understand, let alone manage, the demographic transformation now unfolding in America.

The Color Line in Twenty-first-Century America

Whether the color line will disappear in the twenty-first century is linked to what is happening along the nativity line. We return below to that truth, but first briefly review the color line as it was historically understood—a line separating the "superior" white race from the "inferior" black and red races.

A reader of newspapers in America is unsurprised by headlines reporting that African Americans on average have lower levels of education, lower income, lower employment rates, less access to the voting booth, poorer access to health care, and less success even in settings where you would expect it. Racial disparities are an old story. They are also a new story.

The new story is that disparities *within* each of our race categories are becoming as great as the disparities *between* any of them and whites. When civil rights laws opened opportunities in higher education, employment and property markets, political careers, and the military, ambitious and talented minorities quickly succeeded, often with assistance from affirmative action policy. But this did not end racial inequality. In a popular book about African Americans the journalist Eugene Robinson writes, "it's right there, documented in census data, economic reports, housing patterns, and a wealth of other evidence."[27] What is it that is "right there?" Evidence that there are four black Americas.

> An abandoned inner-city minority with little hope of escaping poverty and dysfunction.
>
> A mainstream middle class with full ownership in American society.

Two emergent groups—mixed-race and recent black immigrants—doing well.
A small transcendent elite with enormous wealth, power, and influence—including the current president of the United States.

"These four black Americas," Robinson writes, "are increasingly distinct, separated by demography, geography, and psychology. They have different profiles, different mind-sets, different hopes, fears and dreams."[28]

Of course, these differences are equally true within the Asian, Hispanic, Native American, Pacific Islander, *and* White population groups. America's class system has always interacted with its racial hierarchy, but how race and class intersect varies across time and differently from one group to another. An influential study, published in 1980, was provocatively titled *The Declining Significance of Race*. William Julius Wilson did not argue that racial discrimination had ended. He did show that comparing employment disparities before and after the civil rights era revealed substantial change in the relative importance of race and social class in determining job success for blacks. By 2010, Wilson could cite research showing that race had less impact than education in explaining success in black employment.[29] That the importance of social class increases, and that of race decreases, does not prove the absence of discrimination; it is only evidence that racial discrimination is not the sole or even predominant force at work.

The declining significance of race means internal variation. This is happening in each of the statistical races, leading to the conclusion that in explaining disparities "the case for classifying and counting Americans by the large, panethnic categories is not as obvious as it once was. The lines between the five color-coded groups are becoming less distinct. The internal diversity of these groups has become harder to ignore."[30]

In chapter 8, I quoted Senator James Webb's assertion that white America is diverse. "One strains to find the logic"—he editorializes in the *Wall St. Journal*—that lumps whites together in making public policy. His target is affirmation action, especially for immigrant groups that he insists have no more right to special government attention than poor whites. Of course the "logic," as we noted, is an archaic statistical category lumping all persons considered white into one race category. But the vast majority of public policies have nothing to do with affirmative action. These polices separate Americans into different groups unrelated to race: by age, health status, geography, gender, education, and so on. Webb's unassailable point is that these other distinctions also reveal disparities—inner-city schoolchildren, on average, fare less well than suburban schoolchildren; access to health care is less available in rural than in urban America; men are paid more than women, and so forth. Webb's argument is that insofar as the nation intends to reduce unfair disparities, those within the white population merit notice, statistically and then in responsive policies.

The Uniquely Disadvantaged

The Senator's point can be accepted without losing sight of how American Indians and African Americans have been uniquely disadvantaged. From the nation's beginning these two groups were explicit targets of government-constructed discriminatory, racist policies and practices; this remained the case well into the twentieth century. More than two centuries of cumulative disadvantages continue to influence how American Indians and African Americans fare relative to whites.

American Indians are in one respect different from African Americans in the terms under which they do or do not benefit from government policies. They belong to tribes, of which there are three kinds: tribes recognized by the federal government; tribes recognized only by a state government; and tribes not officially recognized, though with the right to appeal for recognition.[31] The government determines which tribes are officially recognized, and along with recognition determines important benefits such as the right to occupy lands (Indian reservations) and the right to profit from gaming. But when the government recognizes the Cherokee nation, it does not say who is a Cherokee. Tribal membership is controlled by each tribe, based on proof of descent and/or community recognition. Proof is generally blood quantum, with membership restricted to those who have at least one Indian grandparent (25 percent Indian).

Self-identification is *not* a route to tribal membership, but it is, of course, how American Indians claim an identity on a census form. Not surprisingly, the census records a larger number of American Indians, approximately 3.4 million, than there are members of a federally recognized or state-recognized tribe (approximately 2 million). This distinction matters. American Indians are, on average, much less educated, suffer greater health problems, and have significantly higher unemployment rates than any other group in America. The two million Indians enrolled in one of the 565 federally recognized tribes have access to programs, such as the Indian Health Service, not available to nonmember Indians. The latter, however, like any other protected minority, assert their presence in America via the census. When the government, a business, or a university pursues a diversity strategy, for example, the relevant denominator for Indians is derived from census statistics, not tribal membership.

From this perspective, statistics are needed that will allow measurement of variation in education, health, or employment from one tribal group to another, and between tribal members and nonmembers. A few tribes, for example, benefit from the steady source of income earned through gaming, sometimes substantially.[32] But even including these success stories, there is nothing remotely resembling the African American middle class, the average wealth of Cuban Americans, or the educational achievement of many Asian groups. Consequently, as we turn below to recommended modifications in the census question, we keep in mind this special status of the American Indians.

African Americans also require special attention in our statistics. Robinson's book on the splintering of the black population identifies the "abandoned inner-city minority." A few decades earlier this population was labeled the "black underclass," describing self-reinforcing cycles of single-mother parenting, inadequate public schools, high dropout rates, a drug economy, street violence, crumbling public housing, record-setting unemployment, extraordinarily high incarceration rates, and the anger and despair that accompanies life in such circumstances. When in the 1980s the black underclass terminology was in vogue, there was near unanimity among blacks that structural causes were to blame. Whites were more likely to "blame the victim," pointing to such self-inflicted pathologies as drug use or teenage pregnancy. One of the most striking changes over the last three decades is a shift in attitude. A majority of black Americans now hold blacks themselves responsible if they don't escape poverty.[33] Opportunity for the abandoned has to be created, writes Robinson, but first "there is another factor to take into account: personal responsibility. Opening doors only helps those who are ready to walk through. . . . [No one] could deny that wrong choices play a huge role in keeping the Abandoned mired in their plight."[34]

This shift in attitudes does not mean accepting abandonment as a permanent condition. No sensible American of any race wants the dismal statistical picture of inner-city populations to be unchanged when the 2030 census is taken. There is now, however, space for fresh policy responses that approach inner-city conditions less as race discrimination than as a cluster of parenting, education, income, criminal justice, and employment issues caused by many factors and calling for solutions beyond race-sensitive policy. If it is racial discrimination preventing the abandoned from jobs or health care, stronger antidiscrimination policy is needed. If it is social position that keeps them disadvantaged, the policy remedy is better schools or a higher minimum wage.

My interest here is not in specific policies, but in why we still have to carve out a protected space in the statistical system for African Americans and American Indians. Nathan Glazer made a bold suggestion some years back: the census should ask only one question about race: "Do you consider yourself black or African American?"[35] That question, he argued, along with immigration statistics, would give the country what it needed to pursue antidiscrimination policies and to promote effective assimilation. His one-race question was not well received. It implied that all minorities *except* blacks could cross the color line. My recommendations below differ from Glazer's, but I strongly concur that any reengineered statistics must accommodate the persistence of the deep disparities and unique disadvantages of a significant proportion of African Americans and American Indians.

No one can be confident that in another thirty years the dysfunctions and disparities captured in today's poverty statistics in the inner city will have disappeared. It has, after all, been fifty years since the (now discarded) official war on poverty was announced, along with civil rights policies and urban renewal hopes. Some progress along some dimensions—quality of public housing, for example—has occurred, but it has not come close to erasing the stark disparities that civil rights policies were supposed to fix. Perhaps a growing economy and better urban schools can do better over the next thirty years, but it is a safe wager that despite the rise of the black middle class we will still need statistics specific to the conditions of African Americans.

The Nativity Line, the Color Line, and White Attitudes

The discussion thus far has ignored a critical issue: how will white racial attitudes change in the coming decades? I pose this question not because I can answer it, but to emphasize that white attitudes continue to shape the color line and the nativity line. We best see this by returning to the issue of "whitening" briefly introduced in chapter 9. Sometimes called *deracializing*, it refers to whites changing how they see a given population group, initially as nonwhite but subsequently as white—Benjamin Franklin's Germans, for example, whose complexion he found distasteful, or the swarthy Italian immigrants disembarking at Ellis Island who were viewed as a separate and untrustworthy race by Anglo-Saxon whites. Both, of course, have been viewed as white for decades. Herbert Gans describes "a process which begins when one group ceases to stigmatize the phenotypical distinctiveness of another, continues when it no longer views the other as a race, then ceases to pay attention to phenotypical difference and eventually stops noticing these."[36] Will many of today's immigrants travel this same route?

Researchers have "a special responsibility to follow where Whites will position Black and hybrid populations in coming decades. . . . Monitoring whom Whites will treat more equally is particularly important, because in the right political climate, public policy could encourage this process."[37] Gans offers two hypotheses to explain whitening. First, it is possible that the white population, because it would otherwise become a minority, will "whiten" light-skinned children of biracial marriages or successful professionals from the subcontinent in order to protect its majority status. It was probably no coincidence "that White ethnics were fully whitened when large numbers of African Americans and dark skinned Puerto Ricans came to the cities dominated by White ethnics. Perhaps today the speed with which Asian Americans are being whitened is connected to the concurrent large immigration of Mexicans, especially undocumented ones. . . ."[38] Of course if that process unfolds it will not fully erase the color line. Gans does, however, emphasize, "Deracialization is a process that has no intrinsic connection to phenotype. It is therefore entirely possible, at least in theory, that someday Blacks and other very dark skinned peoples could be deracialized as well." At some distant point in the future, the idea "that people once distinguished themselves from others by selected differences in facial appearance could become a historical curiosity."[39] This, of course, is the acid test of whether America becomes postracial.

His second hypothesis reintroduces the race-class distinction. In constructing the racial hierarchy, is it race or class that dominates? The underclass concept of Wilson and the abandoned minority category introduced by Robinson suggest that class will dominate. If so, any successful black, whether light-skinned or dark-skinned, will be readily accepted by the white majority. But if color trumps class, "very dark skinned people will continue to be ranked lower and possibly discriminated against more severely regardless of their class status."[40]

How much "whitening" is occurring, targeted to which groups, and over what time frame are processes that can be facilitated or retarded depending on how the government records races in our statistical system. The current race and ethnic questions give us an unclear picture of what is happening. The changes I recommend will provide a clearer picture, one that is needed to design policies that can prevent the merger of the color line and nativity line in ways that risk creating a permanent underclass.

Specific Recommendations

I proposed in chapter 1 that it was time to break free of an eighteenth-century race science that has structured how we have understood and experienced race across our history, bequeathing to us the familiar statistical races. They will not easily be dislodged, but there is a strategy that can do so. I lay it out in three realistic steps. They lead us to specific questions (figure 6, p. 202) that have the great merit of meeting technical criteria set by OMB and the Census Bureau. The three strategic steps focus on gaining political acceptability. They involve removing race and ethnic/national origin questions from the decennial census form itself, incrementally introducing change attuned to generational turnover, and postponing disruptions in policy uses.

One: Do Not Ask Any Ethnic or Race Question in the Decennial Census

The first step is to stop asking any ethnic or race question in the decennial census itself.[41] This will strike many as a radical and unnecessary change, but there are strong reasons to consider this. Several were discussed in chapter 10, all pointing to the merit of making the American Community Survey (ACS) the primary data source for key policy issues in the twenty-first century.

Neither scholars nor policy makers dispute the continuing presence of racial disparities in American society; only the causes are in dispute. Do disparities result from racial discrimination, or from characteristics unrelated to present-day discrimination, such as economic disadvantages or substandard education? The census form used once every ten years to do a basic population count does not measure education, income, or employment and cannot untangle the complex sources of persistent disparities. The ACS does include the variables needed. Insofar as the nativity line is implicated in disparities, information on the foreign born and second-generation matter, and the ACS is the appropriate source. Analysis and policy could draw, of course, on the ACS even if race questions remained on the decennial census. But something is gained by removing them, and nothing is lost.

The decennial census form sends a powerful signal. The form "is the piece of official government paper that is probably seen by more Americans than any other, surpassing in the extent of its distribution the income tax forms. It is a message to the American people, and like any message it educates them to some reality."[42] For instance, in 2000, shortly before the census was to be fielded, then senator Jesse Helms irately demanded that a question on marital status be reinstated to the short form (it was on the 1990 form). His argument? "It is irresponsible for the U.S. government to suggest or imply that marriage is no longer significant or important, but that is precisely the message that will go out if marital status is eliminated from the short form."[43] The Census Bureau said it was too late, so the senator introduced an angry "sense of the Senate" resolution, which ninety-four senators supported and none opposed. A "sense of the senate" resolution is nonbinding, and the Census Bureau did not alter the form. But this was the Senate sending its own strong message repudiating the wrong message conveyed by the census form.

It is not just the Senate but large numbers of citizens who can be irritated. Hundreds of bloggers and media commentators attacked the census in 2010, complaining about the race question. The sizable numbers of Americans who oppose policies that favor racial minorities don't appreciate learning that the race question "helps identify areas" in need of "services of particular interest to certain racial and ethnic groups."[44] It should be an easy call. The decennial census is not the platform on which to debate the importance of reducing racial inequalities or integrating the foreign born. The decennial census itself should signal that its sole purpose is the constitutional mandate to provide statistics for reapportionment and redistricting. This requires a correct address and the number of people living in the household at that address, and other questions needed for quality control. It does not require race or national-origin questions.

The country can get better information from the ACS, with less public resentment. It is the appropriate survey for race, national origin, and immigration statistics, which will keep the nation informed about our nativity line and color line.

Two: No Abrupt Change; Phase Change in Incrementally

Abolishing slavery required nearly a century of political pressure, and then a costly Civil War. This did not end racism, which was more deeply embedded in American culture and politics than the progressive forces of the time imagined. There was another century of racial injustice until the remarkable push forward in the civil rights policies of the 1960s. And yet still there is the legacy of cumulative disadvantages now joined by new discriminatory practices targeted at recent immigrants. Seen in the context of 200 years of effort to end racism, a victory in the next twenty-five years (p. 183) seems implausible. But if we take that twenty-five years metaphorically, translating it as "within the next generation or so" and become more specific about what *is* plausible, we can map a path to an equitable future and provide relevant statistical tools to help get us there.

Use Generational Turnover Strategically

When it comes to race statistics, incorporate generational turnover as a deliberate and strategic component of change. The idea is simple enough. The views of Americans sixty-five and older are relevant today but will be irrelevant by 2040. In the meantime, the views of today's youth carry little weight now, but will matter in 2040 when they will be politically active, socially engaged, economically important, and in leadership positions. For today's preadults, the civil rights era is already a historical footnote. They are forming their attitudes in the context of biracialism, diversity rhetoric, identity politics, and demographic transformation. In 1960, five percent of Americans approved of interracial marriage; today the approval rate is 75 percent, and even higher among those under fifty years of age (85 percent).[45] Such transformations are propelled by two factors: first, a gradual shift in perceptions of race as Americans of all ages became accustomed to seeing an integrated society including African American athletic stars, celebrities and blacks of influence in almost all domains of national life, as well as dramatic successes by Asians and Latinos. Second, the transformative effects of generational change as older people who had only known the Jim Crow racial order passed from the scene. Middle-aged Americans were born into a world of antidiscrimination law and racial integration—the civil rights racial order.[46] "When a collective memory fades and fragments, the moral force of the associated racial order is weakened. . . ."[47] Each generation expects statistics to align with its social realities—not with statistics anchored in the realities of its grandparents.

Figure 5 illustrates generational change, extending the time frame back to 1960 and forward to 2130, highlighting key shifts in the census years of 2000, 2020, 2040, and 2060. I label each of five generations according to the racial order it primarily encounters at a formulative age. The first generation came of age in the civil rights era, when statistical proportionality dominated race policy. The next generation, born about 1970, came of age late in the civil rights era, as attention shifted from social justice to biraciality, diversity, and identity politics. The third generation, born in 2000, the year that "mark one or more" was first on the census, is labeled the "transition generation" to emphasize the arrival of a new racial order accompanied by major reforms of the census questions to be implemented in 2020 and 2040. These reforms will mark the transition from five statistical races to national origin statistics. The generation born in 1930 will grow up knowing that system, and by the time it reaches adulthood in 2060, we can hope (but not be certain) that both the color line and nativity line will have disappeared. If so, the generation born in 2060 will be the first in the nation's history to know a truly postracial America.

Three: Introduce a Major Modification in 2020 *without* Disrupting Current Policy Uses

The "mark one or more" option of the 2000 census did not disrupt established policy. This is its genius. Even as the government upended

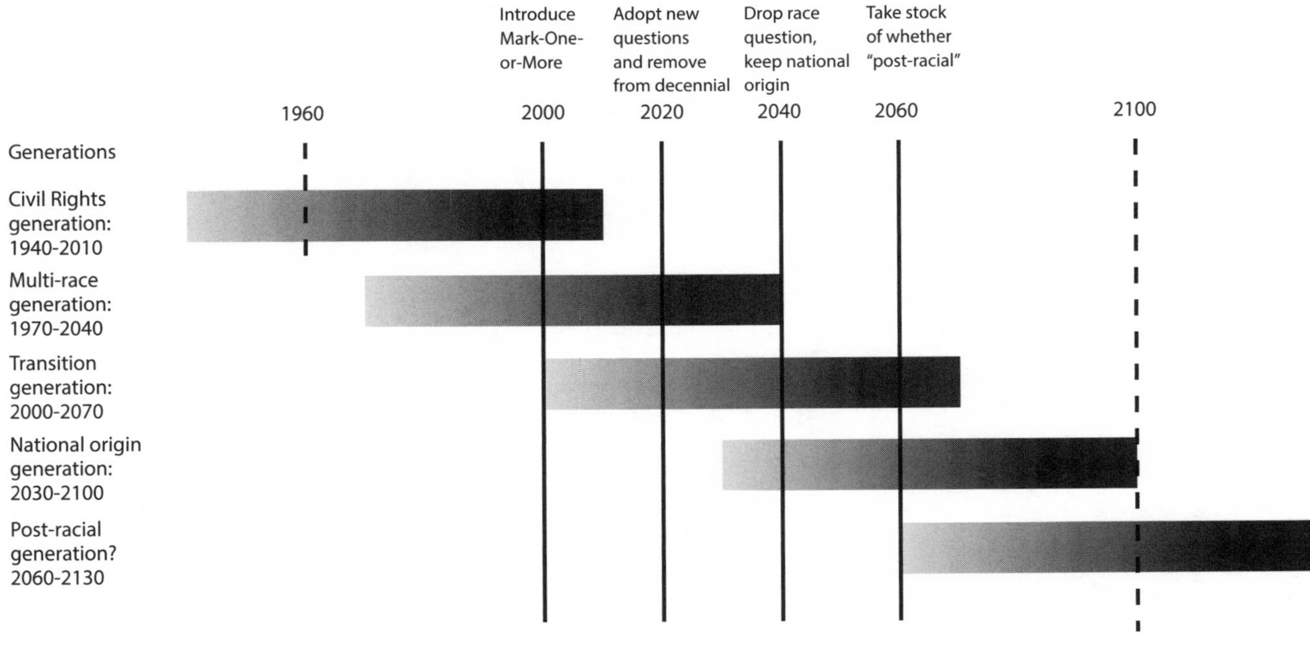

Figure 5. Generational turnover and the race question.
Notes: Light gray = youth years; medium gray = adult years; dark gray = late-adult years. Based on an image by Polina Viro.

century-old cultural beliefs it carefully protected current practice in the policy arena. For policy purposes, the government reassigned persons who reported two or more races to one of the standard single race categories.[48] There was scattered grumbling that this echoed the one-drop rule of the nation's racist past, but reassignment was politically possible because the multiple-race respondents were fewer than 3 percent of the population,[49] and because those politically affected—minorities bringing discrimination complaints to the courts—were protected by the reassignment formulae. Until the multiple-race population grows to a significant percent of the population, 10 percent or so, "mark one or more" will remain a change that points to the future without disrupting the present. When the multiple-race population becomes so numerous that reassignment is technically unworkable or politically unacceptable (at the current rate of growth, approximately a generation from now) any policy use of "mark one or more" will be easily accepted by the generation that grew up with it.

The intense politics that surround racial measurement make it virtually impossible to debate two issues simultaneously: "What are the nation's races?" and "How should race statistics be used in policy?" The political debate over affirmative action was fraught from the outset, but the country nevertheless adopted successful civil rights policies and major social change occurred. This was possible only because racial classification itself was *not* a target. The statistical races were familiar, politically taken for granted. The races—especially in color-blind politics—became a target only when immigrants in large numbers were assigned to those races, thereby disrupting the consensus that affirmative action was a policy for descendants of enslaved Africans. Barring some similar anomaly, by the time there is debate about the policy uses of "mark one or more" statistics, the statistics themselves will be taken for granted. This lesson bears directly on how I believe the country can proceed.

Taking Advantage of the 2010 Census Experiment

My interest has been in articulating a rationale for any racial or national origin questions on the American census (chapter 9), detailing inadequacies in the current questions (chapter 10) and, in this chapter, with the rationale and the inadequacies both in mind, to recommend changes. This task became easier when I learned that the Census Bureau was conducting extensive research on alternative ways to ask its race and Hispanic questions, and that it was on a schedule (funds permitting) to finish its research and make a recommendation to the OMB by 2015.

This will permit introducing any changes in the 2020 census (or even earlier on the ACS).

The Census Bureau has tested six different versions of its race and Hispanic questions. Criteria used by the bureau to recommend the "best one" will be largely technical, covering issues such as ease of administration, improving response rates, reducing public confusion, and the like.[50] A scientific agency is guided by technical issues; it does not consider broad political purposes, asking in this instance, whether a question will adequately capture what is happening at the intersection of the nation's color line and nativity line. The OMB, however, is part of the administration. It is likely to hold public hearings where such broader arguments would be invited.[51] It is likely that Congress will hold hearings on the Census Bureau's recommendation, as it did on the "mark one or more" change. Because I expect technical issues to be considered in appropriate settings, I do not focus on them here.[52] I am more concerned with the public purposes that should be served by the census statistics.

From that perspective, one of the six versions being studied by the Census Bureau best matches the rationale outlined in chapter 9. I strongly endorse the race (#8) and national origin (#9) questions reproduced in figure 6.[53] Before considering strengths (and weaknesses) of these questions I emphasize the importance of linking them to improved immigration questions. This involves adding to the ACS a question on parental place of birth.[54] The immigration questions would appear on the ACS as follows:

10. Where was this person born?
    If not in the United States, when did this person come to live in the United States?
11. Where was this person's father born?
    Where was this person's mother born?

The Shortcomings of Questions 8 and 9

I endorse the two questions in figure 6 recognizing that they not ideal. In my view the most consequential shortcomings are these:

a. It is preferable to alphabetize the list of groups in question 8. This would erase any vestiges of the hierarchical ranking intended by Linnaeus and Blumenbach (see chapter 2).
b. Because we know the "some other race" option to be primarily used by Hispanics, retaining it in this format is redundant.[55] However, if the question does retain the "some other race" line, the use will probably drop off dramatically.[56]

➜ **NOTE: Please answer BOTH Questions 8 and 9 about race and origin.**

8. What is Person 1's race or origin? *Mark [X] one or more boxes.*

- ☐ White
- ☐ Black, African Am., or Negro
- ☐ Hispanic, Latino, or Spanish origin
- ☐ American Indian or Alaska Native
- ☐ Asian
- ☐ Native Hawaiian or Other Pacific Islander
- ☐ Some other race or origin

9. Write in Person 1's specific race, origin, or enrolled or principal tribe – *For example, African Am., Argentinean, Chinese, Egyptian, German, Marshallese, Mexican, Mexican Am., Mongolian, Native Hawaiian, Navajo, Nigerian, Tlingit, and so on.*

Write in the specific race(s), origin(s), or tribe(s).

Figure 6. New 2010 questions to replace existing questions.

c. The wording fails to distinguish race and ethnicity from national origin, repeating the latter term in both questions.

The wording suggests that nationalities—Egyptians, Germans, Nigerians, etc.—are races, as is any identity that is written in the three boxes. This is misleading, and I will "correct" the questions when I reference them in the remainder of the chapter, using the term *race* for question 8 and the term *national origin* (and tribe as a national origin for

American Indians) for question 9. The need to make this "correction" for the sake of clarity is unfortunate. I would much prefer that question 8 not have the term origin in the stem, and that question 9 not have the term race in its stem.

This reservation notwithstanding, I seize the opportunity to endorse a question that has performed well technically and is under active consideration by the Census Bureau and OMB. Questions 8 and 9 are far superior to the current race and Hispanic questions. I anchor my recommendations in these questions because they have a realistic chance of being adopted. I turn to what they achieve.

What Is Accomplished by Questions 8 and 9?

The new questions offer several improvements over the current questions (see figs. 3 and 4):

a. There will be critics of question 8 because it merges Hispanics with the five primary races. I see this as positive rather than negative. The question treats the six groups as they are often treated in law and policy, as they appear on many official forms, are described in the media, studied in public health and the social sciences, and understood by the general public.[57] The closer a question comes to common usage, the less public confusion it produces.
b. Both questions allow for "mark one or more"—question 8 specifically and question 9 by virtue of providing three write-in lines. This is consistent with twenty-first-century demographic changes, diversity rationales, and multirace and multicultural habits of mind.
c. Used in conjunction with the (improved) immigration questions, question 9 allows distinctions between place of birth and national origin.
d. Joint examination of questions 8 and 9, and bringing in immigrant status as appropriate, allows for careful analysis of the color line and the nativity line, which is what we expect of twenty-first-century statistics.

There are additional advantages not easily summarized as bullet points, and are considered in the next two sections.

National Origin and Immigration

Readers familiar with the extensive sociological literature on race relations in America will immediately see that if only question 8 were on the census the nation's statistics would be heavily biased toward a racial interpretation of society; if only question 9 were on the census the statistics would bias toward an ethnic and culture interpretation. In fact, in the debate about how best to understand race in America, one line of reasoning holds that emphasizing ethnicity, with its assumption that cultural features of a group fade in significance from one generation to the next, ignores the persistent color line that was and remains racist in its construction, including the American instinct to racialize any new nonwhite immigrant groups.[58] The alternative and equally significant argument holds that the racial lens hides too much about the highly varied way in which different immigrant groups have made a place for themselves in American society.[59] This is an enormously important debate about how to interpret American history and assess its future. Census statistics are not a neutral bystander. Our current statistics favor a racist interpretation and, especially in their lack of detail about national origin and about the second generation, they miss much of importance to a cultural interpretation.

In endorsing questions 8 and 9, and urging that both stay on the census form at least until 2040, I am trying to assure that the nation has the statistics it needs to inform the racist vs. cultural interpretation. Question 9, in conjunction with a second generation question, will allow greater attention to immigration and assimilation than is possible with our current questions. But as the next two sections make clear, question 8 will assure continued attention to issues that have long been racial.

Cumulative Disadvantage

In the national origin question, the first example listed is African American. This initially seems odd given that the prior race question had already asked if the respondent is African American. However, it is essential that African American appear prominently in the national origin question. Glazer explains why: an African American identity "does not fade after a few generations in this country but maintains itself in a varying but full form generation after generation."[60] Whether in another few generations African Americans will reply "American" to the national origin question is a choice available to them. An example is an example, not a check box. In fact, when a significant proportion of the entire population answers "American" to the national origin question, it will be dropped from the census as no longer providing statistics that have policy uses. It is beyond my powers to predict whether that might happen.

As recommended below, by 2040 the race question should be dropped altogether. By then the national origin question can produce the detail needed to understand disparities and inequalities. Between now and 2040, jointly using these two questions along with the immigration questions will lead to extensive scholarship comparing the African

American descendents of slaves with the more recently arrived African immigrants. This analysis will track the differential social and economic conditions of the "abandoned minority" and the diasporic Africans, permitting an informed decision about the statistics still needed. A similar logic operates with respect to American Indians, and justifies listing the term *tribe* in the stem of the national origin question, and a tribe among the examples. For American Indians the term *tribe* is not likely to lose its salience in one or even two generations.

For African Americans and American Indians the heavy burden of cumulative disadvantages practically guarantees that there will remain marked disparities that separate each from the rest of America. And it is possible that other American groups—especially the Mexican American children of today's illegal immigrants, also prominent in the list of examples—will be equally victimized by cumulative disadvantage. Future statistics, whether from a race or a national origin question, will show the magnitude of persisting disparities, and help us understand their sources.

Flexibility

It is obvious but merits emphasis that question 9 allows for aggregation, including assigning all national origin answers to the traditional race categories. David Hollinger, who has proposed a census question similar in purpose to a national origin question, stresses this flexibility, noting, "Any public or private agency that wished for any reason—including the design and enforcement of antidiscrimination remedies—could combine the numbers of people who selected Mexico, Cuba, Puerto Rico, Guatemala, etc., and have a functionally 'Hispanic' set of statistics. Yet such an agency would have the capacity to deselect Portuguese Americans and Spanish Americans, for example, if they choose to do so."[61] Separate counts of Asian nationality groups could "depending on the mission of the agency using the census data and the salience to that mission" be aggregated to identify East Asians, South Asians, and Middle East Asians, or even all Asians, retaining the definition of that term now in place.[62]

The flexibility of a national origin question permits multiple alternative combinations in a way that the fixed, limited categories in the race classification never can. This flexibility is available to any government agency. The Department of Health and Human Services could aggregate data differently in Miami and in Chicago to better specify who has access to health care in cities with very different demographics. School officials could design a classification more sensitive to a local school-age population rather than, as now, being dependent on the proportion of

Hispanics, blacks, and so on. This flexibility is especially valuable to large urban school districts faced with students speaking dozens of different mother tongues in their homes. The Department of Justice could bring cases against the exploitation of non-English-speaking Central Americans by identifying this group in combination with a question on language rather than have Central Americans statistically lost in the more generic Hispanic category. Researchers could reproduce familiar categories to measure trend lines, but also begin to create a much more nuanced theory of educational success or civic engagement. Advocacy groups and government agencies could draw a much more accurate portrait of income and employment disparities than that given by the rigid classification now available. In the spirit of maintaining policy continuity, the availability of aggregation minimizes disruption and facilitates political acceptability.

Flexibility also solve one of the most troublesome issues in the five-race model. Where do Northern Africans and those from the Middle East belong? European, Asian, African? None of those are satisfactory, which has led to the nagging issue of whether they should be their own "race category"; but if so, is the defining characteristic Arab, or something regional, or simply the Middle East? This issue was engaged in the 1990s without resolution. The growing number of immigrants from North Africa and the Middle East have kept the debate alive. Question 9 allows them to identify their national origin as Egyptian or Saudi Arabian, and then select a race (or, "some other race").

This flexibility is consistent with the argument that modifying the census question should minimally disrupt current policy applications even as it allows more nuanced analysis of social conditions, and eventually more nuanced policy making. Indeed, even if question 8 is eventually dropped, its six broad groupings can be reconstructed by aggregating responses to question 9. In this sense, "race" does not disappear even if the race question does. This "have your cake and eat it too" model will help secure political support for the recommended changes.

Phase the Strategy in across the Twenty-first Century

Finally, as now emphasized, it is important to introduce change gradually. Figure 5 lays out a strategy for the twenty-first century. It takes advantage of generational turnover by introducing change in 2020 that anticipates further modification a few decades later. In figure 5, it is the "transition generation" born about 2000 (see the preface), already comfortable with multiraciality and demographic diversity, that will be in a position to make a more far-reaching change by midcentury.

Specifically, I recommend

- By 2020, replace today's Hispanic and Race questions with questions 8 and 9, placing them on the ACS but not on the decennial census form. To provide second-generation statistics, add parental place of birth to the immigration questions.

In the decades that follow there will be extensive analysis by statisticians, demographers, and social scientists. We will learn what the new questions tell us independently, what they tell us jointly, and what they tell us when combined with the immigration questions. This analysis will inform decisions taken in 2040, and eventually, I hope, will unfold more or less as follows:

- In 2040—Drop the race question and use only the national origin question. Continue the immigration questions—in fact, continue those questions as long as there is a measurable flow of new immigrants to America. Retain the option of a separate question for African Americans and/or for American Indians (see above for rationale for these exceptions) if analysis of racial disparities seems to require that.
- In 2060—Determine if the national origin question is producing meaningful statistics. It is possible that the color line will have disappeared but the nativity line will still matter. The immigration questions will provide relevant statistics. It is also possible that "except for African American" and "except for American Indian" will still matter; if so, separate questions for those groups would be retained. However, it is also possible than in the next half century an America transformed by immigration, diversity, and multiraciality—and one in which cumulative disadvantages will have been erased—will no longer require race statistics.

Conclusions

To unify the states as a nation, America's founding fathers in the northern states accepted the deplorable three-fifths compromise in 1787. It is easy to look back today and lament the human damage wrought by the clause, its corrosive effect on our society, and its injury to America's self-image as a nation dedicated to equal treatment before the law. But how might future generations look back on our generation?

The census and other national surveys can facilitate a transition between today—with policies still framed using Blumenbach's five statistical races—and a future with improved statistics. Political leaders, social scientists, and statisticians can find ways to better capture the enormous demographic transformations underway, the cumulative effects of racial disadvantages, any renewal of biological/genomic racism, the emergence of new forms of racism, and the strengths and weaknesses of assimilation policies and practices. If we miss this opportunity future historians will look back in dismay.

The Race and Hispanic Origin Alternative Questionanaire Experiment in the 2010 Census offers an extraordinary opportunity, the kind that comes along at best once in a generation. If the changes it produces are minor and technical but leave intact our current statistical races, I have no doubt that future historians will blame our generation for failure of imagination and political courage. The 2010 experiment puts within reach an opportunity to boldly design statistics that will keep us aware of our past, capture the dynamics of the present, and give us ways to envision and realize a less perniciously racial society for our children.

APPENDIX: PERSPECTIVES FROM ABROAD

WHAT IS YOUR *RACE?* IS AN AMERICAN-CENTRIC LOOK AT ISSUES THAT ARE not unique to America. Countries other than the United States are actively debating whether and how to include race, ethnicity, ancestry, or national origin in their statistical systems and what purposes should drive those decisions. This appendix serves to alert readers that one country, even considered across its entire history, is only a window onto a broad and varied landscape of international efforts to comprehend color lines and nativity lines, each with its history, political debates, public confusions, and unsatisfactory policy results. Each of these countries—and certainly the three reviewed in this appendix—confirm a core argument about America's experience: racial and ethnic classifications used in government statistics create as well as reflect social realities.

A brief consideration of three cases—Brazil, France, and Israel—underscores another conclusion reached in this book: it is easier to identify flaws than to prescribe workable fixes.[1] This is apparent in Brazil and France, where lively debates focus on what to measure and how to apply the statistics to policy. Israel is more settled on both instances, but faces a demographic challenge that requires a nuanced treatment of religion, ethnicity, and citizenship.

BRAZIL

A book about Brazil would not be titled *What Is* Your *Race?* but perhaps *What Is Your Color?* Although Brazil shares with the United States a colonial past in which Europeans overpowered an indigenous Indian population and then imported African slaves in very large numbers, Brazil avoided the rhetoric of racism so pervasive in America's history. In Brazil there was no race science, no insistent and officially sanctioned repetition of racial superiority and inferiority. Population differences were described as shades of color rather than fixed biological races. Almost from the beginning Brazil was home to a sizable, officially recognized and welcomed multiracial population, labeled the Pardo (Brown) group in early census practice. The racially mixed Brazilians resulted from unions between the European and the indigenous Indian. This was deliberate demographic policy.

In 1775, King Dom João VI (John VI) of Portugal encouraged his subjects in the New World to populate with the native inhabitants: "Let it be known to those who hear my decree that *considering its benefits* . . . my subjects residing in America populate themselves and to this end join with the natives through marriage."[2] The "benefits" were, of course, population growth, as the Portuguese were too few to exploit the resources of the vast region that became modern Brazil and, in any case, were soldiers without wives.

Racial mixture between the European and African slave was a different matter. During Brazil's slave era it was prohibited, though Brazil's enforcement of antimiscegenation policy was more lax than that in the United States.[3] Brazilian scientists did not assert the mulatto to be a feeble race that would soon die out, or claim that blacks freed from slavery would go insane. Slave uprisings in the late nineteenth century helped bring about the end of slavery, and though racist thinking among slave owners (and others) was common, unlike in the United States the end of slavery was not followed by decades of legal segregation, one-drop rules, and prohibition of black-white marriage.

By the early twentieth century Brazil welcomed interracial marriage between Europeans and Afro-Brazilians as readily as a century earlier it had welcomed the interracial union of Europeans and the Indians.[4] When the United States was stressing racial purity in its policies, Brazil was emphasizing racial mixture as a "positive national characteristic and the most important symbol of Brazilian culture."[5] The size of Brazil's mixed-race population grew accordingly, quickly becoming the second largest race group in Brazil.

Brazil prided itself on the absence of a color line.[6] The term *racial democracy* was popularized to describe Brazil as a country of various races living harmoniously and as equals. In the early decades of the twentieth century the only thing missing were statistics to confirm the facts of the racial democracy celebrated at home and boasted of internationally. The 1940 census included a question on color listing three categories: White, Black, and Yellow (for the small but well-established Japanese population). The 1950 census added the all-important Brown category to capture the size of the mixed race population. The 1960 census used a five-color classification that found a place for everyone: White, Black,

Yellow, Brown, and Indigenous (*Branca, Preta, Amarela, Parda, Indigena*). But this fuller count did not appear again until 1991, by which time Brazil's racial democracy was much in doubt.

The growing pressure for improved statistics in the second half of the twentieth century came from black activism and international attention. The first of these echoes the American experience with the civil rights movement. The popularization of Brazil as a "racial democracy" did not match the experience of its black and indigenous population, who were not only unequal in all respects but insisted that poor health care, education, and employment were a direct consequence of discrimination. Progressive politicians and academics joined in making these arguments. Statistics, claimed the advocates for racial justice, would show that Brazil's celebrated racial democracy was a myth.

In an unexpected development, international pressure also demanded improved statistics. The first step was a UNESCO-commissioned study of race relations in 1950. UNESCO, expecting to confirm Brazil's racial democracy, complained that compared to nations that practiced racial discrimination (including the United States), "The rare examples of harmonious race relations have not, however, received the same attention either from scientists or the public in general. Yet the existence of countries in which different races live in harmony is itself an important fact capable of exercising a strong influence on racial questions in general."[7]

UNESCO did not find the racial harmony it expected in Brazil. Nor did other sociological studies in the 1950s and '60s. Scholars instead found a "Brazilian racial problem" traceable to a slave-owning past.[8] They also found that the small Native Indian population was severely disadvantaged. The myth of racial democracy unraveled. Racial inequalities came to the foreground. International donor agencies tied development aid to evidence that would show effective antidiscrimination laws and policies.[9] This drove the need for reliable statistics. Brazil's leaders came to terms with mounting evidence that discrimination was more pervasive than had been acknowledged.

Advocates for racial justice drew on privately collected and government provided statistics to advance arguments for remedial policy attention. As Brazil moved into the twenty-first century, affirmative action (*açaõ afirmativa*) emerged as a policy option, especially with respect to university enrollment. In 2004, the federal government established the Programa Universidade para Todos (University for All Program). The government offered private universities generous tax exemptions on the condition that they provide full-tuition scholarships to disadvantaged applicants. The fine print required that the number of scholarships for self-declared *negros* and indigenous applicants would be proportional to the number of "citizens self-declared [as] black, pardo [brown or mixed race] and indigenous in the respective federal entity, according to the latest census."[10] Policy based on statistical proportionality had reached Brazil. Other policies implemented at the state level and targeted to public universities took into account social class as well as color, with some states (six of twenty-seven) only using class. Those states argued that inequalities result less from racial discrimination than from social disadvantage, and searched for policies that would avoid racial quotas.

Affirmative action is far from a settled issue, partly because many think the race classification on which it rests an unsatisfactory measure of "racial realities," especially in its count of the mixed race. Melissa Nobles asks, if Brazil's color identifications "are complex, flexible, and relatively unstable, can public policies reliably be based on them?" Her qualified answer is yes, "the mere existence of color categories on the census is decisive." Although critics of affirmative action deplore this development, advocates are pressing "to refine and revise the categories in order to pinpoint more precisely enduring inequalities."[11] Critics, however, employing arguments similar to those voiced in the United States, are mounting legal challenges to the entire Brazilian project of affirmative action.[12]

With one significant difference, Brazil and the United States are roughly similar. Both have colonial histories of Europeans inflicting great damage on indigenous American people. Both had slave economies. The significant difference is that, with slavery abolished, racist policy was not instituted in Brazil as it was in the United States. Racial mixing was tolerated and in some instances actively encouraged, with the result being a mixed-race population of about 40 percent reported in Brazil's recent census, more than ten times the (reported) U.S. rate.

Despite this large mixed-race population, Brazil is not a color-blind society. It is not free of discriminatory attitudes and practices and the racial inequalities that follow. Americans tempted to interpret a few decades of multicultural diversity and racial intermarriage as evidence that a post-racial society has arrived might ponder why two centuries of public racial mixing in Brazil that led to a dense multicultural society has left intact a color line that still separates whites and blacks.

France

A book about France would not be titled *What Is* Your *Race?* but perhaps *Who Is French?* French law prohibits asking a race, ethnic, religion, or language question on its census. To do so, write David I. Kertzer and Dominique Arel, would contradict the belief that "the republican conception of the 'nation,' defined as the sum of the state's citizens, admits no other public identity than the civic identity of French. Since national identity is deemed indivisible, the only permissible division on the census is between the nationals (les Français) and the resident foreigners (les étrangers). Unaffected by the evolving international discourse sympathetic to minority rights, France continues to cling to a vision of the nation which, by its very essence, leaves no legal space for the existence of a 'minority,' and therefore of ethnically defined groups."[13]

Because France makes *no* policy use of race and ethnic statistics, it is often presented as the antithesis of the United States. This stark difference, however, is complicated by large-scale global immigration in recent decades, from which France is no more immune than the United States. In fact, France, under European Union law that permits open movement among all of its member states, has a much more difficult time policing its borders than does the United States. France shares with the United States a worry that its immigrant population is not assimilating. This worry has pushed the issue of ethnic statistics to the political foreground, focused on France's Islamic immigrants. They come primarily from North Africa, presenting a color line as well as a nativity line and religion line in French social and political life.[14]

Although French law prohibits the census from asking about race and ethnicity, such questions are sometimes permitted on government surveys.[15] In 1992, research institutes affiliated with the French government conducted a broad study of immigrant assimilation in France. The research distinguished by ethnic origin; it went further by taking up issues of strength of ethnic identity—asking, for example, Are marriages a matter of choice or arranged by families? What is the role of religion in daily life? The goal was "a study of immigration and its future, of immigrants and their descendants, and not of the nationality of the population."[16] This effort to distance the study from France's ethnic composition, and hold to the principle that France was indivisible, did not work out. The widely debated findings inevitably focused on France's non-European immigrants and their children, documenting widespread inequalities separating those immigrants from the dominant white population, including immigrants from other European countries. This prompted strong political controversy on whether the census should produce race and ethnic statistics, with the purpose of understanding the extent to which measured inequalities resulted from discrimination against Africans in housing, employment, and education.

France's debate repeats arguments familiar in the United States. From some quarters, there are claims that immigrants are more likely to be criminals, to engage in urban violence, to take jobs away from French workers, and to treat wives and daughters in ways inconsistent with French values of gender equality. Echoing Samuel Huntington's alarm about America's immigrants from Mexico (see p. 154), it is charged that (Islamic) immigrants hold on to their language and customs rather than assimilating. They are not fit for French citizenship; their growing numbers threaten the civic fabric of France.[17] There are calls for deportation and a strong political movement focused on restricting further immigration.

This right-wing political effort is answered by the Left, arguing that it is difficult for Algerians or Malians to integrate into French culture if they are targets of racial discrimination, are forced into segregated housing, are denied places in higher education, and are pushed into low-paying jobs with no prospect of career improvement. These outcomes, it is argued, result from discrimination against blacks. Scattered evidence indicates much higher rates of unemployment for second- and third-generation North Africans compared to those of second- and third-generation Italians or Greeks.

In the absence of time-series statistical data that distinguish among national origin groups in France and track the second and third generations—which altogether constitute a fifth of France's population—there is no way to sort out fact from fiction in claims and counterclaims. The debate about immigration policy and discrimination has, increasingly, become a debate about measurement, and in particular about the use of race and ethnic categories. Patrick Simon writes, "The state of affairs in French statistics-gathering . . . has gotten to the point that it has triggered a controversy of rare violence between those that would like to see statistics take into account the diversity of the population and those who denounce the danger that such statistics might pose of ethnicizing or racializing society." He points out that "the contentiousness of this debate has been such as to sometimes lose sight of the very existence of discrimination and the flaws of the Republican model that are at the root of the controversy in the first place."[18] An American version would be an intense debate about whether and how to count Mexican Americans, and not—as in fact it is—a debate about policing borders or deporting the undocumented.

Proponents of race and ethnic statistics point out that France has strong antidiscrimination law. The state, for example, is given the power to ban groups that promote racism. It is a criminal act to discriminate in employment or in the provision of goods and services.[19] Hate speech, racial defamation, and racially motivated violence are punishable by law. But, note the proponents of ethnic statistics, these laws now in place for four decades have the same weakness as the 1964 Civil Rights Act in the United States (see p. 85). Laws "designed to punish racists committing bigoted acts motivated by racist intent" are ineffectual if, as we saw in the U.S. case, there is institutional racism.[20] Simon extends the point, suggesting that France's antidiscrimination laws are "unable to effectively tackle what is more akin to a discriminatory *system* or *order* than to a succession of isolated cases."[21]

At the international level, the United Nations Committee on the Elimination of Racial Discrimination has expressed concern over the limited ability of France to implement antiracism legislation due to its inadequate ethnic statistics.[22] Michel Wieviorka, a leading French sociologist and a proponent of race and ethnic statistics, concludes that France cannot correct its institutional racism and its pervasive racial inequalities unless it first recognizes these facts, and this requires statistics unavailable under current law.[23]

These assertions do not go unanswered in French politics. Although opponents of race and ethnic statistics agree that there is discrimination, they emphasize the serious downside to collecting race statistics. The introduction of ethnic statistics can create group differences and promote the idea that boundaries separate one member of French society from another, whereas their absence is itself a policy that promotes the social integration of minorities.[24] This is the French version of the *dilemma of recognition* discussed earlier (see p. 145). Opponents also cite dark chapters in French history: the use of ethnic statistics to shape policies targeted at undesirable foreigners and minorities. Nazi statistics were used to facilitate the extermination of French Jews; more recently, the Roma have been targeted for deportation.

The critics are also fearful that race statistics could lead to affirmative action policies, even quotas. They point to the United States as evidence of what can go wrong—the resentment by those edged aside by quotas or made to pay for social inequalities they are not responsible for; the promotion of group-based claims and the resulting growth of advocacy organizations and political mobilization of race and ethnic groups; the inevitable mismatch between the crude statistical taxonomies employed and those most deserving of social support.

In France, no less than in the United States or Brazil, there are no easy solutions. All three nations are debating whether race statistics are a help or a hindrance. I have presented a way forward for the United States, but certainly make no similar effort with respect to Brazil or France. My brief review is for the reader curious to know if the United States is unique. In some respects, yes—especially in its heavy dependence on statistically shaped racial policy. But in light of twenty-first-century challenges the United States is not unique. It is beyond my predictive powers to assess whether Brazil, France, and the United States are on convergent tracks, and will look more similar than dissimilar by midcentury. It is likely that all three countries will still need antidiscrimination policies; it is not certain that all three will construct those policies via race statistics. France is trying to avoid that altogether, and Brazil, in part, is trying to avoid it by giving more emphasis to class than to race.

Israel

A book about Israel would not be titled *What Is* Your *Race?* but perhaps *Are You a Jew?* In chapter 2, I cited *A Nation by Design*, a book title drawing attention to how the early European founders of America used demographic policy to shape the immigrant flows to America, favoring immigrants thought likely to be loyal to the great experiment of creating a republic based on democratic principles, and also having the skills needed to expand a nation across a sparsely populated continent. A nation by design also aptly describes the demographic project of building a Jewish nation in Israel.

The modern nation-state of Israel differs from the earlier American design-a-nation experiment in one powerful way. The land that became Israel in 1948 had been inhabited by Jews continuously for over three thousand years. It had also been continuously inhabited by Arabs over that period. When Israel gained statehood, its small, resident population of less than one million included both Jews and Palestinian Arabs, the latter primarily Muslim, with a small Arab-Christian population in Jerusalem. To design a new Israel for the twentieth century assumed that Jews scattered around the world would in significant number return to their ancestral homeland. The "ethnic" categories were basically Jewish and non-Jewish, with the former also defined as a religion and the latter category simply grouping Arabs, irrespective of their original homelands and family connections, as non-Jewish.

The Zionist ideology was clear about Jewish ethnicity. It was a category to be gradually erased because the places to which diasporic Jews has dispersed—nearly everywhere in the world—were not their true homes. As summarized by Calvin Goldscheider, Jews on returning to their ancestral homeland of Israel would become new Jews—that is, Israeli nationals "untainted by the culture and psychology of exile and freed from the constraints and limitations of experiences in places of previous (non-Israel) residence. Zionism's construction of Jewish peoplehood therefore involves assignment of ethnic origin to the minority experiences of Jews outside of Israel and therefore requires its devaluation . . . . Israel, Zionism posits, is the national homeland of Jews, their ancestry. Their ethnicity is not the source of their identities: Israel is."[25]

This goal was unprecedented in modern nation building. The new nation adopted three key demographic policies to realize it. The Law of Return provided that Jews from anywhere in the world had an unquestioned right to immigrate to Israel and claim citizenship. Although

Arabs, too, had lived in those lands for millennia, there was no Law of Return for them.

The Law of Citizenship outlined separate citizenship provisions for Jews and non-Jews, with Jews—whether already resident or new immigrants—being automatically granted nationality and therefore citizenship. Arabs then living in Israel could claim citizenship, but many refused to do so on grounds that Israel itself was an illegal imposition on an Arab homeland. Non-Jewish immigrants had to apply for nationality status, which was not easily granted. The third fundamental law assigned to the World Zionist Organization the task of "gathering in the exiles—that is, Jews from Europe, the Americas, and elsewhere in the Middle East.

The basic distinction made in Israel's census was Jewish and non-Jewish. Jews were further divided by place of birth or place of father's birth, but this was designed as a temporary distinction. It did not indicate ethnicity, because by definition a Jew returning home could not be an immigrant. The place of birth designation would fade in importance as the third generation was fully absorbed into the "national policy and culture by exposure to educational institutions and the military, and raised in families where the parents are native-born Israelis."[26]

Israel's policy of ethnic erasure was designed to solve any problem of ethnic cleavage. Jewish immigrants from widely different parts of the world—the United States, Poland, Italy, Ethiopia, Argentina, Russia, Arab countries, and so on—were expected to lose any cultural contact with those places and certainly not import into Israel differences or tensions associated with divergent histories. It is doubtful that this policy has fully worked,[27] but it did accomplish the narrow goal of removing national origin identities from third-generation immigrants. It is similar to the desire for color-blind statistics on the assumption that race differences then disappear. If ethnicity is unmeasured, its unwanted identities will drift away. The French model is based on a similar assumption: "immigrants would gradually lose their cultural and linguistic distinctiveness as they progressed on the path to citizenship. There was no need, therefore, to distinguish among French citizens on the basis of their origin."[28]

Israel's founding demographic project was successful. Israel is now a prosperous country of approximately eight million residents, 75 percent Jewish, 20 percent Arab, and 5 percent other. The growth rate of the Jewish population resulted from immigration, mostly European in the early period and primarily Russian starting in the 1990s. However, by the start of the twenty-first century the number of Jews worldwide had leveled out, and Jewish immigration to Israel is no longer a major source of population growth.

The fertility rate of Jewish women in Israel is slightly above replacement level (2.7), and modest growth of the Jewish population continues. But it seriously lags growth rates of Israel's non-Jewish population. Arab fertility rates are extraordinarily high—certainly in the occupied territories of Gaza and Palestine—but even in Israel proper Arab women have a fertility rate (4.8) nearly twice that of Jewish women. Alarmists predict that if current trends continue, Arab Israelis will outnumber Jews.[29] The prospect of a Jewish nation in which Jews are a minority is unacceptable to Israel's political leadership. The Public Council on Demography was established in 2002 with the task of designing policies necessary to preserve a Jewish majority.

This has not been an easy task. Israel's 1948 Declaration of Independence reflected contradictory goals. It established a Jewish state, but also guaranteed that the new nation "will maintain complete social and political equality among its citizens with no distinction based on religion, race, or gender," and although the clause did not specifically include national origin, it was implied.[30] Among these citizens who are to be treated equal are Arabs who for nearly two decades following the 1948 war lived under military rule and were confined to geographic areas.[31] The confinement severely limited their employment, training, and educational opportunities. The government justified these restrictions on security grounds, but the restrictions also prevented Arabs from competing for jobs with the similarly uneducated Sephardic Jews.[32] Although Arab citizens have enjoyed rights such as free speech and access to government services, they have attended different schools, lived in separate areas, and interacted as subordinates to their Israeli counterparts in the workplace. Even with the lifting of many controls in the late 1960s, the cumulative disadvantages functioned—as they have for American blacks—as a barrier to economic and educational success. In addition, the 1967 war brought the Palestinian Territories (the West Bank and Gaza) under military control. Constitutional promises of equal treatment notwithstanding, six decades of Israel's history has not fully reconciled those promises with the construction of Israel as a Jewish state.

Efforts to limit Israel's non-Jewish population are being implemented. For example, Palestinians who marry Israeli citizens cannot become citizens. Because it is Arab Israelis who choose Palestinian spouses, denying citizenship to the spouse is an incentive for the newly married to leave Israel. In 2012, the Israeli Supreme Court upheld this law, ruling that "human rights are not a prescription for national suicide."[33] Marriage choice was framed as a national security issue.

The statistical edifice used to carefully track the growth rates of Jews and non-Jews and citizens and noncitizens is a national registration system, though the Central Bureau of Statistics conducts a basic census and other surveys that add important demographic characteristics to the basic counts. Whether Israel will be able to fashion policies that can ensure a Jewish majority and protect the rights of all of its citizens is a challenge equal to, if not more difficult, than what faces France with its growing Islamic population or Brazil with its long-ignored legacy of racial discrimination.

Israel and the United States share a founding that depended on national statistics to "design a nation" in terms that distinguished persons fit for citizenship from those unfit. In both cases, the categories employed—Jewish/non-Jewish and white/nonwhite—were constitutive of the kind of nation brought into being, determined the lives that people in those nations were allowed to live, and left a legacy of social and economic inequalitie. It will be deep into the twenty-first century before we learn whether that legacy can be erased with thoughtful policy, in either of the countries.

Conclusions

Brazil, France, Israel, and the United States share a commitment to principles of fairness, justice, equality of opportunity, social cohesion, nondiscrimination, human rights, and immigrant assimilation. They also share the challenge of any multicultural democracy—how to apply these principles in populations being transformed by streams of immigrants moving across national borders (United States and France), differential birthrates (Israel), or long-ignored inqualities hidden by claims of a racial democracy (Brazil). From this broad generalization it is a short step to asking what governments need to know in order to govern their changing populations according to the shared principles. No modern country can function without national statistics. But that obvious truth does not tell us which statistics are needed. This book has attempted to answer, for one country, which population statistics its government needs—and how it can go about getting them. There is a larger landscape, however. Multiculural democracies are likely to be the only kind of democracies we have in the world. Each will have to figure out for itself how to protect basic democratic principles; each will have to decide what statistical tools will be an asset in this task. One thing seems certain: the success of multicultural democracies will depend on whether they can minimize, even eliminate, color lines and nativity lines.

NOTES

Preface

1. These included two friends and colleagues, Arien Mack and Aristede Zolberg, from the New School for Social Research, where I was a dean as this project got underway; and a very special friend, Katherine Wallman, who serves the nation as its chief statistician in the Office of Management and Budget. All three commented on draft chapters, Wallman having to instruct me on a few matters more than once. Another "friend of the manuscript" is Richard Gottleib, whose editorial work on the first half of the book greatly livened it and helped me find "my style," as he put it. Two SIPA students, Ellen Johnson and Kim Sykes, provided helpful insights and background research, especially for chapters 7, 8, and 9. Monique Smith, my careful assistant at Columbia, proved her copyediting skills and helped in numerous other ways.

2. The group included Reynold Farley, Ian Haney Lopez, Victoria Hattam, Jennifer Hochschild, David Hollinger, Melissa Nobles, and Kim Williams. Working with this group was a delight and an education, as is evident in the winter 2005 issue of *Daedalus*—"On Race"—to which most contributed. I thank them all, and take note that two of them went the extra mile in reading drafts more than once: Jennifer Hochschild changed my mind about the importance of the aspirational dimension of a census. David Hollinger persuaded me to focus on the purpose of the statistics as the first step in designing improvements. This book would have been far different, and much less satisfactory to its author, had he not heard and tried to heed those arguments.

3. As recently as August 2012, the Census Bureau issued a report on the first phase of its analysis, which I review in chapters 10 and 11. See Elizabeth Compton, Michael Bentley, Sharon Ennis, and Sonya Rastogi, *2010 Census Race and Hispanic Origin Alternative Questionnaire Experiment* (Washington, DC: Decennial Statistical Studies Division and Population Division, U.S. Census Bureau, 2012).

Chapter 1. Introduction and Overview

1. Ian Haney Lopez, "Race on the 2010 Census: Hispanics and the Shrinking White Majority," *Daedalus* 134.1 (2005): 50.

2. The Constitution does not use race terms. It distinguishes population groups as follows: "Representatives and direct Taxes shall be apportioned among the several States which may be included within this Union, according to their respective numbers, which shall be determined by adding to whole number of free Persons, including those bound to Service for a Term of Years, and excluding Indians not taxed, three fifths of all other Persons" (Article I, Section

2, no. 3). The "free persons" meant the white race; by implication taxed Indians were included; and "three fifths of all other Persons" meant the African slaves.

3. The Constitution stipulates, "The actual Enumeration shall be made within three Years after the first Meeting of the Congress of the United States, and within every subsequent Term of ten Years, *in such Manner as they shall by Law direct*" (Article I, Section 2, no. 3); emphasis added.

Chapter 2. Classification before Counting: The Statistical Races

1. Carl Linnaeus, quoted in Audrey Smedley, *Race in North America: Origin and Evolution of a Worldview* (Boulder, CO: Westview, 1993), 164. In addition to the four major race groups, Linnaeus used two other race terms: *Homo monstrosus* to cover what he referred to as exotics, and *Homo ferus* to cover the wild peoples described in travelers' tales.

2. See chapter 6 for a contemporary genetic explanation for the continental origin of five population groups, adding a "brown race," Pacific Islanders, to the Linnaen four.

3. Lawrence A. Hirschfeld, "Natural Assumptions: Race, Essence, and Taxonomies of Human Kinds," *Social Research* 65.2 (1998): 331–50.

4. Arthur Stinchcombe, "The Logic of Scientific Inferences," In *Constructing Social Theories* (Chicago: University of Chicago Press, 1987), 44.

5. Johann Blumenbach, *On the Natural Varieties of Mankind* (New York: Bergman, 1969).

6. Smedley, *Race in North America*, 166.

7. The term *ethnoracial pentagon* in recent social science literature comes from David Hollinger's influential *Postethnic America: Beyond Multiculturalism* (New York: Basic Books, 2006). Hollinger uses four categories—Black, Red, White, and Yellow—the way Blumenbach did, but applies "Brown" to America's large Hispanic population group. Scholars who cite Hollinger repeat this practice. See especially Jennifer L. Hochschild and Brenna Marea Powell, "Racial Reorganization and the United States Census 1850–1930: Mulattoes, Half-breeds, Mixed Parentage, Hindoos, and the Mexican Race," *Studies in American Political Development* 22 (2008): 59–96. This, of course, makes much sense in today's America, but in my focus on the official race classification in the U.S. census, the Blumenbachian pentagon that separates Pacific Islanders from East Asia remains relevant, in ways the next section clarifies.

8. The earlier directive, known as Directive 15, was issued in 1967. It is discussed in detail in chapter 6.

9. The 1997 OMB classification system introduced other important changes: the option to combine two or more races, subdivisions of the five primary races, and the use of the Hispanic designation not as a race but as an ethnicity. I will get to these complexities in subsequent chapters.

10. America's census categories have also been imposed internationally through standards for clinical trials required by the U.S. Food and Drug Administration, as will be discussed in chapter 6.

11. Bernd Wittenbrink, James L. Hilton, and Pamela L. Gist, "In Search of Similarity: Stereotypes as Naive Theories in Social Categorization," *Social Cognition* 16.1 (1998): 49.

12. Paul Starr, "Social Categories and Claims in the Liberal State," *Social Research* 59.2 (1992): 263–95.

13. Ann Morning, "Ethnic Classification in Global Perspective: A Cross-National Survey of the 2000 Census Round," *Population Research Policy Review* 27.2 (2008): 239–72.

14. Ibid., 248.

15. These terms are borrowed from Claire Kim, "The Racial Triangulation of Asian Americans," *Politics and Society* 27 (1999): 103–36. Jennifer L. Hochschild and Brenna Marea Powell, "Racial Reorganization and the United States Census 1850–1930: Mulattoes, Half-breeds, Mixed Parentage, Hindoos, and the Mexican Race," *Studies in American Political Development* 22.1 (2008), make effective use of the two principles in their comprehensive analysis.

16. Frank M. Snowden Jr., *Before Color Prejudice: The Ancient View of Blacks* (Cambridge, MA: Harvard University Press, 1983), 73–74.

17. Ibid., 63.

18. Ibid., 70.

19. George Fredrickson, *Racism: A Short History* (Princeton, NJ: Princeton University Press, 2002), 18.

20. Ibid., 19.

21. Ibid., 20.

22. Ibid., 26–28.

23. Lisa Rein, "Mystery of Va.'s First Slaves Is Unlocked 400 Years Later," *Washington Post*, 3 September 2006.

24. See David M. Goldenberg, *The Curse of Ham: Race and Slavery in Early Judaism, Christianity, and Islam* (Princeton, NJ: Princeton University Press, 2003).

25. See Stephen R. Hayes, *Noah's Curse: The Biblical Justification for American Slavery* (Oxford: Oxford University Press, 2002).

26. Senator Robert Byrd of West Virginia, filibustering against the Civil Rights Act, on 9 June, 1964; *Congressional Record* 1964. 88th Cong., 2nd sess., vol. 110, no. 10. For further discussion, see David Brion Davis, "Blacks: Damned by the Bible," *New York Review of Books*, 16 November 2006.

27. Blumenbach, *On the Natural Varieties of Mankind*, 57.

28. Scott Leon Washington, "Principles of Racial Taxonomy," Paper presented at the Graduate Student Conference on Categories, Columbia University, New York, 22 October 2004.

29. See, in particular, Ian Haney Lopez, *White by Law* (New York: New York University Press, 1996).

30. Although I will frequently reference the American decennial census it should be stressed at the outset that the census is a stand-in for a much broader system of statistical surveys and record-keeping by the government, all of which share with the census a government proscribed racial and ethnic classification system.

31. Starr, "Social Categories and Claims," 264–65.

32. Ibid., 265.

33. Herbert Butterfield, *The Whig Interpretation of History* (London: G. Bell, 1931), 31.

Chapter 3. The Compromise That Made the Republic and the Nation's First Statistical Race

1. Patricia Cohen, *A Calculating People: The Spread of Numeracy in Early America* (Chicago: University of Chicago Press, 1982), 69–70.

2. Aristide Zolberg, *A Nation by Design: Immigration Policy in the Fashioning of America* (New York and Cambridge, MA: Russell Sage Foundation/Harvard University Press, 2006).

3. Ibid., 35–36.

4. Ibid., 40.

5. Benjamin Franklin, quoted in Zolberg, *A Nation by Design*, 46.

6. For a thorough account of how the conflict over immigration and naturalization influenced the movement for independence, see Zolberg, *A Nation by Design*, chap. 1. The phrase cited appears in the Declaration of Independence.

7. Zolberg, *A Nation by Design*, 49.

8. Margo J. Anderson, *The American Census: A Social History* (New Haven, CT: Yale University Press, 1988).

9. John H. Cassidy, *Demography in Early America: Beginnings of the Statistical Mind, 1600-1800* (Cambridge, Mass. Harvard University Press, 1969), 180–205.

10. John Adams to Matthew Robinson, 2 March 1786, in *Works of John Adams*, vol. 8 (New York: AMS Press, 1988), 385.

11. Thomas Jefferson to the Count de Montmorin, 23 June 1787, in *Writings of Jefferson*, vol. 6, ed. A. E. Bergh (Washington DC: Jefferson Memorial Association, 1903), 186.

12. Henry Steele Commager, *Jefferson, Nationalism, and the Enlightenment* (New York: George Braziller, 1975), 27.

13. Ibid., 45.

14. Ibid., 46.

15. George Washington to Gouverneur Morris, 28 July 1791, quoted in James H. Cassedy, *Demography in Early America: Beginnings of the Statistical Mind, 1600–1800* (Cambridge, MA: Harvard University Press, 1969), 219–20.

16. I make no attempt to survey the many issues that swirled around population policy in the founding period. To keep this section to a manageable length I use Jefferson as the primary spokesperson not because he is representative but because he was influential and did write at length. This section summarizes points made at greater length in Kenneth Prewitt, "A Nation Imagined, a Nation Measured: Jefferson's Legacy," in *Across the Continent: Geopolitics, Science and Culture Conflicts in the Making of America*, ed. Douglas Seefeldt, Jeffrey Hantman, and Peter Onuf (Charlottesville: University of Virginia Press, 2005).

17. Thomas Jefferson letter to Governor William Henry Harrison, 27 February 1803, quoted in Joseph Ellis, *American Sphinx: The Character of Thomas Jefferson* (New York: Vintage, 1998), 201.

18. Thomas Jefferson, *Autobiography*, quoted in Peter Onuf, *Jefferson's Empire: The Language of American Nationhood* (Charlottesville: University of Virginia Press, 2000), 151.

19. Thomas Jefferson to Jared Sparks, 1824, quoted in Onuf, *Jefferson's Empire*, 151.

20. Onuf, *Jefferson's Empire*, chap. 5.

21. Commager, *Jefferson, Nationalism, and the Enlightenment*, 21.

22. Edward Morgan, *The Birth of the Republic: 1763–89*, rev. ed. (Chicago: University of Chicago Press, 1977), 139.

23. Onuf, *Jefferson's Empire*, 38.

24. Commager, *Jefferson, Nationalism, and the Enlightenment*, 3.

25. Anderson, *The American Census*, 11.

26. Ibid., 13.

27. Melissa Nobles, *Shades of Citizenship: Race and the Census in Modern Politics* (Stanford, CA: Stanford University Press, 2000), 27.

28. Garry Wills, *"Negro President": Jefferson and the Slave Power* (Boston: Houghton Mifflin, 2003), 56.

29. Ibid., 57.

30. Ibid., 6.

31. Richard H. Brown, quoted in Wills, *"Negro President": Jefferson and the Slave Power*, 7.

32. Wills, *"Negro President": Jefferson and the Slave Power*, 123.

33. Ibid., 125; emphasis in the original.

34. Cohen, *A Calculating People*, 160.

35. For more detail on Madison's effort, see Margo J. Anderson, "(Only) White Men Have Class: Reflections on Early 19th-Century Occupational Classification Systems," *Work and Occupations* 21.1 (1994): 5–32.

36. For more detail, see Carroll Wright and W. C. Hunt, *History and Growth of the United States Census* (Washington, DC: Government Printing Office, 1900), 19–20. See also Michel L. Balinski and H. Peyton Young, *Fair Representation: Meeting the Ideal of One Man, One Vote* (New Haven, CT: Yale University Press, 1982), chap. 3.

37. Cohen, *A Calculating People*, 163.

Chapter 4. Race Science Captures the Prize, the U.S. Census

1. Patricia Cohen, *A Calculating People: The Spread of Numeracy in Early America* (Chicago: University of Chicago Press, 1982), 165.

2. Ibid.

3. Ibid., 166.

4. Adam Seybert, *Statistical Annals*, quoted in Cohen, *A Calculating People*, 168.

5. Thomas Jefferson, "Notes on State of Virginia" (1781), in *Writings* (New York: Library of America, 1984), 143.

6. *New York Tribune*, quoted in Stephen Jay Gould, *The Mismeasure of Man* (New York: Norton, 1981), 83.

7. Gould, *The Mismeasure of Man*, 83.
8. See Gould, *The Mismeasure of Man*, chap. 2.
9. Cohen, *A Calculating People*, 176–77.
10. Ibid., 192.
11. Melissa Nobles, *Shades of Citizenship: Race and the Census in Modern Politics* (Stanford, CA: Stanford University Press, 2000), 32.
12. Cohen, *A Calculating People*, 197.
13. Nobles, *Shades of Citizenship*, 34.
14. Ibid.
15. Cohen, *A Calculating People*, 222.
16. Reginald Horsman, *Josiah Nott of Mobile: Southerner, Physician, and Racial Theorist* (Baton Rouge: Louisiana State University Press, 1987), 88.
17. Josiah Nott, quoted in Nobles, *Shades of Citizenship*, 37; emphasis added.
18. Nott, quoted in Nobles, *Shades of Citizenship*, 37.
19. Joseph Underwood, quoted in Nobles, *Shades of Citizenship*, 40.
20. Ibid., 42.
21. Seven states had seceded from the Union and joined the Confederacy when this ratio was reported. Four more states seceded shortly thereafter.
22. Margo J. Anderson, *The American Census: A Social History* (New Haven CT: Yale University Press, 2006), 64.
23. Ibid.
24. Ibid.
25. Ibid., 66.
26. Ibid.
27. Ibid., 68.
28. Joseph Kennedy, quoted in Nobles 45.
29. Kennedy, quoted in Nobles 46; emphasis added. Kennedy's use of the term "diffused" references biological rather than demographic mixture.
30. Kennedy, quoted in Nobles, *Shades of Citizenship*, 47.
31. Ibid., 46.
32. I was director of the U.S. Census Bureau in 2000, by which time the bureau provided statistics, not opinions. The director could explain how the census was conducted and comment on the bureau's best judgment about the quality of the information, but certainly not hold forth on matters such as the future of America's races.
33. Nobles, *Shades of Citizenship*, 52.
34. Representative Joseph Wheeler, quoted in Jennifer L. Hochschild and Brenna Marea Powell, "Racial Reorganization and the United States Census 1850–1930: Mulattoes, Half-breeds, Mixed Parentage, Hindoos, and the Mexican Race," *Studies in American Political Development* 22 (2008): 68.
35. Nobles, *Shades of Citizenship*, 56.
36. Ibid., 58.
37. Ibid., 60.
38. Dred Scott v. Sandford, 60 U.S. 393 (1856).
39. University of Missouri–Kansas City School of Law, *Lynching Statistics: By State and Race 1882-1968*; http://www.law.umkc.edu/faculty/projects/ftrials/shipp/lynchingsstate.html.

40. Nobles, *Shades of Citizenship*, 72.

41. Francis A. Walker, *Massachusetts Bureau of Statistics of Labor, Fifth Annual Report*, quoted in James Leiby, *Carroll Wright and Labor Reform: The Origins of Labor Statistics* (Cambridge, MA: Harvard University Press, 1960), 63.

42. For more detailed discussion, see Kenneth Prewitt, "Social Science and Private Philanthropy: The Quest for Social Relevance." *Essays on Philanthropy* 15 (1995); and Kenneth Prewitt, "Political Ideas and a Political Science for Policy," *Annals of the American Academy of Political and Social Sciences* 600.1 (2005).

43. Walter Willcox, "Census Statistics of the Negro," *Yale Review* 13 (1904): 274

Chapter 5. How Many White Races Are There?

1. Aristide Zolberg, *A Nation by Design: Immigration Policy in the Fashioning of America* (New York: and Cambridge, MA: Russell Sage Foundation/Harvard University Press, 2006), 180.

2. Ibid., 182.

3. Ibid., 181.

4. Gary Gerstle, *American Crucible: Race and Nation in the Twentieth Century* (Princeton, NJ: Princeton University Press, 2001), 23.

5. Ibid., 1.

6. Arthur M. Schlesinger Jr., *The Disuniting of America: Reflections on a Multicultural Society* (New York: Norton, 1992), 13; emphasis in the original.

7. Gerstle, *American Crucible*, 4.

8. Jennifer L. Hochschild and Brenna Marea Powell, "Racial Reorganization and the United States Census 1850–1930: Mulattoes, Half-breeds, Mixed Parentage, Hindoos, and the Mexican Race," *Studies in American Political Development* 22 (2008): 71.

9. Hawaiians, however, were excluded from the Asian grouping. For more detail, see Hochschild and Powell, "Racial Reorganization," 72.

10. U.S. Senate, 44th Cong., 2nd sess. *Report of the Joint Special Committee to Investigate Chinese Immigration* (Washington, DC: Government Printing Office, 1877), v, vii.

11. U.S. House of Representatives, 51st Cong., 2nd sess. *Chinese Immigration* (Washington, DC: Government Printing Office, 1877), 1238.

12. This is analyzed in detail in Hochschild and Powell, "Racial Reorganization," and in Naomi Mezey, "Erasure and Recognition: The Census, Race and the National Imagination," *Northwestern University Law Review* 97.4 (2003): 1701–68.

13. Mezey, "Erasure and Recognition," 1730.

14. Zolberg, *A Nation by Design*, 195.

15. Ibid., 209–10.

16. Richman Mayo-Smith, quoted in Zolberg, *A Nation by Design*, 212.

17. Victoria Hattam, *In the Shadow of Race: Jews, Latinos, and Immigrant Politics in the United States* (Chicago: University of Chicago Press, 2007), 41.

18. Zolberg, *A Nation by Design*, 214.

19. Ibid., 211.

20. Paul Schor, *Mobilizing for Pure Prestige? Challenging Federal Census Ethnic Categories in the USA (1850–1940)* (Oxford: Blackwell, 2005), 90.

21. Zolberg, *A Nation by Design*, 232.

22. Ibid., 234.

23. For this and other immigration statistics cited in the section, see Campbell J. Gibson and Emily Lennon, *Historical Census Statistics on the Foreign-born Population of the United States: 1850–1990*, Population Division Working Paper 29 (Washington DC: U.S. Bureau of the Census, 1999); http://www.census.gov/population/www/documentation/twps0029/twps0029.html.

24. Zolberg, *A Nation by Design*, 246.

25. Eugenics, of course, sustained biologically based science through the 1920s and '30s. Because my focus is with racial statistics, I do not take up the eugenics story.

26. George W. Stocking, *Race, Culture, and Evolution; Essays in the History of Anthropology* (New York: Free Press, 1968), 264.

27. William Z. Ripley, *The Races of Europe*, quoted in Hattam, *In the Shadow of Race*, 30.

28. W. I. Thomas, "The Mind of Woman and the Lower Races," quoted in Hattam, *In the Shadow of Race*, 33.

29. Progressive social reformers were also advancing arguments about the importance of these institutions to the improvement of society. The early Russell Sage Foundation was a venue linking progressive social reform with a progressive social science. See Alice O'Connor, *Social Science for What?* (New York: Russell Sage Foundation, 2007).

30. Hattam, *In the Shadow of Race*, 34.

31. Stocking, *Race, Culture, and Evolution*, 263.

32. This is lesser known except, of course, to historians of the census. For the most complete account, see Margo J. Anderson, *The American Census: A Social History* (New Haven, CT: Yale University Press, 1988). I draw heavily from her excellent account of the failure to reapportion.

33. Roy Garis, writing in *Scribner's* magazine, September 1922, quoted in Anderson, *The American Census*, 144. This paragraph summarizes Anderson's account.

34. Anderson, *The American Census*, 145.

35. *Congressional Record*, 68th Cong., 1st sess., 1924, pp. 5469–71. Cited in Anderson, *The American Census*, 145.

36. Mae N. Ngai, "*The Architecture of Race in American Immigration Law: A Reexamination of the Immigration Act of 1924*," *Journal of American History* 86.1 (1999): 71.

37. Ibid., 73.

38. Roy Garis, quoted in Zolberg, *A Nation by Design*, 245.

39. Ibid., 256.

40. Schor, *Mobilizing*, 92; emphasis in the original.

41. Anderson, *The American Census*, 148.

Chapter 6. Racial Justice Finds a Policy Tool

1. Lyndon B. Johnson, "To Fulfill These Rights," in *Public Papers of the Presidents of the United States: Lyndon B. Johnson*, vol. 2 (Washington, DC: Government Printing Office, 1966), 635–40.

2. See Ira Katznelson, *When Affirmative Action Was White* (New York: Norton, 2005), 11, for a discussion of Johnson's speech as providing the "first draft" of how government might remedy "the cumulative history of racial disadvantage."

3. Hugh Davis Graham, *Collision Course: The Strange Convergence of Affirmative Action and Immigration Policy* (New York: Oxford University Press, 2002), 77; emphasis in the original.

4. Daniel Bell, *The Coming of the Post-industrial Society* (New York: Basic Books, 1973), 425.

5. Hugh Davis Graham, *The Civil Rights Era* (New York: Oxford University Press, 1990), 34–35.

6. *Congressional Record*, 88th Cong., 2nd sess., vol. 110 (1964), 5:6549.

7. This is discussed in Graham, *Civil Rights Era*, 111.

8. Congress of Racial Equality, quoted in Graham, *Civil Rights Era*, 105.

9. John F. Kennedy, quoted in Graham, *Civil Rights Era*, 106.

10. The next sections of this chapter are indebted to and largely summarize the pioneering work of Graham, *Civil Rights Era*; and the imaginative treatment in John D. Skrentny, *The Ironies of Affirmative Action* (Chicago: University of Chicago Press, 1996); and John D. Skrentny, *The Minority Rights Revolution* (Cambridge, MA: Belknap Press of Harvard University Press, 2002).

11. National Advisory Commission on Civil Disorders, *Our Nation Is Moving toward Two Societies, One Black, One White—Separate and Unequal* (New York: Bantam Books, 1968).

12. Lester A. Sobel, ed., *Civil Rights: 1960–1966* (New York: Facts on File, 1967), 254–56.

13. California Governor's Commission on the Los Angeles Riots, "144 Hours in August 1965," in *Violence in the City: An End or a Beginning?* (Los Angeles: California Governor's Commission on the Los Angeles Riots, 1965).

14. Doug McAdam, *Political Process and the Development of Black Insurgency 1930–1970* (Chicago: University of Chicago Press, 1982), 182.

15. Nicholas Katzenbach, quoted in Skrentny, *The Ironies of Affirmative Action*, 84–85.

16. *U.S. News and World Report*, quoted in Skrentny, *The Ironies of Affirmative Action*, 90.

17. Particularly noteworthy was the testimony of Eli Ginzberg, an economics professor at Columbia University and the chairman of the National Manpower Advisory Committee.

18. A few months later, after the assassination of King, this author and a talented group of Stanford University undergraduates drew heavily on the Kerner Report in publishing the first book that explicitly addressed institutional racism. See Louis Knowles and Kenneth Prewitt, *Institutional Racism in American Society* (Englewood Cliffs, N.J.: Prentice-Hall, 1969).

19. Patricia Cohen, *A Calculating People: The Spread of Numeracy in Early America* (Chicago: University of Chicago Press, 1982).

20. Samuel R. Gross and Barbara O'Brien, "Frequency and Predictors of False Conviction: Why We Know So Little, and New Data on Capital Cases," *Journal of Empirical Legal Studies* 5.4 (2008): 927–62; D. Michael Risinger,

"Innocents Convicted: An Empirically Justified Factual Wrongful Conviction Rate," *Journal of Criminal Law and Criminology* 97 (2007): 761–807.

21. "Statement by the President upon Signing Order Establishing the President's Committee on Equal Employment Opportunity," 7 March 1961, In *Public Papers of the Presidents of the United States: John F. Kennedy* (Washington, DC: Government Printing Office, 1962), 150.

22. Graham, *Civil Rights Era*, 42.

23. Ibid., 62; emphasis in the original. It was in this context that Whitney Young supported government racial counting, as noted on p. 85.

24. Graham, *Civil Rights Era*, 62.

25. See Skrentny, *The Ironies of Affirmative Action*, chap. 7.

26. Skrentny, *Minority Rights*, 13.

27. Ibid., 89.

28. *Congressional Record*, 88th Cong., 1st sess. (8 April 1965): 7214.

29. Graham, *Civil Rights Era*, 191.

30. Ibid., 192.

31. Ibid., 242.

32. The exception to this generalization is the Fair Housing Act of 1968, which was in part a response to the urban violence following King's assassination.

33. The use of statistical proportionality to discover and correct gender discrimination, and later discrimination toward the disabled, are important to any larger treatment of affirmative action. Because my focus is on racial counting and not on affirmative action more generally, I do not review the role of statistical proportionality for the rights of women and of the disabled.

34. Arthur Fletcher, quoted in Skrentny, *The Ironies of Affirmative Action*, 144.

35. Graham, *Civil Rights Era*, 280.

36. Richard Nixon, quoted in Graham, *Civil Rights Era*, 325.

37. Graham, *Civil Rights Era*, 327.

38. Ibid., 327.

39. Hugh Davis Graham, "The Origins of Official Minority Designation," in *The New Race Question: How the Census Counts Multiracial Individuals*, ed. Joel Perlmann and Mary C. Waters (New York: Russell Sage Foundation, 2002), 293.

40. Kenneth M. Davidson, Ruth Bader Ginsburg, and Herma Hill Kay, quoted in Graham, *Civil Rights Era*, 343.

41. Griggs v. Duke Power Co., 401 U.S. 424 (1971). The Court deferred to the EEOC's expertise in employment policy, including its concept of statistical underutilization.

42. Alan Freeman, "Antidiscrimination Law from 1954 to 1989: Uncertainty, Contradiction, Rationalization, Denial," reprinted in *The Politics of Law: A Progressive Critique*, 3rd ed., ed. David Kairys (New York: Basic Books, 1989), 296.

43. The role of electoral forces, legal strategies by civil rights organizations, public opinion, and other features of American politics relevant to this remarkable policy transformation is the subject of dozens of books. See especially Robert C. Lieberman, *Shaping Race Policy: The United States in Comparative Perspective* (Princeton, NJ: Princeton University Press, 2005).

44. Katznelson, *When Affirmative Action Was White*, 170.

45. See especially Christopher Edley Jr., *Not All Black and White: Affirmative Action, Race and American Values* (New York, NY: Hill and Wang, 1996).

46. The place of Jews in racial classification is carefully described in Victoria Hattam, *In the Shadow of Race: Jews, Latinos, and Immigrant Politics in the United States* (Chicago: University of Chicago Press, 2007).

47. For discussion, see Katherine K. Wallman, "Data on Race and Ethnicity: Revising the Federal Standard," *American Statistician* 52.1 (1998): 31–33. When the OMB issued the standards in 1977, they were not at that time known as Directive 15. Rather, they were issued as part of the OMB Circular No. A-46, *Standards and Guidelines for Federal Statistics*, section 7(h) and Exhibit F. When the statistical policy authority was transferred in October 1977 from the OMB to the Department of Commerce, Office of Federal Statistical Policy and Standards, the Department reissued in May 1978 the various standards/guidelines as separate numbered directives. And so it happened that the standards for data on race and ethnicity became Directive 15.

48. Because my focus is on race classification, I do not cover gender discrimination. Of course, a question on gender appeared on every census, and gender data have been routinely collected by the government in other major surveys and across the administrative record keeping system. When the Civil Rights Act prohibited discrimination based on gender, women quickly found ways to turn affirmative action programs to their advantage. Equal treatment of women—statistical proportionality—has been one of the great achievements of the civil rights era.

49. For discussion of the background to the development of Directive 15, see Katherine K. Wallman and John Hodgdon, "Race and Ethnic Standards for Federal Statistics and Administrative Reporting," *Statistical Reporter*, July 1977, 450–54.

50. Directive No. 15, quoted in *Federal Register* 59.110 (1994): 29834.

51. In lawmaking about race in America, Congress prefers vague language—such as "minorities historically discriminated against"—rather than identifying specific races. This prudent tendency goes back to the Constitution. It was politically more palatable to use civil status, rather than a color or race term, to instruct the census no how to produce the race count for the three-fifths clause. One of the few instances in which Congress was bold enough to identify a specific group occurred in 1976. Congress mandated that information on Hispanics, defined as an ethnic and not racial group, be collected by government agencies in order to "assist state and federal governments, and private organizations in the accurate determination of the urgent and special needs of Americans of Spanish origin or descent." (Public Law 94-311).

Chapter 7. When You Have a Hammer: Statistical Races Misused

1. The discussion of the census undercount draws heavily from—and in places directly quotes—the more extended treatment in Kenneth Prewitt, *Politics and Science in Census Taking* (New York and Washington, DC: Russell Sage Foundation/Population Reference Bureau, 2003).

2. George Washington, *The Writings of George Washington* (Washington, DC: Government Printing Office, 1939), 31:329.

3. The efforts in the American 2000 census are documented in D. Sunshine Hillygus, Norman Nie, Kenneth Prewitt, and Heili Pals, *The Hard Count: The Political and Social Challenges of Census Mobilization* (New York: Russell Sage Foundation, 2006).

4. Censuses can also overcount if duplicate forms are submitted; historically this was assumed to be a much smaller number than the undercount. As census practice has improved, the Census Bureau has found ways to find duplicates in the census record and to lower the overcount.

5. The actual calculation is more complicated. It has to estimate the completeness of birth and death records by age, gender, and race. And allowance has to be made for imprecise estimates of immigration, especially the probable number of undocumented residents, and the estimates of outmigration, for which records are incomplete.

6. Except that no state, however small its share of the total national population, can have fewer than one seat in the House, the result being that the least populated state, Wyoming, gets a seat even though its population in 2000 was approximately 150,000 fewer people than that of congressional districts elsewhere in the country.

7. In the 2000 reapportionment the final congressional seat went to North Carolina. The other state in contention for the 435th seat was Utah, whose population was only 857 persons fewer than North Carolina's. Utah sued to have its Mormon missionaries temporarily stationed overseas included in the census count; had it won that case, the 435th seat would have gone to Utah.

8. David Heer, ed., *Social Statistics and the City* (Cambridge, MA: Joint Center for Urban Studies, 1968), 11.

9. For an excellent nontechnical overview of dual-system estimation, see Tommy Wight and Howard Hogan, "Census 2000: Evolution of the Revised Plan," *CHANCE: A Magazine of the American Statistical Association* 12.4 (1999): 11–19. For more technical treatment see the references in this book or consult the website of the Census Bureau at http://www.census.gov.

10. Margo J. Anderson and Stephen E. Fienberg, *Who Counts? The Politics of Census-taking in Contemporary America* (New York: Russell Sage Foundation, 1999). See also Kenneth Darga, *Sampling and the Census: A Case against the Proposed Adjustments for Undercount* (Washington, DC.: American Enterprise Institute, 1999).

11. Submitting results of a census to political office holders for preapproval was unprecedented. With even less justification this was repeated after the 2000 census. A statistical decision became a political decision, the most serious violation of the basic principle of census independence since the professionalization of census taking. For an account, see Kenneth Prewitt, "What Is Political Interference in Federal Statistics?" *Annals of the American Academy of Political and Social Science* 631.1 (2010): 225–38.

12. A high-level panel of the Committee on National Statistics in the National Academies generally supported dual-system estimation. For its final report, see Constance F. Citro, Daniel L. Cork, and Janet L. Norwood, eds., *The*

2000 Census: Counting under Adversity (Washington, DC: National Academies Press, 2004). A comprehensive summary of the major criticisms of the method is Lawrence D. Brown, Morris L. Eaton, David A. Freedman, Stephen P. Klein, Richard A. Olshen, Kenneth W. Wachter, Martin T. Wells, and Donald Ylvisaker, "Statistical Controversies in Census 2000." *Jurimetrics* 39 (1999): 347–75.

13. Jim Nicholson, "Memo from the Chairman of the Republican National Committee, 20 May 1997," in author's collection. This assertion of how many seats would be "lost" was never documented. Given the numbers involved, it is somewhere between highly implausible and impossible for census adjustment to move this many seats, and certainly impossible a priori to calculate partisan shifts in legislatures resulting from a decennial census.

14. Leadership Conference, "The Census 2000 Education Kit," in *Census 2000 Everyone Counts* (Washington, DC: Leadership Conference Education Fund, 2000).

15. The census short form questions are asked of every household in the country. What in 2000 (and in censuses of the second half of the twentieth century, which is the period on which this discussion focuses) was called the long form went to approximately one-sixth of the households. In addition to the standard short form questions, the long form asked about education, health, income, marital status, housing, and other topics. Data from the long form is relevant to analyzing census coverage, but could not be used in dual-system estimation because estimates from long form data are not statistically reliable at the block level. In the decennial of 2010, the long form questions appear on the American Community Survey, and the decennial census itself was just the short form delivered to every household.

16. A thorough study of census cooperation in 2000 found that marital status and whether the respondent had family members living in the community, an indicator of strong community ties, did predict cooperation after controlling for race. See Hillygus et al., *The Hard Count*.

17. Person characteristics were language isolation, unemployment, poor mobility, living below poverty level, receiving public assistance, and lack of a high school diploma. Housing characteristics were crowded housing, multiunit buildings, lack of telephone in home, vacancy rate, renter occupation, and complex households. See http://2010.census.gov/partners/research/.

18. Source: Peter P. Davis and James Mulligan, *Census Coverage Measurement Estimation Report: Net Coverage for the Household Population in the United States* (Washington, DC: Census Bureau, Decennial Statistical Studies Division, 2012).

19. American Anthropological Association, *Race: Are We So Different?* Washington, DC: American Anthropological Association, 2010; http://www.understandingrace.org/home.html.

20. A useful website that traces the material summarized in this paragraph, and from which the dates are taken, is http://www.bradshawfoundation.com/journey/.

21. For a convenient summary, see Constance Holden, "Race and Medicine," *Science* 302.5645 (2003): 594–96.

22. H. Allen Orr, Review of *Talking Genes*, by Nicolas Wade, *New York Review of Books*, 21 September 2006, 20.

23. Eric Jorgenson et al., "Ethnicity and Human Genetic Linkage Maps." *American Journal of Human Genetics* 76.2 (2005). Only 5 of the 3,636 subjects had DNA that matched a group different from the race box they had checked at the beginning of the study.

24. The costs and a time frame for bringing personalized medicine to the nearly seven billion people of the world has, in the material I have reviewed, not even been estimated.

25. David Goldstein, quoted in Holden, "Race and Medicine," 596; emphasis added.

26. Paul Martin, Richard Ashcroft, George T. H. Ellison, Andrew David Smart, and Richard Tutton, *Reviving 'Racial Medicine'? The Use of Race/Ethnicity in Genetics and Biomedical Research, and the Implications for Science and Healthcare* (London: Faculty of Health and Social Care Sciences, University of London, 2007), 1. The project was sponsored by the Wellcome Trust.

27. Ibid., 6.

28. Ibid.

29. Ibid., 4.

30. Ibid., 5.

31. I have no information on how widespread the risks put forward in the report are shared across the scientific community in the United Kingdom.

32. Martin et. al, *The Use of Race/Ethnicity in Genetics and Biomedical Research*, 5; emphasis added.

33. Orr, Review of *Talking Genes*, 20.

34. Neil Risch, Esteban Burchard, Elad Ziv, and Hua Tang, "Categorization of Humans in Biomedical Research: Genes, Race and Disease," *Genome Biology* 3 (2002); http://genomebiology.com/2002/3/7/comment/2007; emphasis added.

35. Ibid.

36. Ibid.

37. Ibid.

38. Neil Risch, quoted in Nicholas Wade, "Race Is Seen as Real Guide to Track Roots of Disease," *New York Times*, 30 July 2002.

39. Francis Collins, "What We Do and Don't Know about 'Race,' 'Ethnicity,' Genetics and Health at the Dawn of the Genome Era," *Nature Genetics* 36 (2004).

40. R. C. Lewontin, "Confusions about Human Races." Paper presented as part of the Social Science Research Council Web Forum "Is Race Real?," 7 June 2006; http:/raceandgenomics.ssrc.org/Lewontin.

41. David Goldstein, quoted in Wade, "Race Is Seen as Real Guide."

42. Troy Duster, "Race and Reification in Science," *Science* 307.5712 (2005): 1050.

43. Risch et al., "Categorization of Humans in Biomedical Research." The "mark one or more" option is described in detail in chapter 8. Risch also overlooks the fact that the population groups of India and Pakistan were counted as "white" by the census in the first half of the twentieth century, and then were counted as Asian. Where to draw the line between the European and Asian races is no easy matter.

44. http://africandna.com/ (January 23, 2013). See also Ancestry.com.

45. Claudette Bennett, "Exploring the Consistency of Race Reporting in Census 2000 and the Census Quality Survey," paper presented at the Joint Meetings of the American Statistical Association, San Francisco, 3–7 August 2003. The author was an analyst in the Racial Statistics Branch of the Population Division, U.S. Census Bureau.

46. Joan H. Fujimura and Ramya Rajagopalan, "Different Differences: The Use of 'Genetic Ancestry' versus Race in Biomedical Human Genetic Research." *Social Studies of Science* 41.1 (2001): 7.

47. Ibid, 20.

48. Kahn, Jonathan. "Race in a Bottle," *Scientific American*, 15 July 2007.

49. For reservations about the promises of genetic medicine, see James P. Evans, Eric M. Meslin, Theresa M. Marteau, and Timothy Caulfield, "Deflating the Genomic Bubble." *Science* 331.6019 (2011).

50. Fujimura and Rajagopalan, "Different Differences," 22.

51. Human Genome Project, "Human Genome Research Sites"; http://www.ornl.gov/sci/techresources/Human_Genome/research/centers.shtml.

52. Human Genome Project, "Who Are Members of the SNP Consortium?" http://www.ornl.gov/sci/techresources/Human_Genome/faq/snps.shtml #whoare.

53. James H. Bullard and Sandrine Dudoit, "R / Bioconductor: A Short Course," presented at the Division of Biostatics, University of California–Berkeley, 21–25 January 2008; http://wiki.biostat.berkeley.edu/~bullard/courses/T-mexico -08/lectures/hapmap/slides- 2x2.pdf.

54. Leslie Roberts, "How to Sample the World's Genetic Diversity." *Science* 257.5074 (1992): 1204–6; Catherine Bliss, "Genome Sampling and the Biopolitics of Race," unpublished manuscript, 2010.

55. National Institutes of Health, "NIH Guidelines on the Inclusion of Women and Minorities as Subjects in Clinical Research," *NIH Guide* 23.11 (1994); U.S. Food and Drug Administration, "Guidance for Industry: Collection of Race and Ethnicity Data in Clinical Trials" (Washington, DC: U.S. Food and Drug Administration, 2005); Mary E. Peters, "Determination of Reasonable Rates and Terms for the Digital Performance of Sound Recordings by Preexisting Subscription Services," *Federal Register* 68.20 (2003); U.S. Food and Drug Administration, "Investigational New Drug Applications and New Drug Applications"; http://www.fda.gov/oashi/patrep/demo.html.

56. Fujimura and Rajagopalan, "Different Differences," 22, notes, "Although we have identified new actors—both human and technical—working to avoid the use of race categories in biomedical genetics research, it is not clear how much they can change . . . institutionalized and historical practices. . . ."

57. Richard J. Herrnstein and Charles Murray, *The Bell Curve: Intelligence and Class Structure in American Life* (New York: Free Press, 1994).

58. Charles Murray, "Jewish Genius," *Commentary* 123.4 (2007): 29–35.

59. Ann Morning, *The Nature of Race* (Berkeley and Los Angeles: University of California Press, 2011).

60. The drug, under the trade name BiDil, was approved the Food and Drug Administration in June 2005. It is the first race-based prescription in the United States.

61. Evan Charney and William English, "Candidate Genes and Political Behavior," *American Political Science Review* 106.1 (2012): 6.

62. Evelynn M. Hammonds, "Straw Men and Their Followers: The Return of Biological Race," paper presented as part of the Social Science Research Council Web Forum "Is Race Real?, 7 June 2006.

63. Freeman Dyson, "Our Biotech Future." *New York Review of Books*, 19 July 2007, 4.

64. Ibid., 4.

65. Ibid., 4. Attaching his quotation to the "winner of science fair" is not in the text, but is consistent with Dyson's example.

66. Harold Varmus, *The Art and Politics of Science* (New York: Norton, 2009).

67. Risch et al., "Categorization of Humans in Biomedical Research."

68. Barkan Elazar, *The Retreat of Scientific Racism* (Cambridge: Cambridge University Press, 1992); Edwin Black, *War against the Weak: Eugenics and America's Campaign to Create a Master Race* (New York: Four Walls Eight Windows, 2003).

69. Ira Katznelson, *When Affirmative Action Was White* (New York: Norton, 2005), 72–73.

70. Katherine K. Wallman, Suzann Evinger, and Susan Schechter, "Measuring Our Nation's Diversity: Developing a Common Language for Data on Race/Ethnicity," *American Journal of Public Health* 90.11 (2000): 1707.

71. Risch et. al., "Categorization of Humans in Biomedical Research."

Chapter 8. Pressures Mount

A version of this chapter also appears as "The Danger of Misusing Race Statistics," *Du Bois Review* 9.2 (2012): 281–301.

1. Katherine K. Wallman, "Data on Race and Ethnicity: Revising the Federal Standard," *American Statistician* 52.1 (1998): 31–33.

2. U.S. House of Representatives, 150th Cong., 1st sess. *Federal Measures of Race and Ethnicity and the Implications for the 2000 Census: Hearings before the Subcommittee on Government Management, Information, and Technology of the Committee on Government Reform and Oversight, April 23, May 22, and July 25, 1997* (Washington, DC: Government Printing Office, 1998), 263.

3. See David Hollinger, "Amalgamation and Hypodescent: The Question of Ethnoracial Mixture in the History of the United States," *American Historical Review* 108.5 (2003): 1363–90.

4. Victoria Hattam, *In the Shadow of Race: Jews, Latinos, and Immigrant Politics in the United States* (Chicago: University of Chicago Press, 2007).

5. These rates are calculated on the basis of the five primary race groups, and do not include intermarriage between Hispanic and non-Hispanic groups, or marriages within the Asian race—for example, between a South Asian Indian and a Korean.

6. Kim Williams, *Mark One or More: Civil Rights in Multiracial America* (Ann Arbor: University of Michigan Press, 2006).

7. U.S. House of Representatives, *Federal Measures of Race and Ethnicity and the Implications for the 2000 Census*, 662.

8. Susan Graham, quoted in Williams, *Mark One or More*, 43.

9. National Association for the Advancement of Colored People, quoted in Williams, *Mark One or More*, 308.

10. U.S. House of Representatives, *Federal Measures of Race and Ethnicity and the Implications for the 2000 Census*, 383.

11. For an extensive review, see Naomi Mezey, "Erasure and Recognition: The Census, Race and the National Imagination," *Northwestern University Law Review* 97.4 (2003): 1705.

12. See Jennifer L. Hochschild, "Multiple Racial Identifiers in the 2000 Census, and Then What?" in *The New Race Question: How the Census Counts Multiracial Individuals*, ed. Joel Perlmann and Mary C. Waters (New York: Russell Sage Foundation, 2003), 340–53.

13. C. Matthew Snipp, "American Indians: Clues to the Future of Other Racial Groups," in *The New Race Question: How the Census Counts Multiracial Individuals*, ed. Joel Perlmann and Mary C. Waters (New York: Russell Sage Foundation, 2003), 33–61. The OMB discussed whether the "mark one or more" option might also be appropriate for the Hispanic question, but insufficient research had been conducted to justify that change in time for the census in 2000.

14. The Census Bureau website has notes explaining why every question on the decennial form is asked, and lists statutory and program needs associated with each question. For the question on race and Hispanic ethnicity, see http://www.census.gov/dmd/www/pdf/03b_ba.pdf.

15. Paul Gewirtz, memo to President Clinton and others, quoted in Christopher F. Edley, *Not All Black and White: Affirmative Action and American Values* (New York: Hill and Wang, 1998), 77.

16. Regents of the University of California v. Bakke, 438 U.S. 265. 287. (1978).

17. Grutter v. Bollinger, 539 U.S. 306 (2003).

18. Ibid.

19. This appeared in an advertisement, under the heading, "Diversity in the Education Workplace," *New York Times*, 12 September 2010.

20. Justice Lewis Powell, quoted in Ian F. Haney Lopez, "'A Nation of Minorities': Race, Ethnicity, and Reactionary Colorblindness," *Stanford Law Review* 59.4 (2007): 1042.

21. Students for Academic Freedom, "Academic Bill of Rights—Basic Texts—Documents," 26 August 2010; http://www.studentsforacademicfreedom.org/documents/1925/abor.html.

22. This list is taken from the Rutgers University website: http://www.newark.rutgers.edu/diversity-rutgers.

23. Justice Potter Stewart was unable to define hard core pornography, but said: "I know it when I see it." Jacobellis v. Ohio, 378 U.S. 184 (1964).

24. Russell Sage Foundation, *Visiting Fellow Application Form, 2008*; http://www.russellsage.org/about/whatwedo/howtoapply/scholar/070501.352646.

25. I was a Visiting Scholar at the Russell Sage Foundation when the question cited here was adopted. I was consulted by the foundation's president as to how best frame the question and do not escape criticism for my failure to provide a suitable alternative for the specific requirements of the foundation.

26. Plessy v. Ferguson, 163 U.S. 357, 559 (1896).

27. Thurgood Marshall, arguing before the Supreme Court in Sipuel v. Board of Regents of University of Oklahoma, 332 U.S 631. 27. (1948) (no. 369).

28. McLaurin v. Oklahoma, 339 U.S. 637 (1950).

29. Justice Thurgood Marshall, Regents of University of California v. Bakke, 438 U.S. 265, 401 (1978).

30. Haney Lopez, "'A Nation of Minorities,'" 995. This work offers an extended and nuanced treatment of how racial justice discourse has been weakened by a view of America as a nation of minorities in which African Americans have a history of oppression not unlike that of other minorities, including various groups that comprise America's white population. Under this reasoning, privileged treatment of blacks comes at the expense of white ethnic groups no less deserving of compensatory policies.

31. Adarand Construction, Inc. v. Pena, 515 U.S. 200, 240–41 (1995). This is discussed more completely in Haney Lopez, "'A Nation of Minorities,'" 987.

32. Fullilove v. Klutznick, 448 U.S. 448 (1980), cited in Haney Lopez, "'A Nation of Minorities,' " 1046.

33. Haney Lopez, "'A Nation of Minorities,' " 1046–47.

34. City of Richmond v. J. A. Croson Co., 488 U.S. 469 (1989).

35. City of Richmond v. J. A. Croson Co., 521.

36. Hernandez v. New York, 500 U.S. 375 (1991).

37. Haney Lopez, "'A Nation of Minorities,' " 1062; emphasis in the original.

38. Known as the Racial Privacy Initiative, the Proposition was defeated 64 percent to 36 percent. As is common with California propositions, there was an explanation to help voters understand its impact: "Amends Constitution to prohibit state and local governments from using race, ethnicity, color, or national origin to classify current or prospective students, contractors or employees in public education, contracting, or employment operations. Does not prohibit classification by sex." California Secretary of State, *Proposition 54: Official Voter Information Guide* (Sacramento: California Secretary of State, 2003).

39. Exemptions were allowed, including "medical data; law enforcement descriptions; prisoner and undercover assignment; actions maintaining federal funding." The exemptions were in response to arguments by public health and criminal justice officials that without racial data they could not do their jobs, and also to assure voters that California would not lose federal funding if the proposition passed; in fact, the state informed voters that the measure would not have a significant fiscal impact.

40. California Secretary of State, *Proposition 209: Prohibition against Discrimination or Preferential Treatment by State and Other Public Entities* (Sacramento: California Secretary of State, 1996).

41. Zogby International, *Racial Identity Survey*, March 10, 2000, submitted to the American Civil Rights Institute (Utica, NY: Zogby International, 2000).

42. Pew Research Center, "Blacks See Growing Gap between Poor and Middle Class," *Pew Research Center's Social and Demographic Trends*, 13 November 2007; http://www.pewsocialtrends.org/2007/11/13/blacks-see-growing-values-gap-between-poor-and-middle-class/.

43. On a question using the phrase *affirmative action* rather than *preferential treatment*, support is much higher across all groups.

44. Sean Alfano, "High Court Limits Race in School Choice," *CBS News,* 28 June 2007; http://www.cbsnews.com/stories/2007/06/28/supremecourt/main2991748.shtml?tag=contentMain;contentBody.

45. Frank de Zwart, "Ethno-statistics in the Netherlands: Some Unintended Consequences of Institutionalization," unpublished manuscript, July 2010, 137.

46. That whites were the historic beneficiaries of group-based rights is true but not a persuasive argument to the opponents of affirmative action. For detailed treatment of "white affirmative action" in government programs see Ira Katznelson, *When Affirmative Action Was White* (New York: Norton, 2005).

47. James Webb, "Diversity and the Myth of White Privilege," *Wall Street Journal*, 22 July 2010.

48. Gregory Rodriguez, "Affirmative Action's Time Is Up," *Los Angeles Times*, 2 August 2010.

49. Donald R. Kinder and Lynn M. Sanders, *Divided by Color* (Chicago: University of Chicago Press, 1996), 105–6.

50. Steven A. Tuch and Michael Hughs, "Whites' Racial Policy Attitudes in the Twenty-First Century: The Continuing Significance of Racial Resentment." *Annals of the American Academy of Political and Social Science* 634 (2011): 142.

51. Lawrence D. Bobo, James R. Kluegel, and Ryan A. Smith, "Laissez-Faire Racism: The Crystallization of a Kinder, Gentler Antiblack Ideology." In *Racial Attitudes in the 1990s: Continuity and Change*, ed. Steven A. Tuch and Jack K. Martin (Westport, CT: Praeger, 1997), 38.

52. European Commission against Racism and Intolerance, *Third Report on the Netherlands*, 29 June 2007; https://wcd.coe.int/ViewDoc.jsp?id=1231525.

53. Anne Phillips, *Multiculturalism without Culture* (Princeton, NJ: Princeton University Press, 2007), 7–8.

54. De Zwart, "Ethno-statistics in the Netherlands," 2–3.

55. Ibid., 5.

56. All quotes in this paragraph are taken from Arthur M. Schlesinger Jr., *The Disuniting of America: Reflections on a Multicultural Society* (NY: Norton, 1991), 24, 26, 130.

57. J. Hector St. John de Crevecoeur, *Letters from an American Farmer*, quoted in Schlesinger, *The Disuniting of America*, 12.

Chapter 9. The Problem of the Twenty-first Century Is the Problem of the Color Line as It Intersects the Nativity Line

1. W.E.B. Du Bois, *The Souls of Black Folk*, ed. D. W. Blight and Robert Gooding-Williams (Boston: Bedford, 1997).

2. Abigail Thernstrom and Stephen Thernstrom, *Beyond the Color Line* (Stanford, CA: Hoover Institution Press, 2002).

3. Eduardo Bonilla-Silva, "From Bi-racial to Tri-racial," *Ethnic and Racial Studies* 27.6 (2004): 931–50.

4. Herbert J. Gans, "'Whitening' and the Changing American Racial Hierarchy," *Du Bois Review* 9.2 (2012); prepublication manuscript courtesy of the

author. See also Herbert J. Gans, "The Possibility of a New Racial Hierarchy in the Twenty-first Century United States," in *The Cultural Territories of Race: Black and White Boundaries*, ed. Michele Lamont (Chicago and New York: University of Chicago Press/Russell Sage Foundation, 1999), 371–90.

5. Benjamin Franklin, "Observations Concerning the Increase of Mankind, Peopling of Counties, etc.," in *The Papers of Benjamin Franklin,* vol. 4 (New Haven, CT: Yale University Press, 1961), 234; emphasis in the original; http://www.digitalhistory.uh.edu/documents/documents_p2.cfm?doc=233.

6. Arthur M. Schlesinger Jr., *The Disuniting of America: Reflections on a Multicultural Society* (NY: Norton, 1991), 15.

7. Samuel P. Huntington, *Who Are We? The Challenge to America's National Identity* (New York: Simon and Schuster, 2004).

8. Samuel P. Huntington, "The Special Case of Mexican Immigration: Why Mexico Is a Problem," *American Enterprise* 11.8 (2000): 20–22.

9. Samuel P. Huntington, "The Hispanic Challenge," *Foreign Policy*, March–April 2004; http://www.foreignpolicy.com/articles/2004/03/01/the_hispanic_challenge.

10. Patrick Buchanan, *State of Emergency: The Third World Invasion and Conquest of America* (New York: St. Martin's, 2006), 128.

11. These figures can be found at http://www.census.gov/population/www/pop-profile/natproj.html.

12. These estimates can be found at http://www.census.gov/compendia/statab/2012/tables/12s0697.pdf.

13. This information can be found at http://www.census.gov/compendia/statab/2012/tables/12s0229.pdf.

14. Prior to 1960, the census would have counted them as white.

15. Gans, "'Whitening' and the Changing American Racial Hierarchy."

16. Huge Davis Graham, "Affirmative Action for Immigrants: The Unintended Consequences of Reform," in *Color Lines*, ed. John David Skrentny (Chicago: University of Chicago Press, 2001), 55.

17. Senator Ted Kennedy, U.S. Senate, Subcommittee on Immigration and Naturalization of the Committee on the Judiciary (Washington, DC: U.S. Senate, 1965), 1–3.

18. This is a higher absolute number but a slightly lower rate than the approximately 15 percent reached in the late nineteenth century.

19. U.S. Census Bureau, "An Older and More Diverse Nation by Midcentury," news release, August 14, 2008; http://www.census.gov/newsroom/releases/archives/population/cb08-123.html. This estimate treats Hispanic whites as among the minority population.

20. A convenient summary of public opinion toward Muslims post-9/11 and toward undocumented immigrants can be found in Jennifer L. Hochschild, Vesla Weaver, and Traci Burch, *Creating a New Racial Order: How Immigration, Multiracism, Genomics, and the Young Can Remake Race in America* (Princeton, NJ: Princeton University Press, 2012), 153–63.

21. Victoria Hattam, *In the Shadow of Race: Jews, Latinos, and Immigrant Politics in the United States* (Chicago: University of Chicago Press, 2007).

22. Richard Alba and Victor Nee, *Remaking the American Mainstream: Assimilation and Contemporary Immigration* (Cambridge, MA: Harvard University Press, 2003), 10.

23. Ibid., 11.

24. Luis R. Fraga and Gary M. Segura, "Culture Clash? Contesting Notions of American Identity and the Effects of Latin American Immigration," *Perspectives on Politics* 4.2 (2006): 279–87; Richard Alba, "Mexican Americans and the American Dream," *Perspectives on Politics* 4.2 (2006): 289–96.

25. An extensive research literature documenting these employee attitudes and practices is summarized in John D. Skrentny, "Are America's Civil Rights Laws Still Relevant? *Du Bois Review* 4.1 (2007): 119–40.

26. Ibid., 123; emphasis in the original.

27. Ibid., 134.

28. For further documentation, see Skrentny, "Are America's Civil Rights Laws Still Relevant?" 128–30.

29. Philip Kasinitz, John H. Mollenkopf, Mary C. Waters, and Jennifer Holdaway, *Inheriting the City: The Children of Immigrants Come of Age* (New York: Russell Sage Foundation, 2008). The major field period was 1998–2000, but the investigators did reinterview some respondents in 2002 and 2003, after the shock of 9/11. The major findings from the reinterview appear in Philip Kasinitz, John H. Mollenkopf, and Mary C. Waters, *Becoming New Yorkers* (New York: Russell Sage Foundation, 2004).

30. Ibid., 1.

31. Ibid., 13.

32. Ibid., 303.

33. Ibid., 343.

34. Ibid., 352–53.

35. Ibid., 353.

36. Ibid., 355.

37. Richard Alba, "Mexican Americans and the American Dream," *Perspectives on Politics* 4.2 (2006): 289.

38. Charles Hirschman, "Immigration and the American Century," *Demography* 42.4 (2005): 601.

39. Jennifer Lee and Frank D. Bean, *The Diversity Paradox: Immigration and the Color Line in Twenty-first Century America* (New York: Russell Sage Foundation, 2010).

40. Mark A. Leach, Susan K. Brown, Frank D. Bean, and Jennifer Van Hook, *Unauthorized Immigrant Parents: Do Their Migration Histories Limit Their Children's Education*, U.S. 2010 Project (New York: Russell Sage Foundation/Brown University 2012).

41. For a useful summary, including commentary on measurement challenges, see Rebecca M. Blank, Marilyn Dabady, and Constance F. Citro, eds., *Measuring Racial Discrimination* (Washington, DC: National Academies Press, 2004), 223–46.

42. Lawrence D. Bobo, "Somewhere between Jim Crow and Post-racialism," *Daedalus* 140.2 (2011): 15–16.

43. See Hochschild et al., *Creating a New Racial Order*.

44. A 2008 Pew Research Center study of America's 3.8 million marriages found record levels of interracial marriage for every race group: 31 percent of Asian-Americans married non-Asians, 26 percent of Hispanics married non-Hispanics, and 16 percent of blacks married nonblacks. See Jeffrey S. Passel, Wendy Wang, and Paul Taylor, *Marrying Out: One-in-Seven New U.S. Marriages Is Interracial or Interethnic*; http://pewresearch.org/pubs/1616/american-marriage-interracial-interethnic.

45. John Hope Franklin, "The Two Worlds of Race: A Historical View" (1965), reprinted in *Daedalus* 140.1 (2011): 28–29.

46. David A. Hollinger, "The Concept of Post-racial: How Its Easy Dismissal Obscures Important Questions." *Daedalus*, 140.1 (2011): 175.

47. President Barack Obama, quoted in Eugene Robinson, *Disintegration: The Splintering of Black America* (New York: Doubleday, 2010), 162.

Chapter 10. Where Are We Exactly?

1. The ACS Questionnaire can be found at http://www.census.gov/acs/www/Downloads/questionnaires/2011/Quest11.pdf.

2. Karen R. Humes, Nicolas A. Jones, and Roberto R. Ramirez, *Overview of Race and Hispanic Origin: Census 2010 Brief* (Washington DC: U. S. Census Bureau, 2011); http://www.census.gov/prod/cen2010/briefs/c2010br-02.pdf.

3. Ian Haney Lopez, "Race on the 2010 Census: Hispanics and the Shrinking White Majority," *Daedalus* 134.1 (2005): 50.

4. U.S. Census Bureau, "Frequently Asked Questions"; http://www.census.gov/population/www/ancestry/anc-faq.html.

5. Ibid.

6. United Nations Statistics Division Social and Housing Statistics Section of the Demographic and Social Statistics Branch, *Ethnicity: A Review of Data Collection and Dissemination* (New York: United Nations, 2003), 6.

7. Angela Brittingham and C. Patricia de la Cruz, *Ancestry: Census 2000 Brief*, June 2004; http://www.census.gov/prod/2004pubs/c2kbr-35.pdf, 3.

8. The Negro classification remains on the form because for many elderly African Americans it is the term that best describes them, and that they prefer. That population dwindles in number, and it is unlikely that the term will appear on the 2020 census questionnaire. The Census Race and Hispanic Origin Alternative Questionnaire Experiment determined that removing Negro from the question did not reduce the number of respondents selecting the category; see Elizabeth Compton, Michael Bentley, Sharon Ennis, and Sonya Rastogi, *2010 Census Race and Hispanic Origin Alternative Questionnaire Experiment* (Washington, DC: Decennial Statistical Studies Division and Population Division, U.S. Census Bureau, 2012), xi.

9. U.S. Census Bureau, "Overview of Race and Hispanic Origin"; http://www.census.gov/prod/2001pubs/cenbr01-1.pdf.

10. Brittingham and de la Cruz, *Ancestry: Census 2000*, 3–4.

11. U.S. Census Bureau, "Overview," 2.

12. Margo Anderson, personal communication with the author, August 11, 2012. For more detailed discussion of the ancestry question and its flaws, see

Anthony Daniel Perez and Charles Hirschman, "The Changing Racial and Ethnic Composition of the United States," *Population and Development Review* 35.1 (2009): 1–51.

13. Chapter 6 reviewed the use of block-level race data in dual-system estimation, but that technical procedure is unlikely to be reintroduced in census taking. If it is, it should not rely on race data for the reasons reviewed herein.

14. This is a highly condensed treatment of a large, complicated issue. For additional information on the Voting Rights Act, see Leadership Conference, "Voting Rights Act Frequently Asked Questions"; http://www.civilrights.org/voting-rights/vra/faq.html. For additional information on redistricting, see Stephen Ansolabehere, Nathaniel Persily, and Charles Stewart III, "Race, Region and Vote Choice in the 2008 Election: Implications for the Future of the Voting Rights Act," *Harvard Law Review* 123 (2010): 1385–1435.

15. Laura Zayatz, *Disclosure Limitation for Census 2000 Tabular Data* (Washington, DC: Department of Commerce, Bureau of the Census, Statistical Research Division, 2003).

16. Katherine Wallman, personal communication with the author, August 12, 2012.

Chapter 11. Getting from Where We Are to Where We Need to Be

1. Grutter v. Bollinger, 539 U.S. 306 (2003).

2. Sonia Sotomayor, quoted in Ross Douthat, "Race in 2008," *New York Times*, 20 July 2009.

3. Benedict Anderson, *Imagined Communities*, rev. ed. (London: Verso, 1991). For case studies that elaborate on this perspective, see David I. Kertzer and Dominique Arel, eds., *Census and Identity: The Politics of Race, Ethnicity, and Language in National Censuses* (Cambridge: Cambridge University Press, 2002).

4. Pierre Bourdieu, *Language and Symbolic Power*, ed. John B. Thompson, trans. Gino Raymond and Matthew Arnold (Cambridge, MA: Harvard University Press, 1991).

5. Ibid., 306; emphasis in the original.

6. Jennifer L. Hochschild, Vesla Weaver, and Traci Burch, *Creating a New Racial Order: How Immigration, Multiracism, Genomics, and the Young Can Remake Race in America* (Princeton: Princeton University Press, 2012), 9. See also Brenna Powell, "A New Comparative Agenda for Ethno-Racial Politics," unpublished manuscript, Harvard University Government and Social Policy Program, 2010; and Jennifer L. Hochschild and Brenna Marea Powell, "Racial Reorganization and the United States Census 1850–1930: Mulattoes, Half-breeds, Mixed Parentage, Hindoos, and the Mexican Race." *Studies in American Political Development* 22.1 (2008): 59–96.

7. Hochschild et al., *Creating a New Racial Order*, 10.

8. Ibid.

9. Ibid., 9.

10. Scott Leon Washington, "Principles of Racial Taxonomy," paper presented at the Graduate Student Conference on Categories, Columbia University, New York, 22 October 2004.

11. Hochschild et al., *Creating a New Racial Order*, 10.

12. Ibid., 9. The other two components are relative positions of the racial and ethnic groups and the social relations within and among groups. This, of course, leads to the question of what role the state plays in determining relative positions and social relations. As soon as that is asked, we are back to the prior question of how in the first instance the groups are defined (constituted) in law and policy, which in American history gets us to the statistical races.

13. Hochschild et al., *Creating a New Racial Order*, 10–11.

14. Ibid., 11.

15. Kenneth Prewitt, "Race in the 2000 Census: A Turning Point," in *The New Race Question: How the Census Counts Multiracial Minorities*, ed. Joel Perlmann and Mary C. Waters (New York: Russell Sage Foundation, 2002), 354–62.

16. Hochschild et al., *Creating a New Racial Order*, 69.

17. Walter F. Willcox, quoted in Stephanie M. DiPietro and Robert J. Bursik Jr., "Studies of the New Immigration: The Dangers of Pan-ethnic Classifications," *Annals of the American Academy of Political and Social Science* 641.1 (2012): 248; from Walter F. Willcox, "Foreword," in *Immigrants and Their Children 1920: Census Monographs VII*, by Niles Carpenter (Washington D.C.: Government Printing Office, 1927), xv.

18. DiPietro and Bursik, "Studies of the New Immigration," 263.

19. Philip Kainite,, John H. Mollenkopf, Mary C. Waters, and Jennifer Holdaway, *Inheriting the City: The Children of Immigrants Come of Age* (New York: Russell Sage Foundation, 2008).

20. Paul Taylor, Mark Hugo Lopez, Jessica Hamar Martínez, and Gabriel Velasco, *When Labels Don't Fit: Hispanics and Their Views of Identity* (Washington, DC: Pew Research Center, 2012); http://www.pewhispanic.org/2012/04/04/when-labels-dont-fit-hispanics-and-their-views-of-identity/.

21. Pew Hispanic Center, *Between Two Worlds: How Young Latinos Come of Age in America* (Washington, DC: Pew Research Center, 2009); http://www.pewhispanic.org/2009/12/11/between-two-worlds-how-young-latinos-come-of-age-in-america/.

22. Jocelyn Kaiser, "10 Billion Plus: Why World Population Projections Were too Low," interview with John Bongaarts, *Science Insider*, 4 May 2011; http://news.sciencemag.org/scienceinsider/2011/05/10-billion-plus-why-world-population.html.

23. Pew Research Center, *The Rise of Asian Americans*, June 19, 2012; http://www.pewsocialtrends.org/2012/06/19/the-rise-of-asian-americans/?src=prc-newsletter.

24. Ibid. This finding is sourced to the 2010 American Community Survey, Integrated Public Use Microdata Sample.

25. Pew Research Center, *The Rise of Asian Americans*; emphasis added.

26. Charles Hirschman and Morrison G. Wong, "The Extraordinary Educational Attainment of Asian-Americans: A Search for Historical Evidence and Explanations," *Social Forces* 65.1 (1986): 1–27.

27. Robinson, *Disintegration*, 5.

28. Ibid.

29. The original study was William Julius Wilson, *The Declining Significance of Race: Blacks and Changing American Institutions* (Chicago: University of Chicago Press, 1978). The updated argument is William Julius Wilson, "*The Declining Significance of Race*: Revised and Revisited," *Daedalus* 140.2 (2011).

30. David Hollinger, *Post-ethnic America: Beyond Multiculturalism*, 3rd ed. (New York: Basic Books, 2005), 237.

31. The application process is managed by the Bureau of Indian Affairs. Of the 237 tribes that have petitioned or filed papers indicating intent to petition, 15 have been approved, whose total population is less than eight thousand. See C. Matthew Snipp, "American Indians: Clues to the Future of other Racial Groups," in *The New Race Question: How the Census Counts Multiracial Minorities*, ed. Joel Perlmann and Mary C. Waters (New York: Russell Sage Foundation, 2002), 197.

32. Naomi Mezey, "The Distribution of Wealth, Sovereignty, and Culture through Indian Gaming," *Stanford Law Review* 48. 3 (1996): 711–37.

33. A 2007 Pew survey of African-Americans report that 53 percent hold blacks responsible for their failure to "get ahead," and 30 percent cite discrimination as the primary factor. Cited in Robinson, *Disintegration*, 226.

34. Robinson, *Disintegration*, 197.

35. Nathan Glazer, "On the Census Race and Ethnic Categories," in *Double Exposure: Poverty and Race in America*, ed. Chester Hartman (Armonk, NY: Sharpe, 1997).

36. Gans, "'Whitening' and the Changing American Racial Hierarchy."

37. Ibid.

38. Ibid.

39. Ibid.

40. Ibid.

41. This recommendation and its reasoning would apply irrespective of whether future censuses keep the current questions or, as recommended below, modify them in the phased strategy outlined herein.

42. Nathan Glazer, "Reflections on Race, Hispanicity, and Ancestry in the U.S. Census," in *The New Race Question: How the Census Counts Multiracial Individuals*, ed. Joel Perlmann and Mary C. Waters (New York: Russell Sage Foundation, 2003), 318.

43. "Senate Assails Census Decision to Drop Query on Marital Status," *Washington Times*, September 19, 1999.

44. U.S. Census Bureau, *Race, Hispanic Origin and Ancestry* (Washington, DC: U.S. Census Bureau, 2000); http://www.census.gov/dmd/www/pdf/d3249c.pdf.

45. Hochschild et al., *Creating a New Racial Order*, 113.

46. Joseph Carroll, "Most Americans Approve of Interracial Marriages," Gallup.com, August 16, 2007; http://www.gallup.com/poll/28417/most-americans-approve-interracial-marriages.aspx.

47. For treatment of cohort change and public attitudes, see Hochschild et al., *Creating a New Racial Order*, 132–35.

48. The Office of Management and Budget suggested rules for allocating multiple race responses when a claim of discrimination is brought by one racial

minority that generally require that the complaining minority be allocated all those who have indicated they are any part of that racial minority. Office of Management and Budget, *Guidance on Aggregation and Allocation of Data for Use in Civil Rights Monitoring and Enforcement*, Bulletin 00-02 (Washington DC: Office of Management and Budget, 2000).

49. In the 2000 census this was 2.4 percent, and even with a 30 percent increase by the 2010 census, the number only reached 2.9 percent.

50. See Elizabeth Compton, Michael Bentley, Sharon Ennis, and Sonya Rastogi, *2010 Census Race and Hispanic Origin Alternative Questionnaire Experiment* (Washington, DC: Decennial Statistical Studies Division and Population Division, U.S. Census Bureau, 2012).

51. The Census Bureau will not focus on broad purposes because those purposes are inevitably political in nature. The bureau is a scientific, technical agency.

52. The Census Bureau will convene expert panels, conduct internal tests, and consult broadly on technical issues. The OMB may do the same.

53. Other alternatives have attractive features, and if one were eventually adopted by the Census Bureau and the OMB, much of the rationale used to endorse this particular format might still be relevant. However, the Bureau's preliminary analysis of its 2010 alternative questionnaire experiment does indicate substantial technical improvement in a question that merges Hispanic into the race question, as in figure 6. For example, the number not responding to the race question, what is known as "item nonresponse," drops from about 5 percent to less than 1 percent. See Compton et al., *2010 Census Race and Hispanic Origin Alternative Questionnaire Experiment*, viii.

54. I also recommend dropping the ancestry question; it does not produce useful statistics and having it on the same form as question 9 can easily confuse the public.

55. The Census Bureau appreciates the redundancy, but it is currently precluded by law from dropping the "some other race" option. This law could and should be changed.

56. See Compton et al., *2010 Census Race and Hispanic Origin Alternative Questionnaire Experiment*, ix.

57. Ian Haney Lopez, "Race on the 2010 Census: Hispanics and the Shrinking White Majority," Daedalus 134.1 (2005): 47 notes that "because race and ethnicity are already effectively fungible under antidiscrimination law, combining these questions on the census would not have a deleterious effect on civil rights enforcement." This sentence was written in the context of my recommendation that the Hispanic and race questions now on the census be merged. See Kenneth Prewitt, "Racial Classification in America: Where Do We Go from Here?" *Daedalus* 134.1 (2005): 5–17.

58. A strong representation of this argument is Michael Omi and Howard Winant, *Racial Formation in the United States*, 2nd ed. (New York: Routledge, 1994).

59. For an excellent summary of the debate in general and an argument in favor of ethnicity, see Mario Barrera, "Are Latinos a Racialized Minority?" *Sociological Perspectives* 51.2 (2008): 305–24.

60. Glazer, "Reflections on Race," 321.

61. David Hollinger, *Post-ethnic America: Beyond Multiculturalism*, 3rd ed. (New York: Basic Books, 2005), 238.

62. Ibid.

Appendix. Perspectives from Abroad

1. Ethnoracial statistics in these three countries were compared to those of the United States in the seminar Statistical Races and Public Policy, taught at the School of International and Public and Affairs, Columbia University, Spring 2012. Student teams prepared the following case studies: Carolina Escalera, Alexander Foard, and Brittany Fox, "Counting Colors: Implication of Racial Mixing and Public Policy in Brazil"; Christopher Mitchell, Vanessa Ohta, and Nicolas Rodriquez, "Ethnic Statistics in France: Ethnicity in the Census, the Influence of Immigration, and the Current Debate"; and Senna Georges, Nancy Leeds, Cindy Love, and Nicole Manna, "A Religious Democracy: The Case of Israel." My review of these cases is heavily indebted to the work of these ten students.

2. King Dom João VI, quoted in A.J.R. Russell-Wood, *The Black Man in Slavery and Freedom* (London: Macmillan, 1982), 173; emphasis added.

3. Carl N. Degler, *Neither Black nor White* (Madison: University of Wisconsin Press, 1971), 214–16.

4. Mara Loveman, "The Race to Progress: Census-taking and Nation-making in Brazil (1870–1920)," *Hispanic American Historical Review* 89.3 (2009): 207–34; Edward E. Telles, *Race in Another America: The Significance of Skin Color in Brazil* (Princeton, NJ: Princeton University Press, 2004), 25.

5. Telles, *Race in Another America*, 33.

6. Gilberto Freyre, *Casa Grande e Senzala* (1933); trans. Samuel Putnam as *The Masters and the Slaves: A Study in the Development of Brazilian Civilization* (Berkeley and Los Angeles: University of California Press, 1986).

7. Alfred Metraux, "An Inquiry into Race Relations in Brazil," *Courier* 5.8–9 (1952); http://unesdoc.unesco.org/images/0007/000711/071135eo.pdf, 6.

8. Yvonne Maggie and Claudia B. Rezende, *Raça como retórica: a construção da diferença* (Rio de Janeiro: Civilização Brasileira, 2002), 13.

9. Liv Sovi, *Aqui ninguém é branco* (Rio de Janeiro: Aeroplano Editora, 2009), 67–68.

10. Brazilian Law No 11.096, 2005; http://www.planalto.gov.br/ccivil_03/_Ato2004-2006/2004/Mpv/213.htm. Brazil's 2000 census reports a population of 170 million—54 percent white; 39 percent brown; 6 percent black; and less than 1 percent other (includes Japanese, Arab, Amerindian); See Index Mundi, "Brazil Demographics Profile 2012"; http://www.indexmundi.com/brazil/demographics_profile.html.

11. Melissa Nobles, "The Myth of Latin American Multiracialism," *Daedalus* 134.1 (2005): 86.

12. Andrew Downie and Marion Lloyd, "At Brazil's Universities, Affirmative Action Faces Crucial Tests," *Chronicle of Higher Education*, global ed., 2 July 2012; http://chronicle.com/article/At-Brazils-Universities/123720/.

13. Daniel I. Kertzer and Dominique Arel, "Census, Identity Formation, and the Struggle for Political Power," in *Census and Identity: The Politics of Race, Ethnicity, and Language in National Censuses*, ed. Daniel I. Kertzer and Dominique Arel (Cambridge: Cambridge University Press, 2002), 24.

14. France had sizable immigrant flows from other European countries across the twentieth century—after World War I immigration from southern Europe helped France compensate for its low fertility rate and loss of life in the war and after Word War II immigration from Northern Africa as labor for a rebounding economy.

15. There are no restrictions on private surveys, though there are, of course, cost constraints.

16. Alain Blum, "Resistance to Identity Categorization in France," in *Census and Identity: The Politics of Race, Ethnicity, and Language in National Censuses*, ed. Daniel I. Kertzer and Dominique Arel (Cambridge: Cambridge University Press, 2002), 131.

17. In the absence of census statistics, the number of Muslims in France is an estimate. France's metropolitan population is sixty-three million; the government estimates five to six million immigrants from Muslim countries, or 8 to 10 percent. It is estimated than one-third are practicing Muslims. See "How Does France Count Its Muslim Population?" *Le Figaro*, April 2011.

18. Patrick Simon, "The Choice of Ignorance: The Debate on Ethnic and Racial Statistics in France," *French Politics, Culture and Society* 1 (2008): 7.

19. For a discussion, see Erik Bleich, "Race Policy in France," Brookings Institution, 1 May 2001; http://www.brookings.edu/research/articles/2001/05/france-bleich.

20. Erik Bleich, "Antiracism without Races: Politics and Policy in a 'Color-Blind' State," *French Politics, Culture, and Society* 18.3 (2000): 51. In any case, conviction rates for direct discrimination are strikingly low, averaging in the single digits every year; see Andrew Geddes and Virginie Guiraudon, "Britain, France, and EU Anti-Discrimination Policy: The Emergence of an EU Policy Paradigm," *West European Politics* 27.2 (2004): 340.

21. Simon, "The Choice of Ignorance," 23; emphasis in the original.

22. Vernellia R. Randall, "Racial Discrimination: The Record of France," executive summary, September 2001; http://academic.udayton.edu/race/06hrights/georegions/Europe/France01.htm.

23. Michel Wieviorka, "Should France Collect Race Statistics?" in Hervé Le Bras, Jean-Luc Racine, and Michel Wieviorka, *National Debates on Race Statistics: Towards an International Comparison* (Paris: Fondation Maison des Sciences de l'Homme, 2012), 6.

24. Hervé Le Bras, "Ethnic and Racial Statistics and the Structure of the French Nation-state: A Contradiction," in Hervé Le Bras, Jean-Luc Racine, and Michel Wieviorka, *National Debates on Race Statistics: Towards an International Comparison* (Paris: Fondation Maison des Sciences de l'Homme, 2012), 10.

25. Calvin Goldscheider, "Ethnic Categorizations in Censuses: Comparative Observations from Israel, Canada, and the United States," in *Census and Identity: The Politics of Race, Ethnicity, and Language in National Censuses*, ed. Daniel I. Kertzer and Dominique Arel (Cambridge: Cambridge University Press, 2002), 75.

26. Ibid., 76.

27. See Calvin Goldscheider, *Israel's Changing Society: Population, Ethnicity and Development* (Boulder, CO: Westview, 1996).

28. Simon, "The Choice of Ignorance," 7.

29. Phil Brennan, "Israel's Population Bomb in Reverse," Newsmax.com, 19 October 2002; http://archive.newsmax.com/archives/articles/2002/10/18/181802.shtml.

30. Ian Peleg, "Jewish-Palestinian Relations in Israel: From Hegemony to Equality," *International Journal of Politics, Culture, and Society* 17 (2004): 416.

31. Barbara S. Okun and Dov Friedlander, "Educational Stratification among Arabs and Jews in Israel: Historical Disadvantage, Discrimination, and Opportunity," *Population Studies* 59.2 (2005): 163–80.

32. Sephardic Jews descended from or mixed with people from modern Spain and Portugal. They were forced out of Spain in the late fifteenth century, many fleeing to North Africa or the Middle East. Ashkenazic Jews, originating in Central and Eastern Europe, are generally more prosperous and hold most leadership positions in Israel.

33. African Refugee Development Center, *Israel's Violation of the Convention on the Elimination of All Forms of Racial Discrimination with Respect to Asylum Seekers and Refugees in Israel* (Tel Aviv: African Refugee Development Center, 2012); http://www2.ohchr.org/english/bodies/cerd/docs/ngos/ARDC_Israel_CERD80.pdf.

BIBLIOGRAPHY

Adams, John. "Letter to Matthew Robinson." In *Works of John Adams*, vol. 8. New York: AMS Press, 1988.

African Refugee Development Center. *Israel's Violation of the Convention on the Elimination of All Forms of Racial Discrimination with Respect to Asylum Seekers and Refugees in Israel.* Tel Aviv: African Refugee Development Center, 2012. http://www2.ohchr.org/english/bodies/cerd/docs/ngos/ARDC_Israel_CERD80.pdf.

Alba, Richard. "Mexican Americans and the American Dream." *Perspectives on Politics* 4.2 (2006).

Alba, Richard, and Victor Nee. *Remaking the American Mainstream: Assimilation and Contemporary Immigration.* Cambridge, MA: Harvard University Press, 2003.

Alfano, Sean. "High Court Limits Race in School Choice," CBS News, 28 June 2007. http://www.cbsnews.com/stories/2007/06/28/supremecourt/main2991748.shtml?tag=contentMain;contentBody.

American Anthropological Association. *Race: Are We So Different?* Washington, DC: American Anthropological Association, 2010. http://www.understandingrace.org/home.html.

Anderson, Benedict. *Imagined Communities.* Rev. Ed. London: Verso, 1991.

Anderson, Margo J. *The American Census: A Social History.* New Haven, CT: Yale University Press, 1988.

——. "(Only) White Men Have Class: Reflections on Early 19th-Century Occupational Classification Systems." *Work and Occupations* 21.1 (1994).

Anderson, Margo J., and Stephen E. Fienberg. *Who Counts? The Politics of Census-taking in Contemporary America.* New York: Russell Sage Foundation, 1999.

Balinski, Michel L., and H. Peyton Young. *Fair Representation: Meeting the Ideal of One Man, One Vote.* New Haven, CT: Yale University Press, 1982.

Barrera, Mario. "Are Latinos a Racialized Minority?" *Sociological Perspectives* 51.2 (2008): 305–24.

Bell, Daniel. *The Coming of the Post-industrial Society.* New York: Basic Books, 1973.

Bennett, Claudette. "Exploring the Consistency of Race Reporting in Census 2000 and the Census Quality Survey." Paper presented at the Joint Meetings of the American Statistical Association, San Francisco, 3–7 August 2003.

Black, Edwin. *War against the Weak: Eugenics and America's Campaign to Create a Master Race.* New York: Four Walls Eight Windows, 2003.

Blank, Rebecca M., Marilyn Dabady, and Constance F. Citro, eds. *Measuring Racial Discrimination.* Washington, DC: National Academies Press, 2004.

Bleich, Erik. "Antiracism without Races: Politics and Policy in a 'Color-Blind' State." *French Politics, Culture, and Society* 18.3 (2000).

——. "Race Policy in France." Brookings Institution, 1 May 2001. http://www.brookings.edu/research/articles/2001/05/france-bleich.

Bliss, Catherine. "Genome Sampling and the Biopolitics of Race." Unpublished manuscript, 2010.

Blum, Alain. "Resistance to Identity Categorization in France." In *Census and Identity: The Politics of Race, Ethnicity, and Language in National Censuses*, ed. Daniel I. Kertzer and Dominique Arel. Cambridge: Cambridge University Press, 2002.

Blumenbach, Johann. *On the Natural Varieties of Mankind.* New York: Bergman, 1969.

Bobo, Lawrence D. "Somewhere between Jim Crow and Post-racialism." *Daedalus* 140.2 (2011).

Bobo, Lawrence D., James R. Kluegel, and Ryan A. Smith. "Laissez-Faire Racism: The Crystallization of a Kinder, Gentler Antiblack Ideology." In *Racial Attitudes in the 1990s: Continuity and Change*, ed. Steven A. Tuch and Jack K. Martin. Westport, CT: Praeger, 1997.

Bonilla-Silva, Eduardo. "From Bi-racial to Tri-racial." *Ethnic and Racial Studies* 27.6 (2004).

Bourdieu, Pierre. *Language and Symbolic Power.* Edited by John B. Thompson, translated by Gino Raymond and Matthew Arnold. Cambridge, MA: Harvard University Press, 1991.

Brennan, Phil. "Israel's Population Bomb in Reverse." Newsmax.com, 19 October 2002. http://archive.newsmax.com/archives/articles/2002/10/18/181802.shtml.

Brittingham, Angela, and C. Patricia de la Cruz. *Ancestry: Census 2000 Brief.* June 2004. http://www.census.gov/prod/2004pubs/c2kbr-35.pdf.

Brown, Lawrence D., Morris L. Eaton, David A. Freedman, Stephen P. Klein, Richard A. Olshen, Kenneth W. Wachter, Martin T. Wells, and Donald Ylvisaker. "Statistical Controversies in Census 2000." *Jurimetrics* 39 (1999).

Buchanan, Patrick. *State of Emergency: The Third World Invasion and Conquest of America.* New York: St. Martin's, 2006.

Bullard, James H., and Sandrine Dudoit. "R / Bioconductor: A Short Course." Presented at the Division of Biostatics, University of California–Berkeley, 21–25 January 2008. http://wiki.biostat.berkeley.edu/~bullard/courses/T-mexico-08/lectures/hapmap/slides- 2x2.pdf.

Butterfield, Herbert. *The Whig Interpretation of History.* London: G. Bell, 1931.

California Secretary of State. *Proposition 54: Official Voter Information Guide.* Sacramento: California Secretary of State, 2003.

——. *Proposition 209: Prohibition against Discrimination or Preferential Treatment by State and Other Public Entities.* Sacramento: California Secretary of State, 1996.

Carroll, Joseph. "Most Americans Approve of Interracial Marriages." Gallup.com, August 16, 2007. http://www.gallup.com/poll/28417/most-americans-approve-interracial-marriages.aspx.

Cassedy, James H. *Demography in Early America: Beginnings of the Statistical Mind, 1600–1800.* Cambridge, MA: Harvard University Press.

Charney, Evan, and William English. "Candidate Genes and Political Behavior." *American Political Science Review* 106.1 (2012).

Citro, Constance F., Daniel L. Cork, and Janet L. Norwood, eds. *The 2000 Census: Counting under Adversity.* Washington, DC: National Academies Press, 2004.

Cohen, Patricia A. *Calculating People: The Spread of Numeracy in Early America*. Chicago: University of Chicago Press, 1982.
Collins, Francis. "What We Do and Don't Know about 'Race,' 'Ethnicity,' Genetics and Health at the Dawn of the Genome Era." *Nature Genetics* 36 (2004).
Commager, Henry Steele. *Jefferson, Nationalism, and the Enlightenment*. New York: George Braziller, 1975.
Compton, Elizabeth, Michael Bentley, Sharon Ennis, and Sonya Rastogi. *2010 Census Race and Hispanic Origin Alternative Questionnaire Experiment*. Washington, DC: Decennial Statistical Studies Division and Population Division, U.S. Census Bureau, 2012.
Congressional Record, 68th Cong., 1st sess., 1924.
Congressional Record, 88th Cong., 1st sess., 8 April 1965.
Congressional Record, 88th Cong., 2nd sess., 1964, vol. 110, no. 10.
Darga, Kenneth. *Sampling and the Census: A Case against the Proposed Adjustments for Undercount*. Washington, DC: American Enterprise Institute, 1999.
Davis, David Brion. "Blacks: Damned by the Bible." *New York Review of Books*, 16 November 2006.
Davis, Peter P., and James Mulligan. *Census Coverage Measurement Estimation Report: Net Coverage for the Household Population in the United States*. Washington, DC: Census Bureau, Decennial Statistical Studies Division, 2012.
Degler, Carl N. *Neither Black nor White*. Madison: University of Wisconsin Press, 1971.
De Zwart, Frank. "Ethno-statistics in the Netherlands: Some Unintended Consequences of Institutionalization." Unpublished manuscript, July 2010.
DiPietro, Stephanie M., and Robert J. Bursik Jr. "Studies of the New Immigration: The Dangers of Pan-ethnic Classifications." In *Immigration and the Changing Social Fabric of American Cities*, ed. John MacDonald and Robert J. Sampson. Annals of the American Academy of Political and Social Science 641. Thousand Oaks, CA: Sage, 2012.
Downie, Andrew, and Marion Lloyd. "At Brazil's Universities, Affirmative Action Faces Crucial Tests." *Chronicle of Higher Education*, global ed., 2 July 2012. http://chronicle.com/article/At-Brazils-Universities/123720/.
Du Bois, W.E.B. *The Souls of Black Folk*. Edited by D. W. Blight and Robert Gooding-Williams. Boston: Bedford, 1997.
Duster, Troy. "Race and Reification in Science." *Science* 307.5712 (2005).
Dyson, Freeman. "Our Biotech Future." *New York Review of Books*, 19 July 2007.
Edley, Christopher Jr. *Not All Black and White: Affirmative Action, Race and American Values*. New York: Hill and Wang, 1996.
Elazar, Barkan. *The Retreat of Scientific Racism*. Cambridge: Cambridge University Press, 1992.
Ellis, Joseph. *American Sphinx: The Character of Thomas Jefferson*. New York: Vintage, 1998.
European Commission against Racism and Intolerance. *Third Report on the Netherlands*. Strasbourg: European Commission against Racism and Intolerance, 2007.
Evans, James P., Eric M. Meslin, Theresa M. Marteau, and Timothy Caulfield. "Deflating the Genomic Bubble." *Science* 331.6019 (2011).

Fraga, Luis R., and Gary M. Segura. "Culture Clash? Contesting Notions of American Identity and the Effects of Latin American Immigration." *Perspectives on Politics* 4.2 (2006).

Franklin, Benjamin. "Observations Concerning the Increase of Mankind, Peopling of Counties, etc." In *The Papers of Benjamin Franklin*, vol. 4. New Haven, CT: Yale University Press, 1961.

Franklin, John Hope. "The Two Worlds of Race: A Historical View." Cambridge, MA: MIT Press, 1965.

Fredrickson, George. *Racism: A Short History.* Princeton, NJ: Princeton University Press, 2002.

Freeman, Alan. "Antidiscrimination Law from 1954 to 1989: Uncertainty, Contradiction, Rationalization, Denial." In *The Politics of Law: A Progressive Critique*, 3rd ed., ed. David Kairys. New York: Basic Books, 1989.

Freyre, Gilberto. *Casa Grande e Senzala* (1933). Translated by Samuel Putnam as *The Masters and the Slaves: A Study in the Development of Brazilian Civilization.* Berkeley and Los Angeles: University of California Press, 1986.

Fujimura, Joan H., and Ramya Rajagopalan. "Different Differences: The Use of 'Genetic Ancestry' versus Race in Biomedical Human Genetic Research." *Social Studies of Science* 41.1 (2001).

Gans, Herbert J. "The Possibility of a New Racial Hierarchy in the Twenty-first Century United States." In *The Cultural Territories of Race: Black and White Boundaries*, ed. Michele Lamont. Chicago and New York: University of Chicago Press/Russell Sage Foundation, 1999.

———. "'Whitening' and the Changing American Racial Hierarchy." *Du Bois Review* 9.2 (2012); prepublication manuscript courtesy of the author.

Geddes, Andrew, and Virginie Guiraudon. "Britain, France, and EU Anti-Discrimination Policy: The Emergence of an EU Policy Paradigm." *West European Politics* 27.2 (2004).

Gerstle, Gary. *American Crucible: Race and Nation in the Twentieth Century.* Princeton, NJ: Princeton University Press, 2001.

Gibson, Campbell J., and Emily Lennon. *Historical Census Statistics on the Foreign-born Population of the United States: 1850–1990.* Population Division Working Paper. Washington DC: U.S. Bureau of the Census, 1999.

Glazer, Nathan. "On the Census Race and Ethnic Categories." In *Double Exposure: Poverty and Race in America*, ed. Chester Hartman. Armonk, NY: Sharpe, 1997.

———. "Reflections on Race, Hispanicity, and Ancestry in the U.S. Census." In *The New Race Question: How the Census Counts Multiracial Individuals*, ed. Joel Perlmann and Mary C. Waters (New York: Russell Sage Foundation, 2003).

Goldenberg, David M. *The Curse of Ham: Race and Slavery in Early Judaism, Christianity, and Islam.* Princeton, NJ: Princeton University Press, 2003.

Goldscheider, Calvin. "Ethnic Categorizations in Censuses: Comparative Observations from Israel, Canada, and the United States." In *Census and Identity: The Politics of Race, Ethnicity, and Language in National Censuses*, ed. Daniel I. Kertzer and Dominique Arel. Cambridge: Cambridge University Press, 2002.

———. *Israel's Changing Society: Population, Ethnicity and Development.* Boulder, CO: Westview, 1996.

Gould, Stephen Jay. *The Mismeasure of Man.* New York: Norton, 1981.
Governor's Commission on the Los Angeles Riots. "144 Hours in August 1965." In *Violence in the City: An End or a Beginning?* Los Angeles: Governor's Commission on the Los Angeles Riots, 1965. http://www.usc.edu/libraries/archives/cityinstress/mccone/part4.html.
Graham, Hugh Davis. "Affirmative Action for Immigrants: The Unintended Consequences of Reform." In *Color Lines*, ed. John David Skrentny. Chicago: University of Chicago Press. 2001.
——. *The Civil Rights Era: Origins and Development of National Policy.* New York: Oxford University Press, 1990.
——. *Collision Course: The Strange Convergence of Affirmative Action and Immigration Policy.* New York: Oxford University Press, 2002.
Gross, Samuel R., and Barbara O'Brien. "Frequency and Predictors of False Conviction: Why We Know So Little, and New Data on Capital Cases." *Journal of Empirical Legal Studies* 5.4 (2008).
Hammonds, Evelynn M. "Straw Men and Their Followers: The Return of Biological Race." Paper presented as part of the Social Science Research Council Web Forum "Is Race Real?" 7 June 2006.
Hattam, Victoria. *In the Shadow of Race: Jews, Latinos, and Immigrant Politics in the United States.* Chicago: University of Chicago Press, 2007.
Hayes, Stephen R. *Noah's Curse: The Biblical Justification for American Slavery.* Oxford: Oxford University Press, 2002.
Heer, David, ed. *Social Statistics and the City.* Cambridge, MA: Joint Center for Urban Studies, 1968.
Herrnstein, Richard J., and Charles Murray. *The Bell Curve: Intelligence and Class Structure in American Life.* New York: Free Press, 1994.
Hillygus, D. Sunshine, Norman Nie, Kenneth Prewitt, and Heili Pals. *The Hard Count: The Political and Social Challenges of Census Mobilization.* New York: Russell Sage Foundation, 2006.
Hirschfeld, Lawrence A. "Natural Assumptions: Race, Essence, and Taxonomies of Human Kinds." *Social Research* 65.2 (1998).
Hirschman, Charles. "Immigration and the American Century." *Demography* 42.4 (2005).
Hirschman, Charles, and Morrison G Wong. "The Extraordinary Educational Attainment of Asian-Americans: A Search for Historical Evidence and Explanations." *Social Forces* 65.1 (1986).
Hochschild, Jennifer L. "Multiple Racial Identifiers in the 2000 Census, and Then What?" In *The New Race Question: How the Census Counts Multiracial Individuals*, ed. Joel Perlmann and Mary C. Waters. New York: Russell Sage Foundation, 2003.
Hochschild, Jennifer L., and Brenna Marea Powell. "Racial Reorganization and the United States Census 1850–1930: Mulattoes, Half-breeds, Mixed Parentage, Hindoos, and the Mexican Race." *Studies in American Political Development* 27.1 (2008).
Hochschild, Jennifer L., Vesla Weaver, and Traci Burch. *Creating a New Racial Order: How Immigration, Multiracism, Genomics, and the Young Can Remake Race in America.* Princeton, NJ: Princeton University Press, 2012.

——. *Transforming the American Racial Order: Immigration, Multiracism, DNA, and Cohort Change.* Princeton, NJ: Princeton University Press, 2012.

Holden, Constance. "Race and Medicine." *Science* 302.5645 (2003).

Hollinger, David A. "Amalgamation and Hypodescent: The Question of Ethnoracial Mixture in the History of the United States." *American Historical Review* 108.5 (2003).

——. "The Concept of Post-racial: How Its Easy Dismissal Obscures Important Questions." *Daedalus* 140.1 (2011).

——. *Postethnic America: Beyond Multiculturalism.* New York: Basic Books, 2006.

Horsman, Reginald. *Josiah Nott of Mobile: Southerner, Physician, and Racial Theorist.* Baton Rouge: Louisiana State University Press, 1987.

"How Does France Count Its Muslim Population?" *Le Figaro*, April 2011.

Humes, Karen R., Nicolas A. Jones, and Roberto R. Ramirez. *Overview of Race and Hispanic Origin: Census 2010 Brief.* Washington, DC: U. S. Census Bureau, 2011. http://www.census.gov/prod/cen2010/briefs/c2010br-02.pdf.

Huntington, Samuel P. "The Hispanic Challenge." *Foreign Policy*, March–April 2004. http://www.foreignpolicy.com/articles/2004/03/01/the_hispanic_challenge.

——. "The Special Case of Mexican Immigration: Why Mexico Is a Problem." *American Enterprise* 11.8 (2000).

——. *Who Are We? The Challenge to America's National Identity.* New York: Simon and Schuster, 2004.

Jefferson, Thomas. *Writings.* New York: Library of America, 1984.

——. *Writings of Jefferson*, ed. A. E. Bergh. Vol. 4. Washington, DC: Jefferson Memorial Association, 1903.

Johnson, Lyndon B. "To Fulfill These Rights," In *Public Papers of the Presidents of the United States: Lyndon B. Johnson*, vol. 2. Washington DC: Government Printing Office, 1966.

Jorgenson, Eric, Hua Tang, Maya Gadde, Mike Province, Sharon Kardia, Mark Leppert, Nicholas Schork, Richard Cooper, D. C. Rao, Eric Boerwinkle, and Neil Risch. "Ethnicity and Human Genetic Linkage Maps." *American Journal of Human Genetics* 76.2 (2005).

Kahn, Jonathan. "Race in a Bottle." *Scientific American*, 15 July 2007.

Kasinitz, Philip, John H. Mollenkopf, Mary C. Waters, and Jennifer Holdaway. *Inheriting the City: The Children of Immigrants Come of Age.* New York: Russell Sage Foundation, 2008.

Katznelson, Ira. *When Affirmative Action Was White.* New York: Norton, 2005.

Kennedy, John F. "Statement by the President upon Signing Order Establishing the President's Committee on Equal Employment Opportunity," 7 March 1961. In *Public Papers of the Presidents of the United States: John F. Kennedy.* Washington, DC: Government Printing Office, 1962.

Kertzer, Daniel I., and Dominique Arel. "Census, Identity Formation, and the Struggle for Political Power." In *Census and Identity: The Politics of Race, Ethnicity, and Language in National Censuses*, ed. Daniel I. Kertzer and Dominique Arel. Cambridge: Cambridge University Press, 2002.

Kim, Claire. "The Racial Triangulation of Asian Americans." *Politics and Society* 27 (1999).

Kinder, Donald R., and Lynn M Sanders. *Divided by Color.* Chicago: University of Chicago Press, 1996.

Knowles, Louis, and Kenneth Prewitt. *Institutional Racism in American Society.* Englewood Cliffs, N.J.: Prentice-Hall, 1969.

Leadership Conference. "The Census 2000 Education Kit," In *Census 2000: Everyone Counts.* Washington, DC: Leadership Conference Education Fund, 2000.

Le Bras, Hervé. "Ethnic and Racial Statistics and the Structure of the French Nation-state: A Contradiction." In Hervé Le Bras, Jean-Luc Racine, and Michel Wieviorka, *National Debates on Race Statistics: Towards an International Comparison.* Paris: Fondation Maison des Sciences de l'Homme, 2012.

Lee, Jennifer, and Frank D. Bean. *The Diversity Paradox: Immigration and the Color Line in Twenty-first Century America.* New York: Russell Sage Foundation, 2010.

Leiby, James. *Carroll Wright and Labor Reform: The Origins of Labor Statistics.* Cambridge, MA: Harvard University Press, 1960.

Lewontin, R. C. "Confusions about Human Races." Paper presented as part of the Social Science Research Council Web Forum "Is Race Real?" 7 June 2006. http://raceandgenomics.ssrc.org/Lewontin.

Lieberman, Robert C. *Shaping Race Policy: The United States in Comparative Perspective.* Princeton, NJ: Princeton University Press, 2005.

Lopez, Ian F. Haney. "'A Nation of Minorities': Race, Ethnicity, and Reactionary Colorblindness." *Stanford Law Review* 59.4 (2007).

——. "Race on the 2010 Census: Hispanics and the Shrinking White Majority." *Daedalus* 134.1 (2005).

——. *White by Law.* New York: New York University Press, 1996.

Loveman, Mara. "The Race to Progress: Census-taking and Nation-making in Brazil (1870–1920)." *Hispanic American Historical Review* 89.3 (2009).

Maggie, Yvonne, and Claudia B. Rezende. *Raça como retórica: a construção da diferença.* Rio de Janeiro: Civilização Brasileira, 2002.

Martin, Paul, Richard Ashcroft, George T. H. Ellison, Andrew David Smart, and Richard Tutton. *Reviving 'Racial Medicine'? The Use of Race/Ethnicity in Genetics and Biomedical Research, and the Implications for Science and Healthcare.* London: Faculty of Health and Social Care Sciences, University of London, 2007.

McAdam, Doug. *Political Process and the Development of Black Insurgency 1930-1970.* Chicago: University of Chicago Press, 1982.

Metraux, Alfred. "An Inquiry into Race Relations in Brazil." *Courier* 5.8–9 (1952). http://unesdoc.unesco.org/images/0007/000711/071135eo.pdf.

Mezey, Naomi. "The Distribution of Wealth, Sovereignty, and Culture through Indian Gaming." *Stanford Law Review* 48.3 (1996).

——. "Erasure and Recognition: The Census, Race, and the National Imagination." *Northwestern University Law Review* 97.4 (2003).

Morgan, Edward. *The Birth of the Republic: 1763-89.* Rev. Ed. Chicago: University of Chicago Press, 1977.

Morning, Ann. "Ethnic Classification in Global Perspective: A Cross-national Survey of the 2000 Census Round." *Population Research Policy Review* 27.2 (2008).

——. *The Nature of Race.* Berkeley and Los Angeles: University of California Press.

Murray, Charles. "Jewish Genius." *Commentary* 123.4 (2007).

National Advisory Commission on Civil Disorders. *Our Nation Is Moving toward Two Societies, One Black, One White—Separate and Unequal.* New York: Bantam Books, 1968.

National Institutes of Health. "NIH Guidelines on the Inclusion of Women and Minorities as Subjects in Clinical Research." *NIH Guide* 32.11 (1994).

Ngai, Mae N. "The Architecture of Race in American Immigration Law: A Reexamination of the Immigration Act of 1924." *Journal of American History* 86.1 (1999).

Nobles, Melissa. "The Myth of Latin American Multiracialism." *Daedalus* 134.1 (2005).

——. *Shades of Citizenship: Race and the Census in Modern Politics.* Stanford, CA: Stanford University Press, 2000.

O'Connor, Alice. *Social Science for What?* New York: Russell Sage Foundation, 2007.

Office of Management and Budget. *Guidance on Aggregation and Allocation of Data for Use in Civil Rights Monitoring and Enforcement.* Bulletin 00-02. Washington DC: Office of Management and Budget, 2000.

Okun, Barbara S., and Dov Friedlander. "Educational Stratification among Arabs and Jews in Israel: Historical Disadvantage, Discrimination, and Opportunity." *Population Studies* 59.2 (2005).

Omi, Michael, and Howard Winant. *Racial Formation in the United States.* 2nd ed. New York: Routledge, 1994.

Onuf, Peter. *Jefferson's Empire: The Language of American Nationhood.* Charlottesville: University of Virginia Press, 2000.

Peleg, Ian. "Jewish-Palestinian Relations in Israel: From Hegemony to Equality." *International Journal of Politics, Culture, and Society* 17 (2004).

Perez, Anthony Daniel, and Charles Hirschman. "The Changing Racial and Ethnic Composition of the United States." *Population and Development Review* 35.1 (2009): 1–51.

Perlmann, Joel, and Mary C. Waters, eds. *The New Race Question: How the Census Counts Multiracial Minorities.* New York: Russell Sage Foundation, 2002.

Peters, Mary. "Determination of Reasonable Rates and Terms for the Digital Performance of Sound Recordings by Preexisting Subscription Services." *Federal Register* 68.20 (2003).

Pew Research Center. "Blacks See Growing Gap between Poor and Middle Class." *Pew Research Center's Social and Demographic Trends*, 13 November 2007. http://www.pewsocialtrends.org/2007/11/13/blacks-see-growing-values-gap-between-poor-and-middle-class/.

——. *The Rise of Asian Americans.* June 19, 2012. http://www.pewsocialtrends.org/2012/06/19/the-rise-of-asian-americans/?src=prc-newsletter.

Phillips, Anne. *Multiculturalism without Culture.* Princeton, NJ: Princeton University Press, 2007.

Powell, Brenna. "A New Comparative Agenda for Ethno-Racial Politics." Unpublished paper, Harvard University Government and Social Policy Program, 2010.

Prewitt, Kenneth. "A Nation Imagined, a Nation Measured: Jefferson's Legacy." In *Across the Continent: Geopolitics, Science and Culture Conflicts in the Making of America*,

ed. Douglas Seefeldt, Jeffrey L. Hantman, and Peter S. Onuf. Charlottesville: University of Virginia Press, 2005.
——. "Political Ideas and a Political Science for Policy." *Annals of the American Academy of Political and Social Sciences* 600.1 (2005).
——. *Politics and Science in Census Taking*. New York and Washington, DC: Russell Sage Foundation/Population Reference Bureau, 2003.
——. "Racial Classification in America: Where Do We Go from Here?" *Daedalus* 134.1 (2005): 5–17.
——. "Race in the 2000 Census: A Turning Point." In *The New Race Question: How the Census Counts Multiracial Minorities*, ed. Joel Perlmann and Mary C. Waters. New York: Russell Sage Foundation, 2002.
——. "Social Science and Private Philanthropy: The Quest for Social Relevance." *Essays on Philanthropy* 15 (1995).
——. "What Is Political Interference in Federal Statistics?" *Annals of the American Academy of Political and Social Science* 631.1 (2010).
Randall, Vernellia R. "Racial Discrimination: The Record of France." Executive summary, September 2001. http://academic.udayton.edu/race/06hrights/georegions/Europe/France01.htm.
Rein, Lisa. "Mystery of Va.'s First Slaves Is Unlocked 400 Years Later." *Washington Post*, 3 September 2006.
Risch, Neil, Esteban Burchard, Elad Ziv, and Hua Tang. "Categorization of Humans in Biomedical Research: Genes, Race and Disease." *Genome Biology* 3 (2002). http://genomebiology.com/2002/3/7/comment/2007.
Risinger, D. Michael. "Innocents Convicted: An Empirically Justified Factual Wrongful Conviction Rate." *Journal of Criminal Law and Criminology* 97 (2007).
Roberts, Leslie. "How to Sample the World's Genetic Diversity." *Science* 257.5074 (1992).
Rodriguez, Gregory. "Affirmative Action's Time Is Up." *Los Angeles Times*, 2 August 2010.
Russell Sage Foundation. *Visiting Fellow Application Form, 2008*. http://www.russellsage.org/about/whatwedo/howtoapply/scholar/070501.352646.
Russell-Wood, A.J.R. *The Black Man in Slavery and Freedom*. London: Macmillan, 1982.
Schlesinger, Arthur M. Jr. *The Disuniting of America: Reflections on a Multicultural Society*. New York: Norton, 1992.
Schor, Paul. *Mobilizing for Pure Prestige? Challenging Federal Census Ethnic Categories in the USA (1850–1940)*. Oxford: Blackwell, 2005.
"Senate Assails Census Decision to Drop Query on Marital Status." *Washington Times*, September 19, 1999.
Simon, Patrick. "The Choice of Ignorance: The Debate on Ethnic and Racial Statistics in France." *French Politics, Culture and Society* 1 (2008).
Skrentny, John D. "Are America's Civil Rights Laws Still Relevant?" *Du Bois Review* 4.1 (2007).
——. *The Ironies of Affirmative Action*. Chicago: University of Chicago Press, 1996.
——. *The Minority Rights Revolution*. Cambridge, MA: Belknap Press of Harvard University Press, 2002.

Smedley, Audrey. *Race in North America: Origin and Evolution of a Worldview.* Boulder, CO: Westview, 1993.

Snipp, C. Matthew. "American Indians: Clues to the Future of Other Racial Groups." In *The New Race Question: How the Census Counts Multiracial Individuals*, ed. Joel Perlmann and Mary C. Waters. New York: Russell Sage Foundation, 2003.

Snowden, Frank M. Jr. *Before Color Prejudice: The Ancient View of Blacks.* Cambridge, MA: Harvard University Press, 1983.

Sobel, Lester A., ed. *Civil Rights: 1960–1966.* New York: Facts on File, 1967.

Sollars, Werner. "What Race Are You?" In *The New Race Question: How the Census Counts Multiracial Individuals*, ed. Joel Perlmann and Mary C. Waters. New York: Russell Sage Foundation, 2003.

Sovi, Liv. *Aqui ninguém é branco.* Rio de Janeiro: Aeroplano Editora, 2009.

Starr, Paul. "Social Categories and Claims in the Liberal State." *Social Research* 59.2 (1992).

Stinchcombe, Arthur. "The Logic of Scientific Inferences." In *Constructing Social Theories.* Chicago: University of Chicago Press, 1987.

Stocking, George W. *Race, Culture, and Evolution: Essays in the History of Anthropology.* New York: Free Press, 1968.

Students for Academic Freedom. "Academic Bill of Rights—Basic Texts—Documents," 26 August 2010. http://www.studentsforacademicfreedom.org/documents/1925/abor.html.

Telles, Edward E. *Race in Another America: The Significance of Skin Color in Brazil.* Princeton, NJ: Princeton University Press, 2004.

Thernstrom, Abigail, and Stephen Thernstrom. *Beyond the Color Line.* Stanford, CA: Hoover Institution Press, 2002.

Tuch, Steven A., and Michael Hughs. "Whites' Racial Policy Attitudes in the Twenty-first Century: The Continuing Significance of Racial Resentment." *Annals of the American Academy of Political and Social Science* 634 (2011).

University of Missouri–Kansas City School of Law. *Lynching Statistics: By State and Race 1882–1968.* http:/www.law.umkc.edu/faculty/projects/ftrials/shipp/lynchingstate.html.

United Nations, Statistics Division, Social and Housing Statistics Section of the Demographic and Social Statistics Branch. *Ethnicity: A Review of Data Collection and Dissemination.* New York: United Nations, 2003.

U.S. Census Bureau. "An Older and More Diverse Nation by Midcentury." News release, August 14, 2008. http://www.census.gov/newsroom/releases/archives/population/cb08-123.html.

———. *Race, Hispanic Origin and Ancestry.* Washington, DC: U.S. Census Bureau, 2000. http://www.census.gov/dmd/www/pdf/d3249c.pdf.

U.S. Food and Drug Administration. *Guidance for Industry: Collection of Race and Ethnicity Data in Clinical Trials.* Washington, DC: U.S. Food and Drug Administration, 2005.

———. *Investigational New Drug Applications*, 1998. http://www.fda.gov/oashi/patrep/demo.html.

U.S. House of Representatives, 51st Cong., 2nd sess. *Chinese Immigration.* Washington, DC: Government Printing Office, 1877.

U.S. House of Representatives, 150th Cong., 1st sess. *Federal Measures of Race and Ethnicity and the Implications for the 2000 Census: Hearings before the Subcommittee on Government Management, Information, and Technology of the Committee on Government Reform and Oversight, April 23, May 22, and July 25, 1997.* Washington, DC: Government Printing Office, 1998.

U.S. Senate, 44th Cong., 2nd sess. *Report of the Joint Special Committee to Investigate Chinese Immigration.* Washington DC: Government Printing Office, 1877.

Varmus, Harold. *The Art and Politics of Science.* New York: Norton, 2009.

Wade, Nicolas. "Race Is Seen as Real Guide to Track Roots of Disease." *New York Times*, 30 July 2002.

——. "Talking Genes." *New York Review of Books*, 21 September 2006.

Wallman, Katherine K. "Data on Race and Ethnicity: Revising the Federal Standard." *American Statistician* 52.1 (1998).

Wallman, Katherine K., Suzann Evinger, and Susan Schechter. "Measuring Our Nation's Diversity: Developing a Common Language for Data on Race/Ethnicity." *American Journal of Public Health* 90.11 (2000).

Wallman, Katherine K., and John Hodgdon. "Race and Ethnic Standards for Federal Statistics and Administrative Reporting." *Statistical Reporter*, July 1977, 450–54.

Washington, George. *The Writings of George Washington.* Washington DC: Government Printing Office, 1939.

Washington, Scott Leon. "Principles of Racial Taxonomy." Paper presented to the Graduate Student Conference on Categories, Columbia University, New York, 22 October 2004.

Webb, James. "Diversity and the Myth of White Privilege." *Wall Street Journal*, 22 July 2010.

Wieviorka, Michel. "Should France Collect Race Statistics?" In Hervé Le Bras, Jean-Luc Racine, and Michel Wieviorka, *National Debates on Race Statistics: Towards an International Comparison.* Paris: Fondation Maison des Sciences de l'Homme, 2012.

Wight, Tommy, and Howard Hogan. "Census 2000: Evolution of the Revised Plan." *CHANCE: A Magazine of the American Statistical Association* 12.4 (1999).

Willcox, Walter. "Census Statistics of the Negro." *Yale Review* 13 (1904).

Williams, Kim. *Mark One or More: Civil Rights in Multiracial America.* Ann Arbor: University of Michigan Press, 2006.

Wills, Garry. *"Negro President": Jefferson and the Slave Power.* Boston: Houghton Mifflin, 2003.

Wilson, William Julius. *The Declining Significance of Race: Blacks and Changing American Institutions.* Chicago: University of Chicago Press, 1978.

——. "*The Declining Significance of Race*: Revised and Revisited." *Daedalus* 140.2 (2011).

Wittenbrink, Bernd, James L. Hilton, and Pamela L. Gist. "In Search of Similarity: Stereotypes as Naive Theories in Social Categorization." *Social Cognition* 16.1 (1998).

Wright, Carroll, and W. C. Hunt. *History and Growth of the United States Census.* Washington, DC: Government Printing Office, 1900.

Zayatz, Laura. *Disclosure Limitation for Census 2000 Tabular Data.* Washington, DC: Department of Commerce, Bureau of the Census, Statistical Research Division, 2003.

Zogby International. *Racial Identity Survey.* Utica, NY: Zogby International, 2000.

Zolberg, Aristide. *A Nation by Design: Immigration Policy in the Fashioning of America.* New York and Cambridge MA: Russell Sage Foundation/Harvard University Press, 2006.

INDEX